COMPETING
NATIONALISMS

ADVANCE PRAISE FOR THE BOOK

'Rajshree Chandra's fascinating book throws fresh light on the complex journey of Indian nationalism. Its focus is the scholar and freedom-fighter Jagat Narain Lal, a man drawn between the competing, and often conflicting, pulls of faith and politics. Using a wide array of sources, Chandra sensitively narrates the thoughts and struggles of a passionate individual, living through intensely charged times. This richly readable book demonstrates the enormous potential of the biographical genre in illuminating wider historical trends.'—Ramachandra Guha, author of *Gandhi: The Years that Changed the World*

'An extraordinary biography of a man who literally personified the tensions between the competing and conflicting strands of Indian nationalism, which are as much in contention today as they were in his time. Chandra brings to her subject the sensibility of the political theorist as she explores Jagat Narain Lal's inner conflicts, and how he negotiated and reconciled the tensions between contrary strands of nationalism in his political life and thought.'—Niraja Gopal Jayal, former professor, Centre for the Study of Law and Governance, Jawaharlal Nehru University

'A finely written history of a sacrificing patriot, gifted in Sanskrit and Persian, who was enchanted by religion's sacred character but was tempted by its political potential, and who returned to the ethic of equal rights for all in a democratic India.'—Rajmohan Gandhi, historian, biographer, research professor at University of Illinois

'There is much to savour in Rajshree Chandra's detailed, devoted and diligent biography of her grandfather, Jagat Narain Lal, an important figure in Bihar politics in the early twentieth century. The portrait she paints is not of a giant among men—that would be a cardboard cutout of no interest at all. No, she instead tells the story of an ordinary man who finds he lives in extraordinary times; times that make him grapple with conflicting emotions and wrenching questions in himself.

'What is this thing called "nationalism"? What does it demand of him every day? How does it colour morality, faith and even sexual desire? It's Lal's lifelong struggle to face these questions head on that make him such a fascinating character, and make this such an unexpectedly compelling book.'—Dilip D' Souza, columnist; author, *The Deoliwallahs*

'This is an extraordinarily persuasive, rigorous and convincing account, a philosophical portrait and a gripping tale of co-existence of multiple strands of nationalisms in colonial India. Chandra's unusual biography of her grandfather qualifies to be what Stanley Wolpert in his 2010 essay said: "biography is the finest form of history".'—Mohammad Sajjad, professor of history, Aligarh Muslim University.

'A fine and highly readable biography that shows that it was individual lives, actions and ideas that made and transformed India's political history. Through the life of her grandfather, Chandra provides novel insights on how the everyday made the exceptional happen in history. This is a fresh history of India's transition to freedom with an intimate view of the North Indian world of society and family. The contention between religious and inclusive nationalism recounted here through the life of Jagat Narain will resonate widely with readers today.'—Shruti Kapila, associate professor, Faculty of History, University of Cambridge; author of *Violent Fraternity: Indian Political Thought in the Global Age*

COMPETING NATIONALISMS

THE SACRED *and* POLITICAL LIFE *of*
JAGAT NARAIN LAL

RAJSHREE CHANDRA

SUPPORTED BY

THE NEW INDIA
FOUNDATION

PENGUIN
VIKING
An imprint of Penguin Random House

PENGUIN BOOKS

USA | Canada | UK | Ireland | Australia
New Zealand | India | South Africa | China

Penguin Books is part of the Penguin Random House group of companies
whose addresses can be found at global.penguinrandomhouse.com

Published by Penguin Random House India Pvt. Ltd
4th Floor, Capital Tower 1, MG Road,
Gurugram 122 002, Haryana, India

Penguin
Random House
India

First published in Viking by Penguin Random House India 2021

Copyright © Rajshree Chandra 2021

10 9 8 7 6 5 4 3 2 1

ISBN 9780670095490

Typeset in Adobe Caslon Pro by Manipal Technologies Limited, Manipal
Printed at Replika Press Pvt. Ltd, India

www.penguin.co.in

To Jaideep

for the constant light

Nationalism is a matter of historical experience. Neither race, nor lineage, nor country has sufficed to mould a people into nation.

Instead of being united by common historical antecedents, the past of the Hindus and Muslims is a past of mutual animosities and destruction, both in the political as well as in the religious fields . . . the prospects might perhaps be different if the past of the two communities can be forgotten by both. Hence, the importance of forgetfulness as a factor in building a nation.

—Jagat Narain Lal

Contents

Preface

The stories we once belonged to have been lost. Just as you do not know who we are, where we came from or where we are going, you don't even know which part of the story we fit into, and that is even worse. After passing through so many misadventures and catastrophes, after walking such great distances, it is almost as if we too have forgotten our stories, forgotten who we are.

—Orhan Pamuk[1]

About the Book

Most biographies are about men or women who loom large and who have impacted the course of history significantly, if not single-handedly. This one though is a story of a man who was a participant in history, albeit to an extent that he literally embodied and personified it. It would be fair to say that the main protagonist of this story, Jagat Narain Lal, my paternal grandfather, is 'history in person'. He stands as his own evidence of a person continuously

---

[1] Pamuk, *Other Colours: An Essay and a Story*, p. 486–87.

engaged with the nationalist context and practice, charting pathways, shaping and being shaped by new possibilities for the self and the nation.

Jagat Narain Lal was, in Pierre Bourdieu's words, a 'collective individual' who cannot be summarized in a single narrative or viewed through a single ideological lens. Each of the political choices he made, pathways he walked, goals he upheld, is a chronicle of the conflicted life of Indian nationalism.

In straddling the many loyalties and multiple affiliations— as a member of the Indian National Congress and of the Hindu Mahasabha; as a Hindu who wanted to combine *seva* (service), bhakti (devotion) and *sangathan* (organization) and later upheld virtues of civic nationalism; as a Gandhian and as an ascetic nationalist seeking freedom in a political world—Jagat Babu's life becomes a mirror for the times in which the complex of religiosity, cosmology and ritual could not be isolated from either the political or the social field. As I traced his political journey through varied paths, he appeared almost as an embodiment of the various genres and contradictions of nationalist ideology that competed and vied with each other from the 1920s onwards. Importantly and quite uncannily, Jagat Babu's life also holds a mirror to our times, telling us that perhaps we as a nation are destined to keep revisiting and churning the volatile mix of religion and nationalism. This is what makes his political journey uniquely illuminating, and worthy of historical retrieval.

Jagat Narain Lal was a freedom fighter, a professor of economics at Bihar Vidyapith, a practising lawyer, editor of the journal *Mahavir*, a member of the Constituent Assembly and of the first Linguistic Re-organization Commission (1948), a writer, a scholar, and also a very religious and spiritual person—his religiosity marking his place to the ideological right within the Congress. He was also a member of the Hindu Mahasabha and was its general secretary in 1926. He had a conflicted relationship with both the Congress and the Mahasabha and, in his own words, he 'wrestled with many anxieties' throughout his political career.

The aim of this book is to reflect upon Jagat Narain Lal's richly conflictual journey and explore the competing strands of nationalism that intersected not just own life, but also the nationalist world that he was a part of, and that we inherited in 1947. In his anxieties and competing political pursuits lay Indian nationalism's own fraught relationship with questions of identity, faith and nationhood. In his vulnerability, suffering, negotiations and truth-telling lies a story of nationalism's own conflicts and contradictions. In Jagat Narain Lal's small story lies a bigger history of competing nationalisms, as well as a tale that speaks to the present. This is in a sense a chronicle of present-day conflicts foretold, as each of the contradictions and anxieties play out with chilling, uncanny familiarity today.

From his life-world there emerges a possibility of detangling a story of nationalism from its overdetermined, over-compacted historical narratives. I may not be able to free the story from what can be called as the 'gaze of suspicion', but what I will try and do is move away from preoccupations with 'Is a particular piece of knowledge objective?' or 'How can we know?' to further questions of 'What does the receiving again of knowledge do for us?' Can a re-reading of Indian nationalism reveal to us a way of acknowledging our un-negotiated, un-settled, complicated equation between identity and nation-state, and between the sacred and political?

The book travels with Jagat Narain Lal in his journey as a nationalist through four pathways that I characterize as *Ascetic, Hindu Nationalist, Anti-Colonial* and *Civic* nationalisms. His life and times give us a glimpse into the intersecting, competing and mutating idioms of nationalism. Illuminated through his journey, these four idioms form the core chapters of the book. How Jagat Babu traversed these multiple pathways gives us a feel of the textural warp and weft of each of the thematic strands. His journey helps us understand the complexities, unities and divergences of four distinct strands that have somewhere along the way got stapled together and filed under large, unhelpful labels. Four core chapters (chapters 2–5) explore the lived experience (through Jagat Babu's political life) of nationalist thought and practice, the last chapter reflects on the living legacy of these four idioms. How the four genres of nationalism thrived in their ascetic, Hindu nationalist, anti-colonial and civic modes in free India, and how they converged into a potent, hegemonic political practice from 2014 onwards, are reflections you will find in the last chapter.

The four strands are by no means exhaustive of nationalist thought and practice. We can imagine them like railway tracks that sometimes run parallel, seeming to remain separate and unconnected in perpetuity, but suddenly then converging, criss-crossing and emerging into new tracks that can alter the course of a hurtling, serpentine train. Just as tracks repeat the pattern of parallel-ing and converging, separating and meeting, so also do the routes of these nationalist modes. Shaped into idioms that sought India's self-definition as a nation, post-independence nationalist modes continue to draw from the same pool of ascetic, Hindu nationalist, anti-colonial and civic modes. The ideological content, the associated practices, the contradictions and conflicts continue to play out with a sameness that is both reminiscent and unsettling. Progress is often measured as a distance from the past. Absence of that distance is a disconcerting reminder that we are still mired in an older, unchanging time. We seem to be condemned to repeat our past not because we do not remember it, as George Santayana had famously said, but because we remember it only too well.

The Writing of the Book

Every book has a back-story and mine began with an article. A couple of years back while googling my grandfather, Jagat Narain Lal, I came across a piece in Scroll titled, 'How India's founding fathers saw the "nauseating principle of secularity of the State"'.[2] One of the founding fathers quoted in evidence was my grandfather, Jagat Narain Lal. Though I had no memory of him, I cringed at the title of the article and the associations it drew between my grandfather and his alleged abhorrence for secularity. Had he really found secularism and secularity nauseating? I realized much later that I was asking the wrong question, that 'binary questions' only serve to reinforce binaries in which much of our nationalist history is trapped. But what the question did was to activate a search, the result of which is this book.

Thus, strange as it may seem, my search for my *own* grandfather began with a question mark on his secularity. A legacy as rich (and richly conflictual) as his surely should not have needed an allegation to resurrect its memory. The years of inattention indict us as a family for not keeping alive the memory of a man who all-told spent more than eight years in jail, sacrificing his career and family for the greater cause of freedom of his country.

Coincidentally, around the same time as the Scroll article, a few of his diaries and letters came into my possession. Among them was a note requisitioning books from the warden of the Hazaribagh Central Jail in 1929. These included the *Chandogya*, *Kena*, *Isha* and *Mundaka* Upanishads, a book of essays on the *Bhagavad Gita* as also books by Plato, Machiavelli, Carlyle, Rousseau and Bluntschli. The range and depth of his intellectual pursuits triggered in me further curiosity, this time mixed with a new-found pride.

Pride and prejudice are both fertile breeding grounds for curiosity. Almost on a mission, I set out to find more about Jagat Babu. I procured a photocopy of his memoir titled *Light unto a Cell* (1947) from my father, located a short biography

---

[2] Chakravarty, "How India's founding fathers saw the 'nauseating principle of secularity of the State'", Scroll, 2015.

written by my *phua* (aunt), Pratima Verma (herself a prolific writer) and went on to discover over a couple of thousand hand-written pages of his diaries, letters and notebooks at the Nehru Memorial Museum and Library (NMML). I was intrigued. How did these diaries and notebooks, most of which he had written during his years in jail during the 1920s, '30s and '40s, surmount the apathy of the family and reach the NMML archives? On persisting with my query and revealing my relationship with the gentleman in question, I was told that Ram Pyari Devi, my grandmother, had donated them.

It had to be her, I realized. My grandmother had been active on the Bihar political scene and had been a member of the Bihar Legislative Council for many years. A strong, educated lady, she was reputed to be politically more hard-wired than her husband. So, she realized, far more than any of us in the subsequent generations did, that in those papers there lay a legacy that needed to be preserved for posterity. Posterity got to them a little late, but here I am, Jagat Narain Lal's granddaughter, salvaging an inheritance that is both personal and collective.

Reading and writing my grandfather's story has been somewhat of a surreal experience for me, as many narratives that unfolded through his pages were also playing out in front of me in real time. A plethora of issues—cow slaughter, religious conversions, linguistic autonomy, Hindi as a national language, minority appeasement and majority dominance; charges of sedition, public safety, treachery and defamation; allegations that the nation is in danger from its own proselytizing or assertive minorities, or from 'Macaulay's Liberals'; sinister divide-and-rule policies of those in power—eerily resonated and flitted between the two time-frames. On one occasion, as charges of sedition were slapped with indiscriminate alacrity for punishing dissent under Section 124A of the Indian Penal Code (IPC), I was reading about Jagat Narain Lal being charged under the same sedition law, the same section of the same penal code, *a century ago*. In another instance, when the Unlawful Activities (Prevention) Act (UAPA) was being imposed on dissenting citizens with predatory zeal, I was reading about Jagat Babu being hauled up for unlawful activities.[3] In many other instances when puritanical notions of culture, and *'bhartiya sanskriti'*, of what is obscene and profane were playing out in real time ('offensive' depictions of godly characters and deified historical-cum-mythical characters; censorship of films on grounds of 'obscenity'; dress-code prescriptions, etc.), I was simultaneously reading about how Jagat Narain Lal was charged for obscenity because he, as the editor of *Mahavir* magazine, allowed the publication of an advertisement of *Kok Shastra* (translated on Amazon as *Hindu Secrets of Love*) on *Mahavir*'s back-cover. It is quite astonishing that despite so much movement in the fortunes of a nation, there is a part, maybe the very core itself, that seems stuck in an unyielding past.

About the Main Protagonist, Jagat Narain Lal

We are a large family, larger when all my ten aunts and uncles were alive and we had not lost three of our forty-strong contingent of cousins. Considering Jagat Narain Lal was a freedom fighter who spent many years in jail, his tryst with law and the British government should have been a fertile ground for many family stories. But it was not so. Perhaps it was because we (my parents and us siblings) never stayed in Patna where many of my aunts and uncles lived, in or around his house in Kadam Kuan on the present-day Jagat Narain Lal Road. Perhaps the physical distance separated us from collective invocations of memories, stories,

---

[3] On 19 December, the governments of Bihar and Orissa declared the associations like those of the 'Congress Volunteers', the 'Khilafat Volunteers', the 'National Volunteers', the 'Sevak Dal Volunteers' and 'Non-Co-operation Volunteers' to be 'unlawful Associations' under section 16 of the Indian Criminal Law Amendment Act of 1908. Datta, *History of the Freedom Movement in Bihar*, Vol. 1, p. 444.

secrets that are shared with abandon only amongst people who share ties of time or place. But perhaps the absence of stories, and the disinterest in Jagat Narain Lal's legacy, was also because of the uncommonness and oddities of his family, about which I heard in bits from the older generation that remains—my father, my *chacha* and *phupha* (uncle and uncle-in-law, respectively) and two phuas.

My grandmother, Ram Pyari Devi, also took part in the freedom movement and was jailed during the Quit India Movement. In fact, Pratima phua, who as a little child stayed with her mother in the jail, tells me that my dadi was in the late stages of pregnancy then and my youngest phua was born in the jail. After independence, my grandmother remained a member of the Bihar Legislative Council for more than a decade, with one term as the Speaker of the house.

So here was a household of ten children, and a few grandchildren, living with parents who had active political careers, in a family where the main breadwinner had sacrificed his legal career responding to Gandhi's call for Non-cooperation and subsequently spent long periods in jail. Means were meagre and 'parenting' time was sporadic and unpredictable. The children at best thrived on benign neglect though emphasis on their steady education remained a steady component.[4] There is a college he founded in Khagaul, Patna, Bihar—Jagat Narain Lal College— that bears testimony to his abiding interest in education and pedagogy.[5] But pride in their parents' careers and achievements took a backseat to stories of negligence and penury.

---

[4] Two of my phuas went to Prayag Mahila Vidyapith (Allahabad) set up under the headship of Mahadevi Verma, freedom fighter, poet and educationist. Known for his commitment to girls' education, all five phuas received education till graduation. My father studied to be a mechanical engineer, my eldest chacha a lawyer, two chachas trained to be pilots and the youngest was a graduate from Ranchi University.
[5] Wikipedia, Jagat Narain Lal College.

My phua, Pratima Verma, recounts her memories of her mother's meetings and association with many big names of the Indian national movement. She writes: 'We got an opportunity to see and interact with many influential leaders, social workers, stalwarts, but we remained bereft of the security, bonding and the feeling of being nurtured that "ordinary" parents were able to give to their children . . . It also meant that for me I had kind of lost my parents. They belonged more to the nation than to us children.'[6]

This is a feeling echoed by Jagat Babu's other children too. The experience of paucity and neglect is a thread that runs through their memories. So, as a granddaughter, I heard more stories of inattention, grievances and hurt from his children, rather than stories of their parents' role in nation-building. In these stories of neglect, perhaps there is a need for memory—personal and historical—to remember a man with more affection and more credence than has been given to him. It is only when I coaxed my aunts and uncles, during the writing of the book that a few stories emerged out of the recesses of their memories, sometimes with a smile and pride that was reassuring.

My father, Shrish Chandra, narrates this story about the Quit India Movement: Jagat Babu, carrying a reward of Rs 10,000, was fleeing arrest, making his way, in hiding, from Patna to his constituency in Arrah with the Bihar regiment close on his heels. Surrounded from both sides on the Koilvar bridge, he dived into the Son river below, was able to hold his breath for a long time underwater and escaped arrest. Such was his mastery over pranayama and yoga, my father tells us with pride, that he could hold his breath for unusually long periods of time. The story goes that he swam over three kilometres before he came aground, eluding arrest and making his way to Arrah. On reaching Arrah,

---

[6] Verma, *Jagat Narain Lal*, p. iii.

he carried out his mission, handed over charge, gave instructions to members of the local Congress and then surrendered voluntarily.

An elder cousin of mine, Amit Kumar, narrated another detail, possibly of the same incident, and with the flourish that stories gather as they roll along generations. Apparently, Jagat Narain Lal was not fleeing alone. He and his compatriot banked on a secluded shore of the Ganga (the Son is a tributary of the Ganga but note that the river has changed to a holier avatar in my cousin's memory). One day, they climbed a tree to stay in hiding and escape attention. Soon it was dusk and Jagat Babu decided it was time for his *sandhya* puja (evening prayers). His compatriot warned him that this was not a good time for him to come out in the open, but he did—his evening prayers were part of a daily religious ritual that could not be compromised with under any circumstances, even an impending arrest. He got down from the tree, went to the shore of the Ganga, washed his feet and face, spread his *gamchha* under a tree and began his meditation and prayers. As expected, he caught the attention of a British patrol, and a soldier mounted on a horse came up to him and inquired, '*Tum Jagat Babu ko dekha hai?*' (in his anglicized Hindi, my cousin impersonated: 'Have you seen Jagat Babu?'). My grandfather shook his head in denial, with his eyes closed and still in meditative pose. The troops left, after which Jagat Babu must have made his way to Arrah.

Another story narrated by Jagat Narain Lal's daughter, Asha Sinha, was about how during the 1947 riots he disguised himself as a Muslim and tried to calm the community and douse the communal fires. But my favourite story is the one my chacha Sushil Chandra Lal, the youngest of Jagat Narain Lal's offsprings, narrated. As a young boy, he was accompanying his father from Patna to Ranchi (then the summer capital of Bihar and now the capital of Jharkhand state) sometime in the early years after Independence. Travelling along with Jagat Narain were Syed Mahmud (senior Congress leader and member of Krishna Sinha's Bihar Cabinet) and B.N. Azad (the editor of

The Indian Nation) among a few others that my uncle could not recall. The proximate environs of a train compartment led to many a conversation, one such being between Syed Mahmud and Jagat Babu that turned out to be an exegetical commentary on the Bhagavad Gita and the Quran. Interestingly, the expository roles were not as you would expect. It was Jagat Babu with his knowledge of Persian who expounded on the Quran, and it was Syed Mahmud with his knowledge of Sanskrit who held forth on the Bhagavad Gita. Much of the conversation was lost on the young child, but my chacha remembered a headline in the *Indian Nation* the next morning: 'Maulana Jagat Narain Lal debates with Pandit Syed Mahmud'.

Jagat Narain Lal's command over both Sanskrit and Persian was legendary. In his own memoir, *Light unto a Cell*, he narrates an incident from the first session of the Bihar Provincial Hindu Conference in Darbhanga in 1927. Swami Bharti Krishna Tirtha of Shardapith was addressing a large gathering in fluent Sanskrit. A Maharashtrian, who went by the name Barheji, known to have an intimate knowledge of Sanskrit, was translating the speech into Hindi. Jagat Babu found Barheji struggling with the translation and helped him out. He writes: 'My effort impressed the Pandits deeply; they appeared to be overawed by my erudition until I protested that it had only been God's infinite mercy that had carried me through, not any proficiency in Sanskrit.'[7]

Jagat Babu was a learned man with a deep interest in theology and philosophy. His writings and intellectual interests display a staggering repertoire and an impressive oeuvre. Tilak's *Gita Rahasya*, Aldous Huxley's *Ends and Means*, James Allen's *From Poverty to Power* (a treatise on how to find peace and contentment in the material world), Vivekananda, Tagore, Gandhi all became his sources of inspiration for spiritual and intellectual pursuits. In his memoir, he references the Mahabharat, Bhagavad Gita and

---

[7]　Lal, *Light unto a Cell*, p. 54.

Isha Upanishad among others. His writings reflect a similar range of interests—property theory, citizenship, religious rights, Advaita philosophy, *vidya* and *avidya*, reason, unreason and so on. It is personally overwhelming—the range of his interests and the reach of his intellect.

In Pratima Verma's memoir of Jagat Narain Lal, she mentions that during his various prison sojourns, he wrote seven book-length works:

- *Bharat Rashtra ki Avashyak Baatien*
- *Bharat ka Arthik Itihaas*
- *Bhartiya Nagrik Granthmala*
- *Hindu Samaj Darshan*
- *Hindu Dharm ki Pehli Pothi*
- *Light unto a Cell*
- *Jyotsna* (an anthology of poems)

I could not trace copies of these books. Barring *Light unto a Cell*, they may not even have been published, and the manuscripts are probably lost. But one does get a sense of his intent from his notebooks and diaries, which contain extensive notes, sometimes even chapters, perhaps from a draft manuscript, on the aforementioned topics. He wrote a forty-page tract challenging Alfred Marshall's classification of property and associated rights. His interventions in the Constituent Assembly debates on the right to religion (specifically on the right to propagate), citizenship, freedom of press, labour rights, linguistic reorganization, etc, illuminate the world of conflicting ideologies as well as of consensus building.

From the quest for spiritual knowledge, to the tendency towards personal introspection, his diaries and notes give us a glimpse of a man whose quest for self-realization and yearning for freedom, personal as well as political, was boundless. That said, Jagat Babu never quite managed to straddle the two boats of political and spiritual freedom with the depth of a Vivekananda or the wisdom of a Gandhi. His political journey remained conflicted and self-admittedly, riddled with many anxieties.

These memories are poignant even if they are not the most reliable indicator of 'facts' as they stand recorded in history. More often than not, memories are unstable and often unconsciously flawed. They tether somewhere to factual signposts but at the end of the day they are the living imagination of events and people as they once existed. As they re-centre a bygone universe, they re-create not so much the 'facts' as much as the *presence* of those times.

But memories are also significant for another reason: We stand today at the edge of living memories of the freedom movement. With all the participants dead, what remains of their experiences of upheaval, personal loss, trauma, sacrifice, generosity, courage, are diaries, notes, letters, poems and reflections. While freedom movements are complex, protracted events in history, shaping the destiny of something as large as a Nation, they also have within them many personal histories and stories that defy easy pigeon-holing and remonstrations. And small though this story might be, it is large enough for you to want to reopen those boxes into which our nationalist history has been neatly packed.

1

The Shaping of Nationalist Consciousness

This satyagraha is going to be more forceful, more dominant and more dynamic. We need to make ourselves stronger. We have nothing but our resolve to follow the path of Ahimsa and truth in both our deeds and thought.

—Jagat Narain Lal

Writing in 1946, Jagat Narain Lal says in his memoir: 'It was in December 1921, twenty-five years ago that I had the pleasure of becoming His Majesty's guest for the first time, with two other distinguished guests[1] that are alas no more . . . This was to be the beginning of a long and arduous journey through the thorny paths towards the ever-shining, ever-beckoning flag of the Temple of Freedom.'[2] The Prince of Wales was to visit Patna, and as both

---

[1] Late Khurshaid Hussnain and the late Krishna Prakash Sen Sinha; Lal, *Light unto a Cell* [hereafter LUC], p. 3.
[2] Lal, *LUC*, p. 1.

a representative and a symbol of imperial authority, he was to be greeted with hartals and boycotts sending a strong message, as Gandhi put it, of 'strong disapproval of all such efforts to bolster up a system which is tottering to its fall'.[3] Jagat Narain was at the forefront of the boycott of the prince's visit and that, coupled with his cheeky reply to the magistrate, landed him his first jail term. But I move ahead of myself; let me rewind a bit and trace Jagat Babu's journey till here and then from here.

Jagat Narain Lal was born on 21 July 1896 in a small mofussil town of Akhgaon in the district of Arrah, Bihar. His father, Bhagwat Prasad, had a railway job as a stationmaster which was transferable and took him to many places—Ghazipur and Gorakhpur (in the erstwhile United Provinces) finding a mention in Jagat Narain's diaries. In one of his diaries (undated), he fondly refers to his father being a combination of Kabir and Nanak, and his mother, Radhika Devi being a Krishna bhakta. To his parents, he writes, he owes his spiritual inclination, his attraction towards the mystic tradition and devotional spirit. Interestingly, in the same paragraph, Jagat Narain recounts that to the open fields of Ghazipur tehsil (where his father was posted) he owes his love of 'sport and exercise'. The spirit of devotion and pursuit of sports, the discipline of yoga, he writes, made him fearless—'Instead of the diffidence of the meek and submissive, I became fearless in nature.'[4]

Bhagwat Prasad and Radhika Devi had five sons all of whom received elementary education, like many other children of those times, from a maulvi who would come home. In those days, it was not unusual for children born in devout Hindu families to grow up amidst multiples cultural influences. As was the norm in then, Jagat Narain joined a formal school only much later in Gorakhpur

---

[3] *Young India*, 10 July 1921.
[4] Jagat Narain Lal, Private Papers (donated to NMML in 2019), NMML archives: Speeches and Writings, 2 (e), p. 2.

where his father had been posted. He showed great promise as a student. Not only was he a keen learner, but even as a young person, he had a strong moral sense that guided his actions. The story goes that he formed a club of a few students who together took a vow to never use unfair means in examinations.[5] Moved by this child's initiative and commitment, a teacher named Ganpati Rai hugged him and lauded his efforts, predicting that this child would grow up to be a *margdarshak* (pioneering leader).

Young Jagat Narain pursued his higher studies, first in the very reputed, more cosmopolitan Ewing Christian College, Allahabad. After graduating with a first division, he moved to the Allahabad University for his post-graduate studies in economics and law. His devotion to both sports and religion continued here too. He became the captain of the Frontier Club at Ewing Christian College and captain of the hockey team in the final year at Law College, Allahabad.

Unusual mates as they may seem, some form of physical training and religious practice have often cohabited quite naturally in many individuals. For Jagat Narain, sports became the means through which he sought to achieve a balance and unity of physical and mental energies. As Gavin Flood says, 'physical labour becomes the "spiritual core" of a well-ordered social life in so far as it provides the opportunity for transcendence through the individual facing and allowing him or herself to be subjected to the work regime'.[6] The discipline of the body entailed in sports, yoga the production of a bodily habit, is interestingly related to the acceptance of time and necessity.[7] Whatever the body and its social condition, the self finds a resolve to overcome the limited viewpoint of the present.

---

[5] Verma, *Jagat Narain Lal*, p.1.
[6] Flood, *The Ascetic Self*, p. 46.
[7] Weil, 'New York Notebook', *First and Last Notebooks*, p. 83.

So also with Jagat Narain. The 'physicality' of yoga and hockey combined, interestingly, with a growing commitment to social service. 'My spirit of social service', he writes, 'was awakened due to my contact with professors and Principal of the Ewing Christian College who worked with such missionary zeal and so much sacrifice despite being from a far-off country like America. Their zeal and sacrifice created a good deal of reaction in my mind, and I began to feel more and more that we should develop a similar missionary zeal for the propagation of our own Dharma.'[8]

From very early on one can discern that Jagat Narain's admiration for Christian missionaries for their spirit of sacrifice and service lay behind his own need to work for reform. It must have been 1914–15 when he made his first visit to the Kumbh Mela and met many *dharma-gurus* and scholars of religion. Among the many things that influenced him, what stirred him most were the speeches of Annie Besant, who too was camped at the Kumbh, propagating the cause of the Home Rule League movement and mobilizing support for it. The juxtaposition of two images—the multitudinous masses seeking salvation at the Kumbh and Annie Besant inspiring and recruiting people for political action—in a sense foregrounded what was to become Jagat Narain's core political quest. He would go on to fashion a self and a practice of politics that could simultaneously become a means of political freedom and religious regeneration.

Jagat Narain was still a student when he came under the influence of Madan Mohan Malaviya. Malaviya was mobilizing funds for establishing the Kashi Hindu Vishwavidyalaya (Banaras Hindu University). He joined a student group for collecting funds for the university. Lauded for his fund-mobilization efforts, he received a special mention at the inauguration of the Kashi Hindu Vishwavidyalaya in 1916, in the presence of many political

---

[8] Jagat Narain Lal, Private Papers, NMML archives: Speeches and Writings, 2 (e), p. 3.

luminaries including Motilal Nehru and Sarojini Naidu.[9] The Lucknow Congress in December of the same year was to infuse the air of Allahabad with a rush of patriotic fervour. Few remained unaffected by the desire to be associated with a cause as large as the freedom of the country. But for Jagat Narain, the association was to wait for another couple of years.

In 1917, Jagat Narain Lal got married to advocate Balmukund Sahai's daughter, Ram Pyari Devi. In 1918, he moved to Patna where he began his practice in the Patna High Court in the august company of Sir Ali Imam,[10] Syed Hasan Imam,[11] Sachchidanand Sinha,[12] and above all, Rajendra Prasad, who would go on to become the first president of the Indian republic. Under their mentorship, Jagat Narain soon began to make a name for himself. 'In my profession, I felt I was amply equipped for a brilliant career. Other junior lawyers were only overawed when they came face

---

[9] Verma, *Jagat Narain Lal*, p. 2.
[10] Sir Syed Ali Imam (1869–1932), a judge at Patna High Court in 1917, was a law member of the British Imperial Council who played an important part in the constitution of Bihar as a separate province and was conferred knighthood by the British government. A mausoleum for him was built in Patna in 1932.
[11] Syed Hasan Imam (31 August 1871–19 April 1933) was an Indian politician who served as the president of the Indian National Congress. He was regarded as British India's finest barrister by the likes of Chittaranjan Das (C.R. Das) and H.D. Bose.
[12] Sachchidanand Sinha (10 November 1871–6 March 1950) was a barrister, parliamentarian, journalist and member of the Imperial Legislative Council from 1910 to 1920, and member of the Indian Legislative Assembly where he served as the deputy president in 1921. He also held the office of the president in the Bihar and Orissa Legislative Councils. He was appointed executive councillor and finance member of the governments of Bihar and Orissa, the first Indian to be the finance member of a province. Later, he also was a member of the Bihar Legislative Assembly. He was named the interim president of the Constituent Assembly of India on 9 December 1946, but was replaced by Rajendra Prasad after indirect election on 11 December 1946.

to face with a senior lawyer; to me it was a privilege and joy to stand up to a capable senior member of the Bar during a case. And not infrequently did I carry the day against him.'[13] But just as Jagat Narain began making a name for himself as a lawyer, he was sucked into the national movement.

Rajkumar Shukla, who was spearheading the farmers' agitation against the *teenkhatiya* system (where a third of the farmland had to planted with indigo), had invited Gandhi to Champaran. On 10 April 1917, Gandhi came down, and with a small but committed band of local agitators and leaders—Sheikh Gulab, Harbans Sahay, Pir Mohammed Munsi, Sant Rawat Lomrah Singh and prominent layers including Rajendra Prasad, Brajkishore Prasad,[14] Mazharul Haque[15]—launched the Champaran satyagraha. This was, in a sense, India's first civil disobedience movement.

An entire country woke up to the efficacy and immense possibilities of a form of resistance that combined extra-constitutional struggle with the moral force of Ahimsa (non-violence) and Satyagraha (adherence to truth). What made it particularly ingenious was that it was deployed against an

---

[13] Lal, *LUC*, p. 5.

[14] Brajkishore Prasad (1877–1946) was a lawyer inspired by Mohandas Gandhi during the Indian independence movement. He met with Mahatma Gandhi in 1915 and was inspired. He decided to get involved full-time in the freedom struggle and gave up his legal practice. He was instrumental in Gandhi taking up the Champaran and Kheda Satyagraha, in which Gandhi handpicked Rajendra Prasad and Anugrah Narayan Sinha along with him to successfully lead the movement. Gandhi was so impressed by Prasad's dedication that he set aside a full chapter on him in his autobiographical book, *The Story of My Experiments with Truth*, called 'The Gentle Bihari'.

[15] Mazharul Haque was a lawyer who gave up his lucrative legal practice and his elected post as member of the Imperial Legislative Council and turned all his efforts to the freedom struggle. He actively participated in the Champaran Satyagraha for which he was sentenced to three months imprisonment.

adversary whose greatest strength lay in the rule of law and forceful repression. This new vocabulary of protest drew hordes of new supporters. Almost all prominent leaders of Bihar signed up for the Champaran satyagraha. The British government in Bihar responded with more repression and a more divisive agenda.

In 1917, the town of Shahabad (in Arrah district), home to Jagat Narain Lal for many years, saw gruesome and widespread riots. Pratima Verma reported that 'village after village was burnt and scorched down'.[16] She further recounts that in the mofussil town of Arrah, barbed wire had been used to enclose a space within which prisoners could be detained. To look into matters, a tribunal was set up. Stories of police atrocities and tribunal high-handedness spread further unrest and insecurity among people. Well known lawyer, Deshbandhu Chittaranjan Das jumped into the fray and argued in defence of many and secured their acquittal. It was here, in the context of the riots, that Jagat Narain Lal first met C.R. Das. Arrah was in the limelight for another reason. The Maharaja of Dumraon (a place very close to Arrah) filed the famous 'Burma Case' claiming possession of a 15,000-acre estate in Burma, which he stated had been purchased with his money. Many legal stalwarts—Srinivas Iyengar, Sri Vardachari, Motilal Nehru, N.N. Sarkar and Tej Bahadur Sapru—were involved in the case; that is how Jagat Narain ended up meeting and associating with them.

The Champaran satyagraha had brought Bihar under close watch of the nation. Meantime, the Home Rule League movement had spread to various parts of India, including Bihar. Patna, for some reason had shown only a tepid response. Not many people were keen to sign up or be openly associated with the Home Rule League. Only a few—Rajendra Prasad, Mazharul Haque, Brajkishore Prasad and Jagat Narain Lal among them—openly came forward. These small steps paved Jagat Narain's way to a larger involvement in the Non-cooperation movement—the beginning of a journey for which he

---

[16] Verma, *Jagat Narian Lal,* p. 3.

would have to forsake his careers, stake his family life and financial security to become a part of the Indian national movement.

Non-cooperation and Boycott

The years between 1918 and 1920 were a period of ferment. The economy was in the throes of the post-WWI crisis. The humiliation of the Rowlatt Act, the non-representative character of Montague Chelmsford Reforms and the massacre at Jallianwala Bagh had fomented discontent and mobilized masses into the fold of the national movement. Gandhi had drawn up a programme for satyagraha, in response to which people all over the country began to organize protest meetings and hartals.

Protests against the Rowlatt Act began in Bihar in early March 1919. Patna, Mungher, Gaya, Muzaffarpur, Chhapra and Bhagalpur witnessed a groundswell of resistance and nationalist fervour. Patna saw a ceremonial signing of the 'satyagraha *patra*'— Jagat Narain too, along with his senior compatriots, Rajendra Prasad, Mazharul Haque, Syed Hasan Imam and Purnendu Narain Sinha, became a signatory, formally announcing his induction in the mainstream national movement in Bihar. The *pratigya* (vow) was to stand against injustice, stand for truth and adhere to the principles of Ahimsa. The Indian biweekly newspaper, *The Searchlight*, carried extensive coverage and critique of the Rowlatt Act. From here also began the period of newspaper and printed material becoming an influential vector for the dissemination and spread of nationalism.[17] The cold-blooded massacre at Jallianwala Bagh in Punjab united the entire country, bringing Hindus and Muslims onto one platform. This was the time when a staunch Arya Samaji like Swami Shraddhanand, in what was a notable departure from the norm, addressed the masses from the steps of Delhi's Jama Masjid. The Khilafat Committee and the All India

---

[17] Datta, *History of the Freedom Movement in Bihar*, Vol.1, p. 313.

Congress Committee began working under a common leadership. The unity and feeling of oneness that the satyagraha call signalled was without precedent in British India. The many discontents coalesced, forming the socio-political basis for the launch of the Non-cooperation campaign in December 1920. With the Mahatma at the helm, the Congress denounced the British Montague–Chelmsford Reforms, stating that the constitutional concessions granted were woefully meagre and demanded that India be given Swaraj or self-rule. Non-cooperation, put simply, was an act of withdrawing cooperation from a state that, in the non-cooperator's view, had become corrupt. The idea behind it was simple yet potent. Refusal to cooperate would immobilize the British government that sustained itself only through the active or tacit acquiescence of Indian people. If cooperation and obedience were to cease, the British Empire in India would collapse. What seems like a popular idea that expanded the nationalist base and mobilized sections of masses, hitherto indifferent and excluded, went through its fair share of contestations and detractions. Apprehensions were expressed by an influential and vocal group within the Congress about what they essentially saw as a 'non-constitutional method', and this was echoed at the special session of Indian National Congress held at Calcutta (4–9 September 1920) under the presidentship of Lala Lajpat Rai. The momentous resolution on Non-cooperation was passed only after intense debates, discussions, and sometimes opposition by advocates of constitutionalism such as C.R. Das.[18]

In Bihar, the pressure for the launching of Non-cooperation movement had been building up much before it was officially

---

[18] This commitment to constitutional methods may have been a minority opinion and an unacknowledged strand of the Indian National Congress movement, and may have taken a backseat to the very popular and very effective strategies of civil disobedience and non-cooperation, but it was solid and enduring enough to resurface as a form of morality in the making of the Indian constitution.

decided by the Indian National Congress at the Nagpur session in December 1920. The Bihar Provincial Congress Committee (BPCC) approved of the principle of Non-cooperation for the redressal of national wrongs and decided to support the Khilafat movement at its meeting held on 31 July 1920 at the *Searchlight* office in Patna.[19] However, many senior leaders of the BPCC such as Sachchidanand Sinha and Syed Hasan Imam, who were strong believers in the constitutional methods of struggle, opposed the resolution expressing their strong doubts and apprehensions about the strategy of launching such a movement. The resolution could only be passed with the support of students and other members, and that too only when these senior members 'withdrew from the meeting in disgust'.[20]

Again, at the meeting of the BPCC held in Bhagalpur on 28–29 August 1920, Rajendra Prasad, who was presiding over the conference, had to make a strong plea for the approval of the Non-cooperation movement. It was only with the support of the large peasant participation who were attending the conference for the first time,[21] that the resolution was passed.[22]

The Non-cooperation programme envisaged the following: resignation from all government posts and positions, civil disobedience and boycott of courts, government schools, government functions, ceremonies and other government institutions and associations. Paralysing the government machinery seemed like the first step in dismantling a regime that was perceived as unjust and cruel, and that had lost its moral

---

[19] *Searchlight*, 4 August 1920.
[20] Fortnightly Report of Bihar and Orissa for the first half of August 1920, Government of India, Home Department (Political) File no. 111/1920, NAI: AICC Papers, File no. 1920, Part II. Quoted from Datta, *History of the Freedom Movement in Bihar*, Vol.1, p. 307.
[21] This was the first time that delegates other than those from professional classes attended the conference.
[22] *Searchlight*, 3 September 1920.

legitimacy to rule and govern. In Bihar, stalwarts like Mazharul Haque, Rajendra Prasad, Gorakh Prasad, Brajkishore Prasad, Babu Dharnidhar, Md. Shafi and others responded and withdrew their candidature from the forthcoming Council elections.[23] or Jagat Narain, it meant giving up his law practice, which was his main source of livelihood needed to support his own wife and children as well as the extended family.

In the last couple of years, Jagat Narain Lal had established his law practice, bought a house and had been sponsoring the education of two nephews who were staying with him. His father was a railway officer, elder brother was a munsif and the remaining two brothers were also in salaried service. His father-in-law was a well-known lawyer in Gorakhpur. It was not uncommon in those days for members of joint and extended families to be financially interdependent. Despite the shelter of a joint family, to give up one's source of income on which the livelihood of one's family depended could not have been an easy decision. This was not just Jagat Narain's personal problem, but a concern shared by almost all those who were taking the plunge into the Non-cooperation movement. An informal meeting of lawyers was convened at Rajendra Prasad's residence. Among those who attended were Brajkishore Prasad, Mazharul Haque, Gorakh Prasad, Jagat Narain Lal and a few others. It was a gathering to assess each person's financial status, discuss the minimum financial support required (in the absence of their law practice), whether personal wealth and property could fulfil that requirement and so on. Jagat Narain confessed that his financial status and family property were not of the kind that could take care of his family expenses.[24]

In the midst of this predicament and inner turmoil, Jagat Narain came across a pamphlet written by Vitthalbhai Patel, titled

---

[23] See Datta, *History of the Freedom Movement in Bihar*, Vol. 1, pp. 342–343.
[24] Verma, *Narain Lal*. p. 7.

'Non Violent Non-Cooperation in Austria-Hungary'.[25] A reading of this pamphlet erased any doubts he may have had about the efficacy of Non-cooperation as a strategy. He decided to give up his law practice[26] and become a satyagrahi. Two prominent lawyers of Bihar— Gangadhar Das and Md. Hussnain—tried to dissuade him, impressing upon him that his future as a barrister of law was bright. But he had made up his mind by now and resolved to become a part of the Indian National Movement.

Nationalist Education: Jagat Narain Lal Joins as Faculty

Bihar's response to the Non-cooperation movement was noteworthy. Gandhi's short visit to this province in December 1920 not only spread the nationalist fervour but also imbued people with the quintessential Gandhian spirit of renunciation. It was in Bihar that Gandhi announced his programme of triple boycott—boycott of foreign goods, boycott of law courts and boycott of government-controlled colleges and schools—laying the greatest emphasis on

---

[25] Jagat Narain Lal, Private Papers (donated to NMML).
[26] Confidential Report Bihar Special Branch, 8 March 1921, Memo No.3530/36 S.B Pol. Dept. Spl. Section File No. 117(1921) pp. 3530/36 S.B. According to the confidential records, the following lawyers had suspended their practice in Patna:
1. Mazharul Haque, Bar-at-law Patna High Court
2. Rajendra Prasad, MA, BL
3. Anugrah Narayan Singh, MA, BL
4. Baranasi Prasad Jhun Jhunwala, MA, BL
5. R.K.L. Nandkeo, first year
6. Chandra Bans Sahay, Bar-at-law, Patna
7. Maulavi Muhammad Yasin, BL, Judge's Court, Patna
8. Bajrang Sahay, Bar-at-law
9. Jagat Narain Lal, MA, LLB, pleader Judge's Court, Patna
10. Ambica Parsad, Bar-at-law
11. Bipin Bihari Varma, Bar-at-law, Patna High Court

the last.[27] Calling upon the students to withdraw from schools and colleges, Gandhi had strongly advocated setting up an alternative in the form of national colleges for students who would withdraw from British-run colleges and institutions of higher learning. In *Young India* dated 11 August 1920, Gandhi wrote: 'Without vacant schools, there is no sacrifice; if we are not capable of formulating an education system fully independent of the government control, there is no justification of Non-cooperation.'[28] Bihar rose to this call: imbued with the spirit of new patriotism, hordes of students deserted schools and colleges in Patna, Muzaffarpur, Bhagalpur and Mungher to support the national movement.

The call for boycott of government schools and colleges spread to many institutions in Patna and other towns of Bihar.[29] In order to start an alternative teaching programme, a large house was taken on rent in the Bakerganj mohalla in Patna. Everyone knew that this was at best a make-shift arrangement that could accommodate only a few students and that was not adequate. Rajendra Prasad, who was then suffering from an asthma attack had retreated to his home in Chhapra to recuperate. From there he wrote a letter to Jagat Narain directing him to take up a larger house on rent. With Badrinath Verma's help, Jagat Narain found a suitable house, known as '*Babu Lal ki Kothi*' on the Patna–Gaya road for an annual rent of Rs 3,600.[30] It was in this rented house that a national college was started on 5 January 1921 with Rajendra Prasad as principal and Badrinath Varma as vice principal. Other teaching staff included Prem Sundar Bose (philosophy), Jagat Narain Lal

---

[27] Datta, *History of the Freedom Movement in Bihar*, Vol. 1, p. 309.

[28] *Young India*, 11 August 1920. Also see, Ahmad, *Sadaqat Ashram*, pp. 29–30.

[29] For instance, 'the non-cooperators succeeded to a great extent in generating a "considerable amount of unrest" in the educational institutions in the Patna and Tirhut Division.' Singh, *Popular Translations of Bihar*, 2012, p. xx.

[30] Verma, *Jagat Narain Lal*, p. 8.

(economics), Phuldeva Sahaya Verma (chemistry), Moulavi Abdul Bari, Pandit Ram Nirikshan Singh (Sanskrit), Moulavi Tamanna and Krishna Ballabh Sahay.[31] The same subjects were taught in this college as in government-aided colleges. The expenses of the college were met with the amount collected for national colleges during Gandhi's Champaran visit.[32] The Mahatma had given them the much-needed impetus by placing at their disposal 'seven or eight thousand rupees then collected by him in Bihar' for this purpose.[33] The nationalists were sending a message to the British and demonstrating both their academic ability and their financial capacity to run institutions of higher education.

A very significant and dramatic incident happened around this time which led to the establishment of the Bihar Vidyapith in the premises of Patna's Sadaqat Ashram. If a memoir of the Sadaqat Ashram were to be written, this would feature among its most poignant and momentous stories. A large group of engineering students from the Bihar School of Engineering, responding to Gandhi's call for Non-cooperation, left their school with their belongings and flying flags, and came to Mazharul Haque for guidance. They went to him because, as Ayde puts it, 'Haque was not a leader who believed only in giving suggestions and lectures. He was like a soldier who believe[d] in practical demonstration.'[34] Haque rose to the occasion, left his own luxurious and well-furnished residence at Sikandar Manzil and marched with youthful comrades to an orchard at Digha on Patna–Danapur road.[35] With the help of students, Haque got a school building and some sheds constructed over a plot of land donated by one Khairu Mian. Within a few days, this place became a hub of Gandhian "constructive work"

---

[31] Raza, "Mazaharul Haque", *Proceedings of the Indian History Congress*, p. 707.
[32] Ibid.
[33] Prasad, *Mahatma Gandhi and Bihar*, p. 43.
[34] Ayde, *The Message of Ashiana*, p. 26.
[35] Ibid., p.26.

and nationalist activity. Haque named this new place as 'Sadaqat Ashram' (Abode of Truth), symbolizing both in its nomenclature and in its vision the coming together of two religious identities.[36] What began as few sheds and temporary hutments serving as classrooms on the premises of the Sadaqat Ashram, evolved into a national university, the Bihar Vidyapith.[37] Mazharul Haque was appointed chancellor, Badrinath Verma vice chancellor and Rajendra Prasad was appointed as registrar.[38] Teachers and lecturers from other parts of Bihar tendered their resignations to take up faculty positions at the Vidyapith. For example, Prem Sunder Bose, who was a professor of philosophy and the principal of Bhagalpur's T.N. Jubilee College, came to head the philosophy department at Bihar Vidyapith. Maulana Abdul Bari (history), Ram Charit Singh (science), Badrinath Verma (who later became the minister for education) and Krishna Vallabh Sahay (English), Jagatrai Prasad (Sanskrit) and Jagat Narain Lal (economics) were some of the other professors who joined the Vidyapith faculty. A monthly salary of Rs 125 was fixed but seldom did the professors draw their whole salary. Jagat Babu could not forgo the entire amount but settled for a

---

[36] Raza, "Mazaharul Haque", *Proceedings of the Indian History Congress*, pp. 708. He writes that 'Sadaqat' is a Persian word meaning truth and Ashram is a Sanskrit word meaning place. Thus, Sadaqat Ashram is a place where truth does reside.

[37] *The Searchlight* reported the inaugural ceremony of the Vidyapith: 'The opening ceremony of Bihar National University (Bihar Vidyapith) was performed on Sunday the 6th of February [1921] with great eclat by Mahatma Gandhi [and] Maulana Md. Ali...' *Searchlight*, 9 February 1921. The objective of the Bihar Vidyapith was to act an apex university body that was to coordinate, control and regulate the activities of various other nationalist schools and colleges. Report of the Bihar Vidyapith. In Datta, *History of the Freedom Movement in Bihar*, Vol. 1, p. 332.

[38] Raza, "Mazharul Haque", *Proceedings of the Indian History Congress*, Vol. 70, pp. 705–712.

monthly salary of Rs 100, while Rajendra Prasad opted to work pro bono.[39]

Jagat Narain Lal held master's degrees in both law and economics. His jail diaries are replete with notes on property, nature of public property, taxation, finance and so on. The Gandhian vision of 'nationalist education' coincided both with his expertise and his plan to boycott the law courts. Since the law itself had become a tool of repression, as demonstrated by the Rowlatt Act, Jagat Narain resigned from his post as the 'pleader in Judge's Court, and joined the National College and *Bihar Vidyapith* as a teacher of economics'.[40] During this time, Jagat Narain's first-born son died of small pox. His wife's relatives took her away to stay at her parental home for some time. Left alone and all by himself, he packed his books and household things, left them at a friend's place, vacated his home and began staying on the premises of the national college. He started looking after the day-to-day functioning of both the college and the hostel.

Bihar Congress: Jagat Narain Lal's Growing Influence

Jagat Narain Lal was young and a relatively new entrant into politics. He had given up his legal practice in December 1920, but guided by Rajendra Prasad, continued to appear for those cases already under litigation. The courts had started remaining closed for long periods so even with a few pending cases, it became possible for Jagat Narain to devote himself fully to party meetings, conventions and campaigns. As a good orator who was widely read,[41] he started making a mark for himself and soon

---

[39] Verma, *Jagat Narain Lal*, p. 9.
[40] Confidential Report Bihar Special Branch, 8 March 1921, Memo No. 3530/36 S.B. Pol. Dept. Spl. Section File No. 117 (1921), pp. 3530/36 S.B.
[41] Besides his interest in Western and Indic philosophies, Jagat Narain Lal's notes reveal his interest in population studies, citizenship and geographies of the world.

emerged as an influential leader in Bihar. On one occasion, when he accompanied Mazharul Haque to Lai gram in the Danapur division, he was also to give a speech at Sonepur, which was in the same division as his own village. Friends, family, clients and students from nearby villages came in large numbers to hear and support one of their own.[42]

In addition to housing the Bihar Vidyapith, a part of the premises of Sadaqat Ashram also functioned as an office for the Bihar Congress. It became a repository for Congress papers and communication and a meeting place from where the programmes of the freedom movement were planned and launched. When the Non-cooperation movement began, the BPCC was reconstituted and in place of Sachchidanand Sinha, Mazharul Haque was appointed its president. Brajkishore Prasad and Md. Shami became vice presidents, and Rajendra Prasad was the appointed minister. Jagat Narain Lal's name was considered as a joint minister, but it was felt that it would affect his work at Bihar Vidyapith where he had begun teaching economics. He continued to remain a member of the BPCC, but in the interest of his commitment to the Vidyapith, he did not accept any formal post in the committee.

Jagat Narain soon became an indispensable part of the Patna city and district Congress set-up. He did the hard organizational work of going to the interiors, setting up Congress organizational units and reviving existing units. Names and addresses of lawyers who had renounced their legal practice, as per the Nagpur Resolution (1920), were also being collected and responsibilities assigned to them. Md. Khurshaid Hussnain from Patna; Krishna Prakash Sen Sinha and Mukutdhari Prasad from Gaya; Zakariya Hussain Hashmi from Chhapra; Gorakh Prasad from Motihari; Deep Narain Singh from Bhagalpur; Krishna Sinha and Namdhari Singh from Mungher; Atulchandra Ghosh from

---

[42] Verma, *Jagat Narain Lal*, p. 8.

Purulia; Ram Narain Sinha and Bajrang Sahai from Hazaribagh; zamindar Sheikh Saheb from Palamu; Puran Chandra Mishra from Ranchi; Nivarchandra Dasgupta from Manbhumi; Shashi Bhushan Rai and Vinod Anand from Santhal Pargana; and Punyanand from Purnia were some of the *karyakartas* who were recruited by Jagat Narain.[43]

By April 1921, the Non-cooperation campaign was beginning to take a new shape. Concerns were rife not just about the efficacy and capacity of the movement and boycott to sustain itself, but also about the peasant upsurge and its potential to exacerbate class contradictions between peasants and zamindars. Rajendra Prasad expressed this apprehension unequivocally in the Bezwada (Madras Presidency) session of the Congress in April 1921. He said that lawyers in Bihar had not fully accepted the doctrine of civil disobedience and abandoned their practice. Unless the lawyers did so, he said, 'the masses, if aroused, would be without leaders'.[44] Without leaders, he feared, mass activity and revolutionary temper would be directed against their landlords, causing bloodshed and justifying government intervention, resulting in the complete suppression of the movement.[45]

Along with civil disobedience, the Non-cooperation movement in Bihar also incorporated a 'constructive programme' of introducing charkhas, building up Congress membership and collecting money for the all-India Tilak *Swarajya* fund.[46] Boycott of foreign cloth and the production of khaddar became important features of the Non-cooperation movement. Besides this,

---

[43] Ibid., pp. 9–10.
[44] Bihar and Orissa Political Special File no. 178/1921, "Copy forwarded to all Superintendent of Police from 2nd Assistant to the D.I.G. of Police, Crime and Railway, 6 April 1921".
[45] Ibid.
[46] For details see Brown, *Gandhi's Rise to Power*, p. 313.

it was decided to observe 6 April to 13 April (1921)—the second anniversary of the infamous Rowlatt Act and brutal Jallianwala Bagh massacre respectively—as 'Satyagraha Week'. Along with Mazharul Haque and Chandrabansi Sahai, Jagat Narain Lal became one of the signatories of Satyagraha Week.[47]

During this week, all business was to be suspended, all shops were to be closed, *roza* and *vrat* (fasts) were to be observed, and prayers for attaining Swaraj to be offered in temples and mosques. The programme gave a sacred aura to Satyagraha week.[48] In Bihar, notices for the observation of Satyagraha week were printed and distributed in various places. On 4 April, to further build momentum up, just before the Satyagraha week was to commence, Jagat Narain Lal spoke passionately at a public meeting. He said:

'This satyagraha is going to be more forceful, more dominant and more dynamic. We need to make ourselves stronger. We have nothing but our resolve to follow the path of Ahimsa and truth in both our deeds and thoughts. We have not gathered here to understand the meaning and content of Swaraj or to decide whether we want it or not. We have gathered here to be firm in our conviction and resolve to make the Non-cooperation movement a success.'[49] In speech after speech he stressed that the Non-cooperation movement was a form and expression of Gandhian satyagraha. He explained that while satyagraha meant following the path of truth and removal of injustice, the aim of Non-cooperation was to enable freedom, to disable colonial laws and seek freedom from bondage. This was an unprecedented hartal. The elite and the wealthy of the

---

[47] *Searchlight*, 6 April 1921; Bihar and Orissa Political Special File no. 173/1921,

[48] *Searchlight*, 6 April 1921.

[49] Verma, *Jagat Narain Lal*, p. 11.

city, students, shopkeepers, peasants, farmers, government officials, all struck work. As Pratima Verma writes, it seemed as if a surge of electric current had flowed through Patna and the neighbouring villages.[50]

By this time Jagat Narain had moved to the forefront of the boycott and Swadeshi programme of the Indian National Congress (INC). A meeting at Delhi had authorized 'every province on its own responsibility, to undertake civil disobedience, including non-payment of taxes'.[51] In order to put into effect this national programme of civil disobedience, Jagat Narain mobilized his students and party workers, and began his tours to the interiors of Bihar. On one such occasion, he had an unpleasant experience. He realized that it was not just the British against whose imperial authority people had to rise up to; the fight was equally against the zamindars who had been co-opted as allies of the British. From the beginning, writes Verma, they were collaborators of the British and exercised a great deal of power and influence, thanks to the British patronage.[52] In the jurisdiction of the Paliganj thana lay the large zamindaris of Sehda and Bharatpur. Responding to the 'boycott' call of the Congress, when the local shopkeepers observed hartal and put their shutters down, the zamindar of Bharatpur not only threatened them but also made them sign 'bail bonds', something that was clearly beyond the zamindar's remit.[53] Jagat Narain, who was called to intervene, went there with Mazharul Haque, to counter the zamindar's threats, to allay fears and motivate the people to stand up to the atrocities of the British and their allies.

---

[50] Ibid., p. 5.
[51] Datta, *History of the Freedom Movement in Bihar*, Vol. 1, p. 397.
[52] Verma, *Jagat Narain Lal*, p. 13.
[53] Ibid.

Prince of Wales' Visit and Jagat Babu's First Arrest

Of all his early interventions, Jagat Narain's boycott call against the Prince of Wales' visit to India in November 1921 was reported widely. It was originally proposed that His Royal Highness, the Prince of Wales, would formally inaugurate the new legislature and the reform scheme of 1919 in India, both at the centre and in the provinces. The All India Congress Committee (AICC) had already passed a boycott resolution on 28 July 1921,[54] following which Bihar joined the fray. A series of meetings that were held in various parts of Bihar (including the very important meeting of the BPCC in early October 1921 in Arrah under the presidentship of Md. Shafi) supported the resolutions adopted by the AICC.

On this occasion, a special meeting of persons interested in the *Seva Samiti* movement was convened. A strong central committee was formed (with Mahendra Prasad as the president and Jagat Narain Lal as one of the secretaries) pledging to do social service in the districts of Tirhut and Patna divisions, Bhagalpur, Mungher Manbhum and Hazaribagh.[55] The BPCC convention importantly passed a resolution against the Sifton Circular,[56] a resolution in favour of Swadeshi work and propaganda, and also a resolution

---

[54] The AICC resolved that 'it is the duty of everyone to refrain from participating in or assisting in any functions organized officially or otherwise in connection with his visit'. Sitaramayya, *History of the Indian National Congress*, Vol. I, p. 215.

[55] Datta, *History of the Freedom Movement in Bihar*, Vol. 1, p. 392.

[56] On 9 February 1921, J. D. Sifton, Secretary to government, financial department, had issued a circular according to which the officers of the excise department were instructed 'at once to report to the local Magistrates all cases where shops are being picketed and ask for their assistance in preventing restraint and intimidation in order that the excise sales should have a fair chance of success when they are held next month.' For details see, Ibid., p. 378–379.

proposed by Jagat Narain for boycotting the impending visit of the Prince of Wales.[57] The resolution stated:

> That in the event of the British Government persisting in bringing to India His Royal Highness the Prince of Wales against the wishes of the people, to strengthen its disappearing prestige and its policy in the eyes of the people, this meeting of the Bihar Provincial Congress Committee supports the resolutions adopted by the All-India Congress Committee in pursuance of the policy of Non-Co-operation and it further requests the people of the Province not to take part in any party or procession or festivities on the occasion of visit of His Royal Highness the Prince of Wales.[58]

Jagat Narain made a similar call at a public meeting held in Patna's Gulab Bagh in early November to ensure that the boycott of the Prince of Wales' Patna visit was effective. Khurshaid Hussnain and Sriprakash Sen also made speeches and exhorted the people to observe 17 November, when the Prince was due to land in Bombay, as a day of complete hartal.

The presence of royal patronage, no matter how ostensibly benign, was deeply symbolic of imperial subjugation. As Gandhi had expressed it: 'India will refuse to welcome a representative of a system of which she is sick unto death . . . In my humble opinion, the projected visit will be an insult added to injury. And it will be duty of every Non-Co-operator, respectfully but firmly and in no unmistakable manner, to express his strong disapproval of all such efforts to bolster up a system which is tottering to its fall'.[59]

The entire nation observed a day of hartal and boycott on 17 November, putting the colonial government on notice. Under the

---

[57] *Searchlight*, 11 November 1921.

[58] Datta, *History of the Freedom Movement in Bihar*, Vol. 1, p. 383.

[59] *Young India*, 10 July 1921.

watch of Jagat Narain and many other stalwarts, the strike achieved its desired objective of total shutdown. In one instance, Jagat Babu led a group of 400 *sevak dal* volunteers at the Sonepur Mela. Speaking of the Sonepur fair, Babu Nirsu Narayan Sinha stated in the Bihar and Orissa Legislative Council: 'I do not believe that it is due to the duress used by the Non-Co-operators, that hartal was observed in Patna and in other places in the Province. I may tell you, Sir, of my own experience on the 17th of November. I was in the Sonepur Fair and I made it a point to make enquiries from shop-keepers if they were going to observe hartal on account of any duress from the Non-Co-operators. But my enquiry showed that they were willing to do it; they said that "if other people were making sacrifices, they would also make some sacrifice by closing their shops for a day".'[60]

The prince was to visit Patna on 22–23 December. A meeting of the BPCC was held on 27 November, where arrangements in view of Prince of Wales' impending visit were considered. Preparations had been proceeding everywhere for observing a hartal throughout the province on that day, and at this meeting, the leaders decided upon taking all possible precautions to prevent disturbances in that connection.[61] It was at its meeting, that the BPCC, following instructions of the Congress Working Committee, also formed the Bihar National Volunteer Corps (Qaumi Sevak Dal) 'out of the members of the Seva Samitis, Khilafat workers and Congress workers from the whole Province.'[62] When the fixed time came the hartal was observed in a perfectly peaceful manner at all places in the province. The official report asserted that the hartal on this

---

[60] Speech of Babu Firsu Narayan Sinha in the Bihar and Orissa Legislative Council on 25 January 1922. Quoted from Datta, *History of the Freedom Movement in Bihar*, Vol. 1, p. 400.
[61] 'Non-Co-operation and Khilafat Movements in Bihar and Orissa', Government of Bihar and Orissa, 1925, p. 82.
[62] Ibid, p. 79.

occasion was not incidental and called it a strike that had been
'carefully organised beforehand'.[63]

In response, the government unleashed a series of repressive
measures, declaring the Khilafat and Congress volunteers, sevak
dal, volunteer corps and other similar bodies 'unlawful' under
Section 16 of the Indian Criminal Law Amendment Act. Thus
ensued, writes historian K.K. Datta, a period of intensive repression
and countrywide arrests of prominent leaders including Lajpat
Rai, C.R. Das, Motilal Nehru, Abul Kalam Azad, Jawaharlal
Nehru, etc. From Bihar, Khurshaid Hussnain, Mazharul Haque
and Jagat Narain Lal were among those arrested on the charge
of unlawful speech and disrupting public order. None of them
contested the charges, but when Jagat Narain was called upon to
record his statement in front of Magistrate Johnston, he, much
like a precocious student of Gandhi would have, said: 'As a fellow
human, I can only see you with love. But to you as a government
magistrate, I can only express my complete indifference. You are
an instrument of the very same government that has incarcerated
us under false pretexts and charges. What justice can I ever expect
from you?'[64]

Jagat Narain's cheekiness landed him with a greater sentence
than his fellow offenders. The magistrate sentenced him to two
years, Khurshaid Hussnain to one year and Krishna Prakash Sen
to six months in jail. Later, thanks to pressure from the Bihar
Council, their sentences were reviewed by High Court and all
were commuted to six months.

* * *

---

[63] Letter from H.D. Craik, Government of India, Home Department,
Political, addressed to E.L.L. Hammond, Chief Secretary to the
Government of Bihar and Orissa, 19 December 1921, Political Special,
Conf. File No. 643/1921; Datta, *History of the Freedom Movement in
Bihar*, Vol. 1, p. 399.
[64] Verma, *Jagat Narain Lal*, p. 15.

From here on begins his journey on what he calls the 'thorny path of freedom'. What was to make his path 'thorny' from here on was this: In seeking freedom for one's self, and simultaneously for the nation; in seeking solace in the redemptive potential of Hinduism, but politicizing it for political goals; in articulating the politics of both the Indian National Congress (hereafter Congress) and the Hindu Mahasabha, Jagat Narain became a repository of many conflicting strands of Indian nationalism. But neither the conflict nor the reasons were his alone. Like many others of his times, who embodied multiple idioms of nationalism, Jagat Narain Lal traverses the intersecting and competing terrain of nationalism—the ascetic, the Hindu nationalist, the anti-colonial and the civic routes. The book from here on reflects his journey through the conceptual and political labyrinth of Indian nationalism.

2

The Fashioning of an Ascetic Nationalist

Indian nationalist practices of almost all political and ideological hues, adopted the ethic of asceticism as a mode of both defying imperial subjugation as also of refashioning the self in relation to the nation. While the idiom of these ascetic practices usually correlated with the unsettling and remaking of the old self, it was not uncommon to find references to ascetic practice as also a vitally active, rational and political force—the Bhagavad Gita principle of karma yoga (righteous action) being a manifestation of that idea.[1] The tradition of ascetic practices became aligned with an idea of duty to a higher self or entity, like the nation for instance, of selfless action, of sacrifice and renunciation of desires. It became an endeavour to know the extent to which it might be

---

[1] In an incisive reconstruction of early Christian practices, philosopher Michel Foucault has described 'ascesis' as a means of disciplining or even remaking the self. He shifted the focus from external ascetic practices to 'technologies of the self', or 'decentering the self'. Foucault, "Technologies of the Self" in *Ethics: Subjectivity and Truth*, Vol. 1, pp. 223–251.

possible to think differently instead of legitimating what already exists or is known.

For many nationalists (Gandhi being a prime example), ascetic practice became a fundamentally destabilizing deed which had the power to defy both colonial knowledge and rule. In 'sacrificing' themselves for the cause of the nation, nationalists fashioned a sort of 'counter-performance', insofar as they attempted to resist the moral authority of colonial consciousness and rule.[2] Jagat Narain Lal was no exception. In the formation of his ascetic will lay a larger story of ascetic self-fashioning—a practice and a will that shaped and has continued to shape nationalist morality.

Suffering

I was just a gaunt, emaciated person, full of inexplicable fancies.[3]

Jagat Babu spent more than eight years in jail over a period of two decades, starting the winter of 1921 when he was at the forefront of a movement to boycott the visit of Prince of Wales.[4] In a diary entry dated 7 May 1942, he wrote, 'Today marks approximately twenty years of a jail journey I began in Buxar. It was within the precincts of the Buxar jail that my inner eye woke up to the joys of knowledge and the divine experience of bhakti gyan.'[5] For most of these times, Jagat Babu recorded memories in the form of notes or diary entries.

---

[2] For a discussion see, Francesco Tava, "Sacrifice as a Political Problem", *Metodo*, Vol. 6, p. 72, 71–96.

[3] Lal, *LUC*, p. 31.

[4] The Bihar Provincial Conference met at Arrah early in October 1921, under the presidentship of Maulavi Muhammad Shafi. Here the resolution of the Karachi conference was endorsed, and a resolution was passed to boycott the visit of the Prince of Wales. Datta, *History of the Freedom Movement in Bihar*, Vol. 1, p. 432.

[5] Jagat Narain Lal, Private Papers, NMML, Speeches and Writings. 2(f). Translated from Hindi (henceforth translated).

These jail diaries and notebooks not just retrace the steps of India's freedom struggle but also reveal the depth of un-freedom and suffering endured by freedom fighters like him. The rationing of water, soap, paper, oil for lighting lamps; the darkness, the stench and suffocation of dark prison cells; the claustrophobia of solitary cells; prolonged bouts of stomach ailments and illnesses; severance from domestic life and absence at the time of illness, childbirth or death in the family are not dramatic tales of torture and inhuman treatment, but slow, dreary tales of confinement, deprivation and prolonged cycles of bodily and psychological depletion.

Jagat Narain's jail journey began with the eagerness and first flush of a freedom fighter. Soon after the twenty-five-year-old entered the Patna district jail in 1921 with his two companions—M. Khurshaid Hussnain and Krishnaprakash Sen Sinha—he wrote, 'We were served with ordinary jail diet in model iron dishes and experienced the first strange thrill of tasting it. Locked up in one of the barracks early evening without any books or papers, we had to pass our time in chatting and singing, or rather *trying* to sing, till we fell asleep'[6]

But life in prison has little room for such lightness of being. An unexpected turn of events in the summer of 1922, when he was shifted from the barracks to a solitary cell, dramatically altered things for him. His personal relationship with the jail authorities, thus far marked by courtesy on either side, changed abruptly. 'It was summer and the heat was intolerable', Jagat Narain narrates. 'On that particular day matters took a turn for the worse. In the heated exchanges that followed, the assistant jailor got angry and threatened that he would have the inmates locked up by sweepers. The threat, it was evident, was based on how repugnant the idea of being touched by an untouchable would be for higher caste Hindus.'[7] Jagat Narain, who had arrived on the scene after

---

[6] Lal, *LUC*, p. 3.
[7] Ibid., p. 14

hearing loud, agitated voices, replied with insolent calm that 'we as followers of Gandhiji saw no difference between him [the jailor] and a sweeper and would not in the least mind being locked up by sweepers'.[8]

This, he writes in his memoir, annoyed the assistant jailor very much. Jagat Narain was charged with aggression and abusive language, and punished by being shifted from the barracks to a solitary cell. He wondered what it referred to and enquired how it was that he was charged with abusing the assistant jailor. 'For, as a gentleman and the political prisoner belonging to the Gandhian category, I would not brook the charge of abusing anybody . . . my sense of self-respect and the soldier's spirit in me revolted against this suggestion and I asked them to lead me to the cell without any further discussion.'[9]

From here on began Jagat Narain's journey of spiritual and intellectual quest and ascetic practices. There is bound to be a bond, as Nietzsche proposes, between renunciation and intellectual pursuits. A certain asceticism, he proposes, is one of the most favourable conditions for highest intellectualism. He goes on to say that so strong is this connection that there should be no 'surprise at the philosophers in always treating the ascetic ideal with a certain amount of predilection'.[10]

Jagat Babu's story bears out this bond. Soon after he was moved to solitary confinement, he wrote: 'The solitude for which I had been longing was thus arranged for me by the hidden hand of destiny in the shape of this solitary cell given to me as punishment. Here was that solitude in all its plentitude.'[11] With not even a lamp to light the dark cell, and a limited supply of mustard oil, the problem that confronted Jagat Babu most was how to read in

---

[8] Ibid., p. 15.
[9] Ibid., p. 16.
[10] Neitzsche, *The Genealogy of Morals*, p. 143.
[11] Ibid., p. 17.

the dark. At intervals, he read the Gita, *Gitarahasaya*, and a few speeches of Swami Rama Tirath from one of the Hindi booklets he had carried with him. These along with *Isha*, *Chandogaya*, *Kena*, *Mundaka* and *Mundakya Upanishad*s became the texts that helped shape Jagat Narain to fashion a renunciatory self. In that ascetic ideal, he not only found his faith, but also sought new way of purposing himself. In the profound cultural crisis of those times, vitiated by the unprincipled policies and 'modern' life-worlds of the colonial masters, Jagat Narain grappled with questions of identity, religious subjectivity and how 'the self' could be historically reconstituted.

Life in a solitary cell was hard. The romance and the glory associated with becoming a political prisoner soon made way for a body that weakened and depleted in oppressive prison conditions. He often complained of his deteriorating health. 'The heat before the rains set was intense and unbearable . . . I had given up pranayama and steadily my health deteriorated considerably. And now life in this cell during a spell of excessive heat, without any opportunity to exercise in the open air or meeting my fellow prisoners, coupled with the unsatisfactory jail diet, put such an unbearable strain upon it that it broke down completely.'[12]

The pathologies of an imprisoned body are often not recorded for one may be squeamish about divulging graphic details. But not so for Jagat Narain Lal. Over weeks, in the margins of a daily diary, he writes, almost like a refrain—*pet gadbad* (stomach upset). He complains of fever, belching, 'reaching the climax of dyspepsia and constipation', 'burning sensation while passing urine and stool'; he writes of his experiments with Louis Kuhne's system (possibly inspired by Gandhi who was known to practise this system) of water cure to relieve him of the agony, of medicines not being made available in jail, of bouts of fasting, of eliminating pulses

---

[12] Lal, *LUC*, p. 18.

from his diet, and complains often about losing weight, appearing gaunt, emaciated, frail, etc.[13]

'No care was however taken of me. I was never examined by a jail doctor or the Superintendent, nor was I provided with any medicine or diet suited to my medical condition . . . instead of showing concern over the alarming deterioration in my health, he decreed that I should be kept in the [solitary] cell for a month longer. Such is the mental degradation and the sense of irresponsibility that even high officials of the government, particularly of the jail and police departments, develop in this hapless country under foreign rule.'[14] 'I was living alone, utterly segregated from most of my fellow prisoners, and had no means of obtaining or borrowing anything. I had curtailed my requirement to the lowest limit and was living as I have already said, on rice and vegetable, since pulses would not suit me.'[15] On his release from jail in July 1922, Mazharul Haque was deeply affected at the sight of him. In an editorial article in the English weekly, *The Motherland*, Haque said that Jagat Narain Lal had come of the jail a 'physical and mental wreck' and held the government responsible for his condition.[16]

Jagat Narain Lal was imprisoned again in 1928. This time the charges were more serious. He was being tried for allegedly publishing seditious and inflammatory material against Lord Irwin in the weekly *Mahavir*, of which he was both founder and editor. Once again, he describes in some detail his physical ailments and suffering. But this jail term was made harder for he had to become a mute witness to illnesses, sufferings and deaths of his near and dear ones in his family. There are diary entries of his son's sickness, paucity of money, of his wife and children living in Gorakhpur under the care of his father-in-law. Perhaps

---

[13] Jagat Narain Lal, Private Papers, Speeches and Writings, 2(k), 2(l).
[14] Lal, *LUC*, pp. 18–19.
[15] Ibid., p. 24.
[16] *Motherland*, July 1922, p. 32.

a coping mechanism, perhaps the force of his ascetic will, but
Jagat Babu recalls many of these instances with detached and
resigned guilt.[17]

In 1928, while still serving time in Hazaribagh Central Jail
for sedition, his wife died. He was not granted parole to perform
or attend her last rites. There is a curious detachment and almost
an unreal apathy with which he recounts the departure of his
wife—a detachment that surprised even him. 'I received the
news without registering any mental shock or grief whatever.
That surprised me no-end and I went out and sat under one
of the small trees in the compound to ponder the event. The
only thoughts that came to my mind concerned the passage from
the Gita: "Beings are unmanifest in their origin, manifest in the
middle, O Bharata, and unmanifest likewise in their dissolution,
why should there be grief?"'[18]

He further writes, 'When I sat down for my evening prayers
that day, the shadowy figure of my wife seemed to peep through
the passage of the adjoining cell. I was somewhat disturbed as I
reflected [on] how I should feel if her memory were to haunt me
as a shadow. But this experience did not occur more than once or
twice. The only lasting effect this sad event produced upon me
was to bring about a state of utter resignation to the Divine Will.
I felt that God had freed me from this last major bond of earthly
attachment . . .'[19]

Approximately four years later, once again lodged in
Hazaribagh Central Jail in the aftermath of the civil disobedience,
Jagat Narain received news of his father's passing. His jail
diary has an entry dated 12 April 1932: 'I need to record a very

---

[17] *Mahavir* was published by Srikrishna Press which was set up initially
on the premises of Kadam Kuan, Jagat Narain Lal's Patna residence
(on what was later named Jagat Narain Lal Road). More details of the
Mahavir sedition case are provided in the next chapter.
[18] Lal, *LUC*, pp. 69–70.
[19] Ibid.

important episode of my life. My much loved and respected father passed away on 8ᵗʰ April while he was performing his tasks as a station master . . . It was a big blow and my heart felt heavy. I tried to control myself but could not escape feeling an immense sense of loss. A few tears escaped and trickled down, but I soon quelled my heart. I spoke of my father's love for us, his qualities, the sacrifices he made and narrated it to fellow inmates. My heart welled up, but it at least freed me from the restlessness and pain.'[20] It is interesting to note that while there was poetic pathos, of a very personal kind, when his wife died, his father's death triggered more expressive grief that was shared with inmates.

There are other diary entries from various times: of his eldest son's long fever, of his second son's accident and leg injury, his wife's tuberculosis, her suffering from both the disease and his absence. But none of these were a source of any prolonged grief, mourning, regret or even a feeling of guilt associated with reneging on familial duties. He writes, 'I lost so many of my precious ones—those near and dear to me, my father, my wife, my child and others in subsequent journeys . . . but I have never grieved over all these earthly losses—and that not merely because it is a privilege to suffer for the country's freedom and to sacrifice all that one holds dear, but also because destiny has amply repaid me for all this and made me many times richer though not in a worldly sense'.[21]

Jagat Narain turned suffering into a meditative exploration. The physical and material separation from the humdrum and routine spheres of human activity that centre around family, work, desires and wants, presented an opportunity to him, as he writes—of solitude to reflect, ponder, meditate, read and explore

---

[20] Jagat Narain Lal, Private Papers, NMML, Speeches and Writings. 2(k), p. 12.
[21] Lal, *LUC*, p. 1–2.

possibilities of spiritual regeneration. His prison terms became spaces of solitude in which he sought to cultivate the many qualities of his ascetic self—a predilection to deny, doubt, wait, to analyse, search, explore, dare; his tendency to compare and to equalize; a will to be neutral and objective, to be without anger or passion.[22] The very conditions that imprisoned his body became the context of his ascetic self-fashioning and the condition of his intellectual and spiritual 'awakening'.

The words he penned after he was denied parole to perform his wife's last rites, however, are of an anguished soul seeking redemption: 'Let my barque be wrecked and torn to pieces by angry winds in mid-ocean and let me be tossed helpless into the waves, so that, once at least, I may look up to Him . . . and see His hands raised to succour me'.[23] Then again he writes, ten days later: 'O prison! If thou canst offer salvation or even point out the way to it (the salvation of the soul) holding this body in bondage, if thou canst make it possible for me to drink even one drop of the nectar of the Lord's love, thou art a hundred and thousand times welcome . . .'

The quest for purposive knowing and spiritual redemption became the flip side of Jagat Narain Babu's jail journey. Reminiscing twenty years later, he wrote of prison terms as 'the ever-beckoning flag of Freedom' and went on: 'As I look back now on those years of my life, punctuated by frequent terms of imprisonment, arbitrarily decreed by those in whose hands destiny had placed our fortunes from time to time, I rejoice and feel amply recompensed. Not that they did not entail all the earthly suffering and travail, which is the necessary companion of such a life. I have these in no small measure'.[24]

---

[22] Drawn from Nietzsche, *Genealogy*, p. 143.
[23] Lal, *LUC*, pp. 73–74.
[24] Ibid., p. 1.

Renunciation

A feeling of renunciation surged in my breast . . .

There is, in Jagat Babu's writings of the 1920s and early '30s, a constant seeking of detachment and disassociation from desire, pain and attachment. Imprisonment had altered the context of his material realities and he craved to rework the dialectic of the body in relation to the world. He had to reshape himself as a bearer of this new colonized world, a reality that, Jagat Narain realized permeated not just prison life but the existential life of the country itself.

As early as in 1921 when he enters the prison gates for the first time (in the midst of arrests associated with various campaigns of the Non-cooperation movement), he is already aware of the change he is undergoing. 'A feeling of renunciation surged in my breast, and the first thing I did was to put aside the wrist-watch which I always carried on my person. I felt like throwing it away.'[25] The wristwatch anecdote may appear unremarkable but in the context of a 'beginning', of a journey of sacrifice, it becomes an interesting metaphor. It was, in those days, a symbol of affluence, stature, perhaps even of fashion. But in a deeper sense, it is also a keeper of time, the setter of daily rhythms that binds a person to their duties and chores. Jagat Narain sums up the meaning of this moment and feeling: 'I felt a sudden and violent change in me', he notes.[26] It was almost as if he himself was a witness to the dramatic severance of ties from a life he had planned and led thus far. He packed his coat, his wristwatch and 'other superfluous belongings' and gave it to a co-worker engaged in social service.[27]

---

[25] Lal, *LUC*, p. 6.
[26] Ibid.
[27] Ibid., p. 8.

The watch epiphany was a moment of another realization for Jagat Narain: that his decision to forsake his promising career and participate in the national movement had earned him vast popularity. He noted that although this 'served, doubtless, as an additional impetus' it also instilled in him a sense of vanity. 'A sense of vanity also seemed insidiously to have crept into me. For, I felt I could carry all before me, which although is a sign of self-confidence, is perhaps a sign of vanity as well.' Often breaking from prose into verse, he writes:

> *O Vanity! Why dost thou colour and conceal the illusory nature of all things worldly—name, fame, work, writing and renown!* [28]

In another of his revelatory moments he writes:

> *O Sorrows! Anxieties! Troubles! Away! Away!*
> *Yes! Ten honest men can shake the world. No more!*
> *No more! The death-knell has been sounded!*
> *The self must die now! This baser self!*
> *This false self! This serpent of the Ego!*
> *. . . No more of those sordid desires.*
> *Name and fame hunting expeditions!*
> *Cease! Cease All!*
> *Away with the name, away with the body, away with office!*[29]

Jagat Narain listed five vows that he intended to keep for six months, after his release from jail in 1922: (i) to practise *Bramhacharya* or celibacy; (ii) to practice *Aparigraha* ('i.e. not to keep anything that was not absolutely necessary'); (iii) not to ride any conveyance on short journeys up to three miles; (iv) not to ask anything from

---

[28] Lal, *LUC*, p. 68.
[29] Ibid., p. 29.

anybody; (v) not to partake of salt—'all for a period of six months compulsorily, and for further periods to be extended later on, if feasible and necessary'.[30]

Fasting, denial, austerity and celibacy are inseparable elements of the ascetic ideal through which Jagat Narain sought continuous discipline and spiritual transformation. His vows were a set of specific exercises and techniques, or 'technologies of the self",[31] through which he sought to fashion himself. For him, this practical training was an indispensable step in the fashioning of himself as a moral subject.

On his release from jail, he refused to, for example, ride in a carriage, then in a car that some of his co-workers had arranged for him, 'in view of the vow [he] had taken not long before, and also because [he] looked upon Buxar as the sacred place of [his] penance and self purification'.[32] In another example, Jagat Narain says that his father 'could not understand why I should offer him money to buy stamps for me. But how else could I act save in keeping with the vows I had taken, albeit for a limited period?'.[33]

Jagat Babu makes repeated assertions in his diaries and autobiography that he had undergone a transformation that was hard for others to comprehend when they met him after his release from jail—the reaction of his uncle-in-law when Jagat Babu refused to immediately visit his own ailing child in Gorakhpur saying that '[he] was not a doctor and nor could [he] cross the will of God'; or the reaction of his friends who found him 'in a peculiar mental condition, almost beside [himself] with religious fancies'; or of his brother who, though he 'was aware of Jagat Babu's mental condition', was taken aback when

---

[30] Ibid., p. 28.
[31] Foucault, "Technologies of the Self", *Technologies of the Self*, pp. 17–18.
[32] Lal, *LUC*, p. 30.
[33] Ibid., p. 35.

he got off a stationary train in the middle of nowhere and 'seated [himself] on earth and gave [himself] to chanting the *Pranava* and singing [his] favourite songs'; or of his wife who 'could hardly have imagined the transformation I had undergone during my incarceration'.[34]

In a notebook titled *Vicharkan*, carrying the stamp of Hazaribagh Central Jail (issued to him on 7 February; year missing, but likely to be 1929), probably intending to get it published at some point, he writes: '*Aasakti* and *Ahankaar*—attachment and conceit—are two evil enemies that creep on us subtly and inadvertently and infiltrate each of our chores, thoughts, speech, attire, in short affect each of our activities. We should, at all times, guard ourselves against them. Saving ourselves from these two vices is extremely important.'[35] Continuing in a similar vein, in 1932, he writes, 'Man must pass through three gateways of Surrender. The first is the surrender of Desire; the second is the surrender of Opinion; and third is the surrender of the Self . . . passing through this Gate, he adopts a process of self discipline which is the first step in the purification of the Soul.'[36] In his memoir (from sometime in 1928–29 while he was prison) he quotes *Shankara*: 'I am neither the *manas*, neither ego nor *chitta*; neither ears nor tongue nor nose nor eyes; neither sky, nor earth nor water nor air. I am that Consciousness full of Joy—the one, all pervading Soul.'[37]

The purpose of his writing and making extensive notes (on topics that ranged from *karmayoga*, ends and means, *vidya avidya*, vedantic philosophy to notes on digestion, alimentary canal, nervous system, population records and so forth) was to dispassionately

---

[34] Lal, *LUC*, pp. 19–36.
[35] Jagat Narain Lal, Private Papers, NMML, Notebook 12, p. 11. Translated.
[36] Ibid., Notebook 3, p. 35. Translated.
[37] Lal, *LUC*, p. 65.

record and to let himself *only* be altered by the activity of thinking and not by physical suffering. If the mind had to be led towards purposive knowing, the body had to be disciplined through modes of denial and forfeiting bodily pleasures.

Running through his various jail terms, was also the recurrent theme of brahmacharya, a vow that he had taken as early as in 1922, albeit for a short period then.[38] Of his first meeting with his wife (in Gorakhpur, at his father-in-law's house) after a gap of eight months in 1922, Jagat Narain writes: 'When I was about to go to bed, my wife came to join me. This was our first meeting after eight or nine months. She was astonished to see me so weak and thin, with a sickly unclipped beard on my chin. She was shocked too, to find me reclining on a bed spread on the ground. We were young and she had keenly felt our separation . . . Imagine her stupefaction when as she approached me, I quietly and gently remarked that she was not to touch me, but to speak to me from a distance. This would be heartrending enough for any wife in any circumstances—and ours were poignant! . . . Then I explained to her my programme and my mental outlook and we slept on separate beds . . . She bitterly grieved at the thought that I was almost lost to her. And on her account, a great dejection descended upon the family. But for the time being there was no help . . .'[39]

Brahmacharya was a practice Jagat Narain often wrestled with. 'I do not know if I pondered over this question during my previous prison terms of 1931–33, but this time, more than ever before, an important question for me is whether Tolstoy, Gandhiji, rishi (sages), *muni* (hermits), all believe that in the absence of brahmacharya, spiritual life and awakening

---

[38] Celibacy, as an ideal of the *varnashrama* system (that divides the conduct of life into four stages) is indicated at least two of the four stages—brahmacharya and sanyasa).

[39] Lal, *LUC*, p. 36.

is not possible. Tolstoy's *The First Step* and *Man and Woman*, Gandhiji's *Mangal Prabhat*, the teachings of Buddha deva all point towards the centrality of brahmacharya in the conduct of spiritual life.'[40]

He goes on to acknowledge that the practice of brahmacharya is difficult and demanding. 'It is not a practice whose observance should be considered easily achievable.'[41] He writes: 'It is surprising that the observance of the very same brahmacharya that seemed impossible outside, has become so *svabhavik* (instinctive) in confines of the prison . . . My mind often musters up the resolve to climb the third rung. I have already sacrificed domestic life for my country. But my life is still marked by the absence of restraint and meditation. I want to take the plunge so that I lead the rest of my life practising restraint and meditation.'[42]

'Mahatma Gandhi's words— that *pratigya* (vows) cannot be followed by adding adjectives of *yatha sadhya* (if possible)— is imprinted on my mind . . . from now on the adjective of 'if possible' shall be expunged from my resolve. I have noted this in my diary on 10th of last month and also shared and discussed the possibility of practising celibate life with my wife, beginning next *ekadashi*.'[43]

Jagat Narain Lal repeatedly sought to imbibe the Gandhian model of a moral celibate subject, self-admittedly, rather unsuccessfully—'The pursuit of brahmacharya has become the most difficult of tasks for me. My failure to be a true brahmacharya has contributed so much to my moral and spiritual degradation.'[44] He is acutely aware that he must guard

---

[40] Jagat Narain Lal, Private Papers, NMML. Speeches and Writings, 2(f), p. 4.

[41] Ibid., 2(f), p. 6.

[42] Ibid., 2(f), p. 6.

[43] Ibid., 2(f), pp. 5–6.

[44] Ibid., 2(f), p. 5.

himself against own sensations and failures. In a diary entry dated 24 May 1932, he admits that his ascetic morality is a work in progress, that he has not been able to eliminate either 'impulse' or 'passion'. He writes: 'Reading into my nature, I find that I am impulsive both in speech and action. That leads to errors, sometimes indiscretions in speech and action and causes heartaches to others. Remedy is to resist the force of impulse— not to speak or act unless reason has had time to sit in judgement over what impulse dictates.'[45]

He goes on to say that 'The desire to be activated infinitely by love in dealing with others, exists [in me] but not in sufficient degree: (a) firstly, to render disinterested service to others . . . (b) secondly, to enable me to act lovingly even towards those whose attitude is not good or favourable towards me. As soon as I learn that somebody harbours an unfavourable or uncharitable feeling towards me, that somebody has spoken ill of me or acted injuriously towards me, an unwholesome feeling does become seated in my heart towards him . . . I find I allow my heart also to be sufficiently stained . . . How then can I return love for hatred and conquer the hate of another?'[46]

Jagat Babu is acutely aware that his quest for asceticism is marked, often marred, by weakness and failures. In failures perhaps lay a fractured psyche—the suffering/desiring body, the seeking mind; with the absent husband, the unconcerned father, the respectful son, the nationalist, the Congressman, the Hindu Mahsabhaite, the Gandhian, becoming the many aspects of his self. Fractured into many selves, the Self is no longer 'self-centered' or anchored in its own interests. Socially constructed and fragmented into simultaneous beings, the Self is no longer able to, on its own, attain self-mastery and meet the requirements

---

[45] Jagat Narain Lal, Private Papers, NMML. 1(b), p. 9.
[46] Ibid.

of a moral life.[47] Jagat Narain's Self had, in a Foucauldian sense, become 'decentered'.[48]

But this 'decentered' Self realized that in the degrading conditions of the prison, his 'suffering' self would become unworthy, stand condemned and therefore would be in need of radical redemption. His act of writing and recording his own suffering and turmoil became modes through which Jagat Babu sought a displacement and transformation of the limits of his thought—to do something else, to become other than what he was. In fashioning his own self, his asceticism (ascesis)[49] was also a rebellion against life as had been forced on him by the British authorities. It was an art of living that was a counter to the fashioning of the colonial subject.

The twin tracks of suffering and renunciation paired up in his notebooks and diaries, almost as if forged in a relationship. Jagat Babu's ascetic instincts may well have originated in his experience of suffering and pain. Ascetic methods and modes of life become a counter-demonstration of power and will, exercised by a person over his life. How can you inflict pain on a body that refuses to experience the pain? How can the body be made to suffer if it is freed from that which causes pain?

Jagat Narain Lal became a devoted follower of the Gandhian dictum that *there is no independent thing called 'freedom' that is separate from the existence of 'unfreedoms'*. The reality of captivity and the experience of oppression meant that the only available recourse to freedom was detachment from the very source of these unfreedoms, i.e. desire and want. The greater the frequency of his prison terms, the more he sought a disassociated self—a self that

---

[47] For a detailed discussion on decentering of the self, see, Wills, "Ascetic Theology before Asceticism", *Journal of the American Academy of Religion*, Vol. 74, pp. 902–925.

[48] See generally, Foucault, "The Masked Philosopher", *Foucault Live*, pp. 433–458.

[49] Ibid., p. 307.

was not just an inscribed surface of events, but also simultaneously a *knowing self* in the pursuit of truth. He followed the path shown by the Gita —that one should give up Attachment to the objects of Desire, and go on performing all Actions without thinking of the fruits of those Actions.

Jagat Babu's ailing, weakening body suffered and this led him to seek out the meaning in suffering. His problem was not suffering itself, but perhaps the lack of an answer to the crying question: To what purpose do we suffer? 'Man, the bravest animal and the one most inured to suffering, does not repudiate suffering in itself: he wills it, he even seeks it out, provided that he is shown a meaning for it, a purpose of suffering. *Not suffering, but the senselessness of suffering was the curse which till then lay spread over humanity . . .*'[50] This search for meaning also resonated with a kernel of the Nyaya school of philosophy that Jagat Narain Lal cites in his diary— the idea of *anukula vedaniyam sukham*, that suffering made meaningful or purposive could become a source of happiness, even realization. This became an abiding tenet of Jagat Narain Lal's ascetic will.[51]

Jagat Narain Lal's ascetic self was not just a body that renounced and sacrificed pleasure. It was also a knowing self that forged a relation between itself and the nation it sought to free. His ascesis was explicitly linked to the momentous implications colonial servitude had for his own identity both as a Hindu and as an Indian. For him, his philosophy was no longer a set of propositional statements about the 'real' world. It was rather an act of self-disclosure. The turpitude of the British rule, and his own identity as a devout Hindu, created the

---

[50] Nietzsche, *The Genealogy of Morals*, Vol. 8, p. 211. However, it is important to distinguish between Nietzsche's 'ascetic priest' and other forms of the ascetic ideal, forms that are more life-affirming. Emphasis mine.

[51] Jagat Narain Lal, Private Papers (donated to NMML).

possibility of a self-fashioning that entailed both an aesthetics of asceticism and a vision for political action. The ascetic will was to serve as a link between his politics and his religious/ascriptive self, between a Hindu program of cultural regeneration and national liberation. It involved shunning the ethic of *sanyasa* and its renunciatory quest for otherworldliness, and embracing a code of righteous conduct rooted in the wonderfully complex doctrine of karmayoga outlined in the Bhagavad Gita. Because this formed such an important core of his ascetic practice, and because he wrote extensively on and about it, this aspect has been dealt in more detail below.

Righteous Conduct

A true karmayogi is not expected to take up saffron-coloured robes of an ascetic and abandon all Actions.

Jagat Narain Lal's ascetic practice was guided by the Bhagavad Gita and its threefold ethic of 'devotion', 'knowledge' and 'duty' (or 'Action'), against the countervailing ethic of renunciation and otherworldliness of the *Sanyasa* school. The ethic of sanyasa, integral to the four ashrams (brahmacharya, *grihastha*, *vanaprastha* and sanyasa) of the smritis, is a prescription for renunciation of the material world and of all action. The Gita, on the other hand, makes departures and sanctions all actions if made in the greater interest. As Jagat Narain Lal notes, the Gita does not propagate the doctrine of the Sanyasa school, that all Action is faulty and, therefore, such as ought not to be performed.[52]

He writes in his notes on *Gita Rahasya*, 'we cannot accept the dictum of the Sanayasa school that all happiness arises from prevention of pain, desire, "thirst", etc. . . . . The message of the

---

[52] Jagat Narain Lal, Private Papers, Notebook on *Gita Rahasya*, pp. 68–69.

Gita is not that one should do away with all activity or prowess in the world; but, on the other hand, it is stated in the 18ᵗʰ Chapter of the Gita (18.26) that the doer must, side by side with equability of mind, possess the qualities of perseverance and enthusiasm.' A true karmayogi, Jagat Narain Lal writes, 'is not expected to don saffron-coloured robes of an ascetic and abandon all Actions'. The Gita advocates the sanyasa (renunciation) of only kama (desire-prompted) actions. A karmayogi should always practise charity, austerity and sacrifice, but above all, should never abandon karma.

The Gita became Jagat Babu's abiding companion. It helped him fill out the meaning and content of the freedom he sought, political as well as spiritual. In particular, there were two philosophical conceptions that he held closely—*stitha pragnya*, and *anasrita karmaphal*. In many ways, these two ideals formed the core of Gandhi's ascetic practices too. In fact, at one point in his memoir, Jagat Narain writes, 'As I read the Gita and came across the description of the stitha pragnya in the second chapter, I was deeply impressed and meditated on it again and again. When some time after my release, I learnt that this was a portion which formed the chief subject of Mahatma Gandhi's meditation and recitation during his daily prayers, it gave me no small pleasure.'[53]

In a diary full of notes on the *Gita Rahasya*, Jagat Narain describes stitha pragnya as the state of being of an individual who is steady in mind; who is always full of courage; who is indifferent towards the outcome of actions; whom the constituent elements cannot unsettle; who remains steady, performing his duties without emotion; to whom pain and happiness are the same; to whom earth, stone and gold are just the same; to whom what is dear and what is disliked, what is praise and what is criticism, are just the same.[54]

---

[53] Lal, *LUC*, p. 65.
[54] Jagat Narain Lal, Private Papers, Notebook on *Gita Rahasya*, pp. 26–27.

In another notebook titled *Vicharkan,* Jagat Narain writes: 'In the beginning, the mind runs towards desires and is a slave to its senses. The happiness that it seeks is actually transient. Such a mind finds it difficult to experience the joys of detachment and purity of happiness. A person who has adopted the path of *stitha pragnya* will aspire for a state of being where he is detached from his organs and outcomes of desire and is apathetic towards the fruits of his action.'[55]

His notes on *Gita Rahasya* make a clear distinction between the stitha pragnya of the karmayogi and the stitha pragnya of the sanyasi. The latter is merely engrossed in shanti (peace) and does not care for the world; the former, has a responsibility greater than just the responsibility towards one's self. The karmayogi practises control of his sense organs and their desires, and through that control, he continually brings his self-identification into his conduct of ordinary life.[56] Jagat Narain goes on to cite Lord Krishna's sermon when Arjuna asks how one achieves such control and discipline over one's desires. Krishna replies that even the most difficult mountain climb can be achieved by *abhyasa* or the practice, of renouncing desires. He goes on to say that the ethic of abhyasa (practice, action) is a taller ideal than sanyasa.[57]

One finds very few references to the question of means in the Gita, barring that it should be imbued with dispassionate action and capacity for reason. As we will see in the following section, Jagat Narain used his personal judgement to question the Gita's ambivalence towards violence. So while his sense of duty and motivation for action is driven by Gita's idea of a karmayogi, its lack of a clear ethical position on the question of means and violence leads Jagat Narain towards other philosophical sources.

---

[55] Jagat Narain Lal, Private Papers, Notebook 12 (*Vicharkan*), pp. 16–17. Translated.

[56] Ibid., Notebook on *Gita Rahasya*, pp. 69–70.

[57] Ibid., p. 71.

Ends and Means

Violence cannot beget non-violence and cannot bring about a lasting and peaceful society.

Reading and reciting the slokas of the Gita one day in the jail, Jagat Babu pondered over the question of violence. His mind sensed a conflict between the teachings of Gita and the Gandhian principle of non-violence. He wondered why there should be so much insistence on non-violence, when the soul is immortal and the body after all perishable, when the knowledge of this phenomenal world is partial—*avidya*, as he explains in his autobiography.[58] In his reading, the Gita not only excused violence in a just cause, but also held it to be perfectly justifiable. His own leanings, he admitted candidly, 'were strongly towards non-violence. How to reconcile the two conflicting attitudes?'[59]

Jagat Babu's philosophical and normative canvass was vast and eclectic. The conflict in ethics of Action made him seek a resolution through Aldous Huxley's treatise *Ends and Means*. He writes (in a notebook that carries the stamp of Hazaribagh Central Jail, possibly dated sometime in 1943 when he was jailed in the aftermath of the Quit India movement) that almost all countries

---

[58] The *Isha Upanishad* had acquainted him with the distinction between vidya (reason) and avidya (partial knowledge). 'Here was this Upanishad pointing out to me for the first time that what I had acquired was not Vidya but Avidya . . . Avidya is the knowledge of diversity—of diverse objects as manifested on this earth and of their activity. Vidya is the knowledge of the "one essential unity" that pervades all diversity,' Lal, *LUC*, p. 19–20. Jagat Narain Lal goes on to write that 'in reality, we spend all our years in attaining Avidya, or knowledge of those subjects which give us an insight into the diverse affairs pertaining to this life,' Lal, *LUC*, p. 20. We go about our lives, he said, following and obeying masters who masquerade as learned men. In reality, it is 'the blind leading the blind'—*Andhnaiva niyamana vatha andhak.*

[59] Lal, *LUC*, p. 25.

in all times agree on a set of ideals that need to be upheld. 'But the methods differ from country to country, age to age and the results also therefore differ, though the ideals remain the same. The results differ because the means employed are not the same.' He continues, 'People think and say that the "End justifies the Means". But, they forget that it is the means employed which determine the nature of the ends produced. Violence cannot beget non-violence [and] cannot bring about a lasting and peaceful society.'[60]

The second strand that he picks up is that it is the locality of situations that ought to determine our ideals and principles. 'Causation in human affairs is multiple hence there can be no single cure for the disease of body politic.'[61] And therefore, he believes, led by Huxley, that we have to formulate our conception of right and wrong, frame our conduct, in light of our beliefs about the ultimate nature of reality. Good ends are ones that adhere to the truth. *And good ends can only be achieved by the employment of appropriate means.* Quoting Huxley, he writes: 'The end cannot justify the means, for the simple and obvious reason that the means employed determine the nature of the ends produced.'[62] Jagat Narain Lal cites Barthelemy de Ligt's dictum: 'The more violence, the less revolution.'[63] For him, this was a dictum 'worth meditating on'. 'A violent revolution cannot achieve anything except the inevitable results of violence.'[64] He gives examples of the never-ending, self-perpetuating cycles of violence and tyranny perpetrated by Nazism and Bolshevism's quest for nationalist power.[65]

---

[60] Jagat Narain Lal, Private Papers, NMML, Notebook 10, p. 3.

[61] Ibid., Notebook 10, p. 9.

[62] Ibid.

[63] Ibid., p. 14.

[64] Ibid.

[65] Even Harold Laski, 'a highly intelligent man', Jagat Narain Lal writes, made the mistake of regarding the 'iron dictatorship of the Jacobins' as crucial for the resilience of the French Republic, but this was precisely the reason for the demise of the republic. Iron dictatorship led to more wars

The use of violence to reform, or for nationalistic or political ends is 'criminally rash', according to Jagat Babu. Plain common sense, according to him, demands two things. One, that for large-scale reforms we must choose measures that do not require violence to enforce them. And two, that because human conservatism is a fact in any given historical situation, because human beings are resistant to change, 'we must preserve all such constituents of the existing order as are valuable . . . Hence it is very important that social reformers should abstain from making unnecessary changes or changes of startling magnitude. Wherever possible, familiar institutions should be extended or developed so as to produce the results desired; principles already accepted should be taken over and applied to a wider field. In this way, the amount and intensity of opposition to change and, along with it, the risk of having to use measures of violence would be reduced to a minimum'.[66]

In keeping with the path shown by Gandhi, Jagat Narain understood the value of non-violence. He recognized that, in order to avoid the trap of self-conceit, prejudice and tyrannical authority, political participation required, as its own internal principle, regulation and power over oneself. The ability to not inflict violence, to exhibit moderation and toleration, to practice non-violence became aspects of each other, as also of dominion over the self.

The Ascetic Practice of Jagat Narain Lal

It would be a mistake to judge Jagat Babu's ascetic practice in terms of its approximations to an ideal type or against a threshold of renunciatory activities that participants like him

and reactions at home; this led to the creation of military dictatorships and yet more wars. 'These wars served to intensify nationalistic sentiment throughout the whole of Europe. Nationalism became crystallized in a number of new idolatrous religions dividing the world.' Ibid., p. 15.
[66] Ibid., p. 18.

must comply with. Instead, it is more fruitful to read it, in the variety of motivations, reasons and activities described by him, both during the practice itself and as a memory of it, as building of an *ascetic lore* that coexists with the more 'official' traditions.[67] The Bhagavad Gita may have been the font of ascetic inspiration for generations of social reformers and freedom fighters. But its influence is to be judged not in terms of the purity of ideal it sets up, but in the proximations it inspires, in the myriad practices it stimulates, in the diverse ways in which participants negotiated the reality of colonial subjugation and incarceration and in the ascetic lore it weaves.

Jagat Narain Lal and other men and women entered into a lineage of resistance, constituted through the smallest and the most idiosyncratic of practices yet the most ambitious forms of political consciousness. Despite the power of the state to punish, incarcerate and inflict disproportionate repression—denying demands for more soap, or walk-time after dinner, or more books, for example—the psychic rewards cannot be underestimated.[68] Many of Jagat Babu's conduct and practices may have struck as being strange or aberrant, or even pathological. But that is to miss the power of nationalistic ascetic practices in claiming a moral ground against colonial subjugation.

Jagat Narain Lal's ascesis can be seen as combining three sets of practices. First, a practical training in a set of everyday exercises that were indispensable in order for him to form himself as a moral subject was important. Practices of reading, writing, yoga, pranayama, puja (worship), chanting, meditation and so on formed part of his daily rituals. He practised these more or less coordinated exercises in a moral, philosophical and religious system. At the most instrumental level, the claim to spirituality and knowledge served to relieve Jagat Narain Lal of the responsibility of resolving

---

[67] Lobetti, *Ascetic Practice in Japanese Religion,* p. 66.
[68] Ibid., p. 152.

the fractures of his being and burden of circumstances. The need for an escape from the contradictions—familial, religious, political—is indicated as an objective of his spiritual practice and has been elaborated in some detail in his diaries, notebooks and autobiography.

The second strand involved progressing from the exercises themselves (the 'means') towards the virtues of moderation and temperance (the 'ends') for which they were meant to serve as training. The procedures (trials, examinations, self-control) tended to form particular techniques that were more complex than the mere rehearsal of the moral behaviour they anticipated. Jagat Babu believed that with the modification of the adjectival 'everyday'—the everyday life from which he expunged intimacy, closeness and desire—a 'state of knowing', and a fashioning of the knowing self, could be achieved. His ascesis was not just circumvention of conditions of deprivation. It was a quest for a certain transformation, a certain transfiguration of himself as a subject. The physical, material, emotional sacrifices became a form of discipline that enabled him to shrug off 'the conditioning inscribed on and in the body by the social world'.[69]

The third strand of his ascesis sought to combine renunciation with action. Buxar was the beginning of Jagat Narain's self-fashioning in the ascetic mould—into a being with interiority, knowledge, conscience, vows and a certain fastidious desire to exclude whatever appeared extraneous, unnecessary and in excess. But while Jagat Narain Lal looked upon Buxar and the Hazaribagh Central Jails as the sacred places of his 'penance and self-purification', and places 'where he found God'[70], his ascesis was as much about rendering service. 'I felt that my place too was among the poor and wretched, that my Lord wanted me to go

---

[69] Butigan, *Pilgrimage through a Burning World,* p. 28.
[70] Lal, *LUC,* p. 30.

and serve His children, not sink into the solitude of a self-seeking discipline.'[71]

But there is another sense in which Jagat Narain Lal's ascetic practice became 'action-oriented', i.e. in fashioning a *nationalist community*.[72] Being out there in the world, in a non-religious context, in colonial prisons, among the inmates, meant that Jagat Narain Lal was not 'alone' in fasting, meditating, reading, rebelling, talking-back to prison wardens. There were other prison inmates who regarded him as a guru and were witness to Jagat Narain Lal's renunciatory activities. Through his ascetic routine and mundane practices, what got performatively amplified was not just Jagat Narain's personal plight but also the collective plight of the native lot. In that sense, though not unique to Jagat Narain Lal, through the performance of culturally potent rituals and of a *personal* journey in a public sphere, he added to the repertoire of 'renunciation' that crafted new ways of being, of understanding, of disobeying and of oppositional consciousness.

It is thus possible to understand his ascetic practice as a political practice that transformed the Self but also, given the context, added to the 'nationalist solidarities'. 'The ascetic creates more than a basic social identity or role, an articulated self, a persona, or a personality: the ascetic constructs an entirely new agency capable of functioning in a different and resistant way to

---

[71] Lal, *LUC*, p. 30.

[72] I am borrowing here from Chandra Russo's concept of a 'prefigurative community'. Russo argues that a "[p]refigurative community is a key element of ascetic political practice. Through modes of physical and psychosocial discipline, activists create something not merely greater than the individual but expose as well the limitations and kinds of damage that a culture of bourgeois individualism creates. This community, in turn, becomes an experience of transcendence akin to other ascetic processes.' Russo, *Solidarity in Practice*, pp. 123–152.

the dominant culture that defines identity, personality and social functions from hegemonic power.'[73]

* * *

Jagat Narain Lal was in prison because of his own carefully chosen and deliberated actions that adamantly renounced the dominant order at great cost to himself and his family. The personal, physical, financial and social risks he took for a life in prison, the acts of civil disobedience—as major as the boycott of Prince of Wales, the Bardoli Satyagraha or the rejection of the Cripps Mission Proposal, and as small as fasting, giving up salt, etc.—became not just modes of self-discipline that led to personal transformation, but also fashioned a nationalist practice.

However, the fashioning was fraught and riddled with a core tension. The tension was between an ascetic practice of the self, located in the dispassionate, desireless reason in the mould of a karmayogi and the telos of the nation state to which oppositional consciousness attached itself. There is a radical distinction between the two realms of value. On the one hand, *ascetic consciousness* seeks to fashion itself in opposition to the material, to self-interest and to pursuits that serve an egotistical, individualistic, self-centred being. It seeks to free the individual from the sources of unfreedoms—greed, hatred, untruth, attachment and violence. The *nationalist consciousness*, on the other hand, seeks to free the nation. Its pursuit rests on an idea of freedom all right, but freedom itself is conceptualized in the context of freedoms conferred by the state.

The ascetic can fashion himself in a worldly realm—like a karmayogi for instance, taking Vivekananda, Gandhi and Jagat Narain Lal as exemplars—but the world of the nation-state militates against its core existential value: detachment and desireless action. *The ascetic and nationalist genealogies are from*

---

[73] Valantasis, *The Making of the Self*, p. 103.

two different cosmic worlds. One seeks to free the Self through the act of self-knowing or self-realization (where renunciation and finding oneself is an undifferentiated act), the other seeks to institutionalize and entitle the possessive self. Nationalism mobilizes sacrifice but displaces the ascetic individual.

But the deepest fracture stemmed from the role religion was expected to play in the conduct of modern politics and in collective nationalist imagination. The Western construct of the nation state relied heavily on relative uniformity of religious practices and on the separation of religion and politics in the public sphere. This construct assumed axiomatic proportions and became the aspirational default setting for the Indian national movement.

There were two problems here. One, of course, India was not religiously, or linguistically, or ethnically homogeneous. It could not be converted into a similitude of homogeneity by a movement for political freedom and rights, no matter what it chose to call itself and who it claimed to represent. The second issue was that the political culture of asceticism—both Gandhian and Hindu nationalist, and everything in between—continued to use the authentication of traditional rituals and religious motifs—in fashioning and constructing the nationalist self. A political culture needs the authentication of traditional rituals and practices. A viable political community needs the moral sedimentation of tradition. We imported the nation state from the West; we tried to indigenize it; we tried to be secular like them, but we could never displace the authority of religion and replace it with the authority of a secular state. Jagat Narain Lal's own struggle with secular consciousness testifies to this paradox.

3

From Hinduism to Hindu Nationalism

Barring a few atheistic ascetic practices, the connection between religion and asceticism has always been quite strong. In teaching humanity that the material is immaterial, transient, ephemeral, or illusory (maya), religious philosophies have nearly always upheld an ascetic ideal. This is true of those that proliferated during the freedom movement too. Combining nationalist pursuits with a religious consciousness, Jagat Narain Lal, like many of his contemporaries, becomes a repository of this consciousness, almost irrevocably so.

On the cognitive plane, Jagat Babu's ascetic practice was shaped by an enchantment with the metaphysical. It formed the core of his spiritual pursuits and intellectual interests. At the performative level, given the context of colonialism and nationalism, 'being Hindu' and 'being nationalist' became his two most significant identities, at times merging with each other. Admiration for political mentors like M.K. Gandhi, Madan Mohan Malaviya and B.S. Moonje, in their own different and conflictual ways, convinced him that religion was not a contemptible pursuit in the field of politics. From Swami Rama Tirath, who was regarded by Jagat Babu as his spiritual mentor, he imbibed the idea of *spiritual patriotism* which preached that 'you must realize unity with God, realize first your unity with the Whole Nation . . . Through Prana-pratishtha you vitalize an idol of stone or an effigy of clay. How much more worthwhile would it be to call forth the inherent glory and evoke fire and life in the Deity that is Mother India?'[1]

In spiritual patriotism, Jagat Babu found the beckoning order of his early nationalist identity. In its ethos, he discovered an expression of his own identity as a devout Hindu in pursuit of freedom for a 'modern nation. The spiritual guidance of Swami Rama Tirath filled him with a passion for leading the life of a karmayogi. The Vedantic ideal of a multidimensional freedom—individual, political, social and spiritual—had so many contemporary nationalistic articulations, beginning with Vivekananda, that it was not aberrant for Jagat Narain to mix politics with religion, making Hindu nationalism become his chosen route to spiritual patriotism.

Politics was the arena where Jagat Narain sought his own reconciliation of bhakti with nationalism. How fraught that pursuit would be, he did not know at the time. But he was to realize early enough how irreconcilable the ideas of nationalism and bhakti could be. By the mid-1930s, his disillusionment with the Hindu Mahasabha began, and reached a point of severance on the eve of the first provincial assembly elections in 1937. But the unmaking of the unholy mix of bhakti and Hindu nationalism first needs the telling of its making.

Seva: The Construct of Service

I could pledge life-long allegiance only to an institution that stood for the ideal of service to the Hindu Community, to the country and to the world at large in a selfless spirit of dedication to the Lord.

---

[1] Jagat Narain Lal, Private Papers (donated to NMML).

If there was one ethos that cut through the various nationalist-ascetic narratives, it was the idea of seva or service. So integral was the idea of service to both Gandhian and Hindu nationalist practice that it became a core value of nationalist consciousness. Drawing much of its content from Vivekananda's teachings and Gandhi's practice, many freedom-fighters like Jagat Narain believed that in seva lay the route to both individual freedom and social transformation. From Vivekananda, he imbibed that he who directs his activities to the service of man—the manifestation of God upon earth—is a true karmayogi.[2] 'He who sees Shiva in the poor, in the weak, and in the diseased, really worships Shiva; and if he sees Shiva only in the image, his worship is but preliminary.' 'If you want to find God, serve man. To reach Narayana, you must serve the Daridra Narayanas—the starving millions of India . . .'[3] Charles Heimsath reads Vivekananda's Vedantic revivalism as a critical moment in the progress to universal nationhood. The idea that 'service' to humanity, would simultaneously lead to reformation of the social structure and amelioration of the depressed classes and to individual freedom/salvation held tremendous potential as a transformative tool for nationalist aims.[4] However, while Vivekananda focused on grihastha as the site of activism, inheritors like Jagat Narain scaled it up to make the nation a site for service.[5] Seva in the context of the national movement began to embody ideas of the nation and the nation's goals.

Large numbers of students who left educational institutions in response to Gandhi's call for boycott of educational institutions during the Non-cooperation movement (1920–22), began to join *seva samitis*

---

[2] Jagat Narain, Private Papers, NMML, Speeches and Writings, Notebook 12, p. 13.
[3] Vivekanand International Foundation, https://www.vifindia.org/2019/january/17/swami-vivekananda-s-idea-of-service%20
[4] See Heimsath, *Indian Nationalism and Social Reform*.
[5] Vivekananda, 'The Ideal of Karma Yoga'.

and take part in their village organization work. 'By the end of 1920s the Seva Samitis proliferated in every district of Bihar . . . By April 8 [1921] there were 7860 volunteers and by June, the number reached 10,319. Nationalist propaganda work too came to be vested almost entirely in the hands of these volunteers.'[6]

But the shift was not just in scale of seva operations—it was also in its meaning. While the religion-neutral idea of seva— that loosely implied service, welfare, social and constructive work—remained in use,[7] the idea of seva was beginning to get narrowed down. It was beginning to serve and represent various Hindu interest groups and community positions, all geared in different ways to the revivalist ideology of its key actors.[8] Seva may have begun as a form of social work, but soon, in many formative ways, the idea of seva became a 'Hindu practice', *forging a conflation of devotional and religious identity with the aims of the nation.* The idea that 'Hindu interests' on their own formed a nationalist agenda soon crystallized into the more exclusive conception of Hindu nationalism. What started as an idea of seva, a positive sensibility associated with preserving the interests of the community, became a communal concern symbolizing an exclusionary sentiment that aimed to compete with and defeat the 'other community'. For example, in the aftermath of the Kohat Riots of 1924 in NWFP, Lala Lajpat Rai (who had founded the Lok Sevak Mandal in Punjab in 1921) advocated a partition of Punjab along religious lines,

---

[6] Alam, *Government and Politics in Colonial Bihar*, pp. 110.
[7] Examples being the establishment of the Seva Sadan (1908–09) in various cities of Maharashtra for upliftment of widows; Seva Mandir and Deshsevashram being the two names suggested for Gandhi's Sabarmati Ashram; a Marathi weekly called *Bharat Sevak* to which Gandhi contributed an article about the Hindu caste system in 1915; Gandhi Seva Sangh; Bhil Seva Mandal; Gond Seva Mandal, Harijan Sevak Sangh and so on.
[8] See Srivatsan, "The Idea of 'Seva'", *EPW*, Vol. 41, pp. 427–438, 435–436.

suggesting that this would be between a Muslim India and a non-Muslim India.[9] Shortly thereafter Lajpat Rai resigned from the Congress and was nominated as the president of the Hindu Mahasabha in 1925. 'Insisting that "unity cannot be purchased at the cost of Hindu rights"',[10] Lala Lajpat Rai fought the 1926 assembly elections, as the founding member of the Congress Independent Party, along with Jagat Narain Lal, against the Congress on a largely Hindu nationalist plank.

On his release from jail in July 1922, one of the first things Jagat Narain Lal did was to resume his responsibilities at the Bihar Provincial Seva Samiti, of which he had been the general secretary since 1918–19. In his words, 'One of its chief activities was rendering of social service at the great Harihar Khetra fair, held annually in Sonepur on the occasion of Kartik Purnima, some time in November, with the help of several hundred volunteers.'[11] As a member of the Samiti, Jagat Babu also involved himself with the All India Go-Seva Mandal which was concerned with issues of cow protection (*goraksha*). He joined forces with Jagannath Barhe and Lakshman Narayan Garde to make the Harihar Kshetra the all-India centre for goraksha work and to organize an all-India conference under the presidentship of Shankaracharya Bharti Krishna Tirtha.[12]

The religious and socio-cultural aspects seemed to merge in the idea of seva, often abetting a collective psyche of persecution and a shared, exclusive identity. Together with the Hindusthan Seva Sangh, which Jagat Babu founded in 1930, almost all the

---

[9] Nair, *Changing Homelands*, p. 7.
[10] Ibid.
[11] Lal, *LUC*, p. 44.
[12] The Harihar Kshetra was traditionally a place for cow slaughter as it hosted one of the biggest cattle fairs of Asia, some presumably for trade and slaughterhouses. The fair celebrated the legendary *gaj-graha* battle between the elephant and the crocodile and the Lord appearing in the final stages of the battle to rescue the elephant.

existing *seva dals*—Swayam Sevak Dal, Rashtriya Sevak Sangh, Servants of India Society, Servants of Hindu Society (Hindu Sevak Samaj)—took on shades of meaning beyond the idea of simply community service to also include 'religious work'.[13] The call was for a missionary attitude and the spiritualization of public work (the context of Christian missionary conversions often providing the impetus and the provocation, as I shall shortly discuss in the case of Jagat Narain Lal). These seva samitis become essentially 'Hindu' organizations, taking up issues of cow protection, 'music before mosque', Hindi language, and sometimes reform campaigns for the removal of untouchability, *mutt* (temple) reforms and so on.

A word about the Hindusthan Seva Sangh is in order, for it reveals Jagat Narain Lal's vision and version of service. He had long wanted to organize, to quote him, 'a missionary institution working on the lines of the Servants of India Society, founded by late G.K. Gokhale'.[14] He nearly joined Lajpat Rai's Lok Seva Mandal (Servants of People Society) but at the last moment discovered that it would not accommodate anyone with his 'particular views'.[15] In 1932, Jagat Babu joined B.S. Moonje's Servants of Hindu Society, set up after Lajpat Rai's death in 1928 to memorialize him, but he soon 'found it impossible to fit [him]self into the scheme.[16] He goes on to clarify what he was looking for: 'I could pledge life-long allegiance only to an institution that stood for the ideal of service to the Hindu Community, to the country and to the world at large in a selfless spirit of dedication to the Lord. For this I need fearless, god-intoxicated men with a passion for threefold cause, men

---

[13] For a discussion, see Srivatsan, "The Idea of 'Seva'", *EPW*, p. 427.
[14] Lal, *LUC*, p. 92.
[15] Ibid.
[16] Ibid.

who had faith in God and were prepared to die for their ideals—only such as these could be my comrades'.[17] He discussed this project with several of his colleagues in jail, and proceeded to establish the Hindusthan Seva Sangh, soon after his release from jail in 1930.

But what really became the converging point for all these different seva campaigns—were the *shuddhi* (purification and reconversion) and *sangathan* (organizing the Hindus into a band of political volunteers) campaigns. By the mid-1920s, the idea of seva had a acquired a missionary zeal and had aligned with the shuddhi and sangathan campaigns of Hindu right-wing organizations like the Hindu Mahasabha, the RSS and its many affiliates. The belief that Hindu culture, its religious practices, its purity and holiness, was in danger from the political machinations of the British, from the 'evangelical zeal of missionary Christians', from 'virulent Islam' and from Macaulay's 'agnostic liberals' became the ideological impetus for the programme and content of the Hindu Mahasabha, of which Jagat Narain Lal became a member in 1922. That these fault lines would remain embedded in our national bedrock was not imagined at the time.

Between the Sabha, Seva and Congress

That I would separate myself from the Congress and stand with another party [Hindu Mahsabha], *the very thought would disturb me deeply. After all it was on Congress' call that I joined the Non-cooperation movement, altered the trajectory and aims of my life and accepted a new life . . . What a big dharm sankat this is for me.*[18]

---

[17] Lal, *LUC*, p. 92.
[18] Jagat Narain Lal, NMML, Speeches and Writings, 2(i), 30–31.

On the occasion of the Harihar Kshetra fair in 1922, Jagat Babu was summoned to an informal meeting at the conference camp where he was asked to express his views on the one issue that had become a rallying point for many seva dals—cow protection. 'I said', he writes, 'that goraksha was impossible unless Hindus were properly organized, for it was they who championed the cause.'[19] There are two aspects of Jagat Babu's approach to the idea of sangathan which are interesting and may have been at variance with the prevailing ideas then. First, despite being a strong votary of the idea, sangathan, or organization of Hindus (formulated largely in the context of large-scale conversions in Eastern and Central India), Jagat Babu never spoke of shuddhi or reconversions. The second, for him the idea of seva and Swaraj were to be inextricably linked to each other. For example, he reminds Sriyut Narayan Jagannath Barhe, who he described as a 'cultured Brahmin who was obsessed with the cause of goraksha (cow-protection)', that seva and swaraj could not be separated.[20] '[Barhe] tried to enlist my sympathy for this cause. But I was equally obsessed about Swaraj. I told him that goraksha was impossible to achieve without Swaraj. We should all therefore fight for Swaraj before everything else.'[21]

Jagat Narain's views on sangathan probably appealed to the Shankaracharya who told Jagat Narain that he himself had a great interest in the cause of Hindu organization. The idea that the Hindu Mahasabha had formerly been an unrepresentative organization under the guidance of the Liberals and Moderates whose main concern had been the presentation of petitions addressed to the Viceroy and the Provincial Governors, was a matter of great concern. It called for a restructuring of the organization. [22]

---

[19] Lal, *LUC*, p. 45.
[20] Ibid.
[21] Ibid., p. 44.
[22] Ibid., p. 43.

Jagat Narain had an innate talent for organizational work. He was among the foremost fundraisers both for the Congress and the Hindu Mahasabha, as well as for the seva sanghs and samitis he was part of. It was the agenda of 'organization' (sangathan) that motivated him to sign up and offer his services for the upcoming Hindu Mahasabha session that was to be held alongside the Gaya Congress of the INC in 1922. '[A] subcommittee consisting of five persons, including myself, was formed . . . I was asked to accept secretary-ship, but I preferred to remain an ordinary member, though I promised to do all that was necessary for its success,'.[23]

The 1922 Hindu Mahasabha session held in Gaya is an important point in the history of the Indian national movement. It was here that Hindu Mahasabha formally laid the foundation of sangathan, proclaiming the need for the Hindus to unite and organize themselves.[24] The anti-climactic end to the Non-cooperation movement provided an opportunity to the Hindu Mahasabha to revive itself after having lapsed into insignificance in the early years of the Gandhian era.[25] As it geared up to streamline its organizational structure and programmatic content, the Hindu Mahasabha was helped in no small measure by factionalism in the

---

[23] Lal, *LUC*, p. 46.

[24] Sinha, "The Dilemma of Jagat Narain Lal", *Proceedings of the Indian History Congress*, Vol. 76, pp. 481–487, 482.

[25] With Gandhi's entry into politics, many of the Hindu Mahasabha's core programmes found a place in the Gandhian action plan (Hindi and the cow protection plan, for instance), and the Hindu Mahasabha was in organizational disarray and had become quite irrelevant. Gandhi's lead in the formation of the All-India Cow Protection Conference and the One Script and One Language Conference diverted much of the support that the Mahasabha had received from the Hindi and cow protection movements. See Gordon, "The Hindu Mahasabha and the Indian National Congress", pp. 145–20, 161. The Congress–Khilafat unity during the Non-cooperation movement added to its irrelevance. Also see, Tejani, "Re-Considering Chronologies of Nationalism and Communalism", pp. 249–269, 261.

Congress and by the simmering disenchantment with Gandhi's termination of the Non-cooperation movement. Hardening of religious identities was fostered by the strikingly open espousal of the 'Hindu cause', and by the entry of manifestly pan-Islamic aims of many Khilafat leaders.[26] This led several Congressmen to veer towards the Hindu Mahasabha. And Gandhi's approval of many of Hindu Mahasabha key concerns made such divided loyalties lie easier on many Congressmen's conscience.[27]

Disenchantments oftentimes bring out latent, secretly held attachments. This was exactly what happened within the Congress. Freed from the artificial restraints of Gandhian ideals, many Congressmen like Rajendra Prasad, Madan Mohan Malaviya, C.R. Das, Lala Lajpat Rai and Jagat Narain Lal began their formal association with the Hindu Mahasabha, taking advantage of the porous ideological and organizational boundaries. As if on cue to showcase this porosity, the Hindu Mahasabha held its session exactly at the same time and place as the Gaya Congress. Rajendra Prasad served as the chairman of the Hindu Mahasabha reception committee, Mohan Malaviya as the president of the session. Richard Gordon, in his excellent account of Congress–Mahasabha relations, recounts: 'In his presidential address, Malaviya dwelt at length upon the disintegration of the Hindu community, the need for strong communal organization and the revival of the

---

[26] Loose talk of a 'holy war', stories of atrocities on Hindus in the Moplah rebellions ('tactlessly white-washed by the Central Khilafat Committee'—*Leader*, 7 September 1923).

[27] In 1915, Gandhi spoke at Haridwar in support of the All-India Hindu Mahasabha. In December 1916, he presided at the First All-India One Language and One Script Conference at Lucknow. In April 1919, he became president of a subcommittee of the Hindi Sahitya Sammelan, to popularize Hindi in the Bombay and Madras presidencies. He was particularly successful among the Marwari communities in north India. The Marwari Agarwala Conference in 1919 donated Rs 50,000 for the spread of Hindi. Home Poll, File 140 of 1925, NAI; *Leader*, 6 January 1917, 24 April 1919 and 16 June 1920.

Mahasabha, themes which were to become common in the following years.'[28] The presence of both Malaviya and Rajendra Prasad, two stalwarts of the Congress, at the helm of Hindu Mahasabha affairs, signalled the obvious—i.e. *the Congress and Hindu Mahasabha were not radically divided over the fate of Hindus in the nation-in-making.* Reiterated again by Motilal Nehru, at the Ninth Annual Session of the Mahasabha at Delhi in March, that the Congress was and always had been, except during the brief period of Non-cooperation, a predominantly Hindu organization. 'The true remedy', he had suggested, 'lies in the Hindu Sabha as a body joining the Indian National Congress and thereby influencing the whole programme of work in the Councils.'[29]

It was common in those times for Congressmen to hold dual membership. Many like Jagat Babu were members of the Congress as well as of the Hindu Mahasabha (or other organizations like the RSS or the Communist Party of India). At the Banaras session of the Hindu Mahasabha in 1923, held soon after the Gaya Congress, Jagat Narain Lal was appointed as secretary of the Bihar Provincial Hindu Sabha and, to quote him, 'was also asked to serve on the Working Committee of the All-India Hindu Mahasabha'.[30] Thereafter, '[a]t the Calcutta session of the All-India Hindu Mahasabha (1925), [he] was pressed by both Pandit Malaviya ji and Lala Lajpat Rai to accept the Secretaryship of All-India Hindu Mahasabha'.[31]

For many in the two organizational boats, it may well have been a matter of political expediency and ideological predilection. For Jagat Babu, it seems, it stemmed from a deeper place where attachments were not simply political or ideological but more personal and emotional and therefore perhaps also deeply

---

[28] Gordon, "The Hindu Mahasabha", p. 169.
[29] *Leader*, 17 March 1926.
[30] Lal, *LUC*, p. 33.
[31] Ibid.

conflictual. Politically, the conflict manifested for the first time in 1926 on the eve of provincial legislative council elections. Manish Sinha, Jagat Narain Lal's grandson, notes, 'It became very difficult for him to decide whether to stand on the Congress ticket which had already been offered to him, or to stand on another party's ticket, which would allow him to speak independently on the issues of Hindu interest.'[32]

The question of 'Hindu interest' had assumed importance at this juncture. The breakdown of the Non-cooperation movement (and also of the Congress–Khilafat unity) had prised open the fissures of Hindu–Muslim discord. For the Hindu Mahasabha, this was both a vindication of its core ideology, as also an opportunity for resurgence. Jagat Narain corroborates the fact that the Hindu Mahasabha did not see the Congress as an organization that had any interest in privileging Hindu interests. The Hindu Mahasabha was critical of the fact that 'although the numerical weight of the Muslims within the Congress was less, even then the Congress remained partial to their interests and concerns'.[33] Yet, many in the Congress and Hindu Mahasabha, like Madan Mohan Malaviya, Lala Lajpat Rai, Dr Moonje, Jayakar Kelkar, were of the opinion that a cooperative framework ought to be developed between the Congress and Hindu Mahasabha within which seat-sharing and representation of Hindu interest in the Council would be made possible. Jagat Narain also writes that these leaders were in favour of leaving sympathetic Congressmen free to opine and vote on communal questions.[34]

---

[32] Sinha, "The Dilemma of Jagat Narain Lal", *Proceedings of the Indian History Congress*, Vol. 76, pp. 481–487, 482.

[33] Jagat Narain Lal, Private Papers, NMML, Speeches and Writings, 2(i), p. 25.

[34] Ibid.

Jagat Narain Lal's dilemma-ridden journey began roughly from here. He attended the All India Hindu Mahasabha convention at Delhi (1926) where the attendees were completely disunited on the question of whether to participate in the elections independently or to align with other parties, and if the latter, whether with the Congress or with other parties that were openly in support of Hindu interests. In the midst of all the heated parleys and exchange of ideas, the debate took an intractable turn. Congress stalwarts like Motilal Nehru, Vitthalbhai Patel and Rajendra Prasad came to the convention and tried to dissuade the Hindu Mahasabha from participating in the elections, Jagat Narain narrates. Jagat Narain Lal describes the convention in vivid detail—the discord between the various factions led by followers of Shraddhanand, the Arya Samajis and the Sanatanis; the tussle between Lajpat Rai and Malaviya and their reservations about Bhai Parmanand; the selection of Narendra Nath as the president of Punjab Sabha (who went on to become the president of the Hindu Mahasabha in 1926); and Jagat Babu's own selection as the secretary of the Hindu Mahasabha in the executive committee meeting that followed. In the end, Jagat Narain Lal says, the Hindu Mahasabha decided to take part in the elections but declared that 'parties that show open and full support to Hindu interests will receive backing from the Hindu Mahasabha in the next elections'.[35]

On the eve of the provincial elections of 1926, an attempt was made once again, Jagat Narain writes, by many stalwarts—Motilal Nehru, Madan Mohan Malaviya, Lala Lajpat Rai, M.R. Jayakar, N.C. Kelkar, Dr Moonje—to get together in September 1926 to unite the different factions and parties for the upcoming elections, but to little avail.[36]

---

[35] Jagat Narain Lal, Private Papers. NMML, Speeches and Writings, 2(i), pp. 26-28

[36] Lala Lajpat Rai's Independent Congress Party (the electoral front of the Hindu Mahasabha), Malaviya's Nationalist Party, The Responsivist

For Jagat Babu, this discord morphed into his first political predicament. He met Malaviya (who he regarded as his political and ideological mentor) and sought his counsel. 'What should I do?' he asked. 'Many friends in the Hindu Mahasabha are of the opinion that I should not contest Council elections on a Congress ticket because according to them, I will not remain free to speak for or represent Hindu interests. I am facing a big moral quandary for I have already been nominated by the Congress as a potential candidate.'[37] Malaviya advised him to keep his own counsel and come to his own decision. The question of who to go with, as Jagat Narain says, was a difficult one for him, a dharm sankat (moral dilemma) as he describes it. 'On the one hand was the expectation that as a Hindu Mahasabha minister, Congress restraints would be absent, and I would be able to speak for myself and protect Hindu interests freely each time they arose in the Council. On the other hand were my deep associations with the Congress. That I would separate myself from them and stand with another party, the very thought would disturb me deeply. After all it was on Congress' call that I joined the Non-cooperation movement, altered the trajectory and aims of my life and accepted a new life . . . What a big dharm sankat this is for me.'[38]

Eventually, Jagat Narain Lal contested elections as a candidate of the Congress Swatantra Dal (Congress Independent Party), founded by Lala Lajpat Rai in defiance of Congress policy of 'no partiality' to Hindu interest. *He had wanted to join such a party which, he writes, apart from the question of Hindu interest, was a supporter of the Congress on all other issues.*[39] 'In Lala

Party, The Swarajya Party to name a few.

[37] Jagat Narain Lal, Private Papers, NMML, Speeches and Writings, 2(i), pp. 29–30.

[38] Ibid., pp. 30–31.

[39] It is interesting that he doesn't join Malaviya's party. The reason could well be Malaviya's critical stand on Non-cooperation (to which Jagat Narain had been wholeheartedly committed) as inimical to the long-term

ji's Congress Independent Party, I saw the possibility realizing both my aims.'[40] It is interesting to note that Jagat Narain did not join Malaviya's Pratiyogi Sahyog Dal, despite his immense respect for Malaviya. Malaviya, according to Jagat, was never fully a supporter of the Congress strategy of non-cooperation and often fell short of taking a radical stance—his criticism of the Non-cooperation movement was a case in point.[41] For Jagat Babu, the party to be in had to be 'Congress plus Hindu interests', and more importantly, the commitment to national struggle was non-negotiable.

It was not as if in the Congress Independent Party, Jagat Narain Lal found a perfect fit. It was also not as if straddling two ideological and party boats ever became easy. His next political predicament arose after the historic Lahore Congress session of 1929. Jagat Babu had been released from jail just a couple of months before, having been prosecuted and jailed for a year in the 'Mahavir Sedition case' in 1928. At Lahore, Congressmen in the central and provincial assemblies were asked to resign from their seats. 'Pandit Jawaharlal Nehru', Jagat Narain writes, 'was the President-elect, and the Congress had decided to present the national demand on the lines of the Nehru Report in the shape of an ultimatum to Lord Irwin. Both Mahatma Gandhi and Pandit Motilalji went personally to present this ultimatum to the Viceroy. It was the proud privilege of the Lahore session under Pandit Jawaharlal ji's presidentship,

---

interests of the Hindu community of north India. At Allahabad in October 1920, he condemned the boycott of the schools and colleges as educational suicide. It would have been the height of folly to cut off the much-needed government financial aid to expanding educational institutions such as the Benares Hindu University, of which Malaviya was appointed vice chancellor in 1919; Gordon, "The Hindu Mahasabha", p. 194.

[40] Jagat Narain Lal, Private Papers, NMML, Speeches and Writings, 2(i), p. 34.

[41] Ibid.

to adopt the achievement of complete independence, instead of Swaraj (which implied dominion status) as the goal of the Congress . . . But Mahatma Gandhi declared that he did not see light, and for the time being, therefore, he was not in a position to offer the country any programme . . . As a preliminary step, Congressmen in Central and Provincial Legislatures were called upon to resign from their seats.'[42]

Jagat Narain Lal had been elected to the provincial legislature not as a Congress candidate but as a member of Lala Lajpat Rai's Congress Independent Party. 'Technically therefore', he writes, 'I was not bound by the Congress mandate, though on every other issue I had hitherto voted with the Congress Party (*LUC*, 83). There was another problem. Jagat Narain Lal was the sponsor and prime mover of the Hindu Religious Endowment Bill. He writes that 'resignation from the legislature would mean resignation from the Hindu Religious Endowment Committee, the issue being close to my heart. I resolved to hang on until the national struggle had been launched by the Congress and Mahatma Gandhi.' He didn't have to wait long; as he says, 'the hour of trial came sooner than expected'.[43] When Gandhi gave the call for salt satyagraha in 1930, Jagat Narain Lal writes, 'preparations for satyagraha were pushed forward under his leadership and in less than a month it was decided to break the Salt law—the most iniquitous among laws of the land . . . Mahatma Gandhi was to initiate the campaign at Dandi and I lost no time in resigning my seat in the legislature and set about preparing to join the struggle,'.[44]

Jagat Babu writes with the pride of a nationalist and a Congressman. From all his accounts, the Congress still was his primary political location. But on the question of political allegiance, Jagat Narain Lal remained conflicted, his predicaments often

---

[42] Lal, *LUC*, p. 83.
[43] Ibid., p. 85.
[44] Lal, *LUC*, p. 85.

making his politics ambivalent and prone to vacillation. He had joined the Hindu Mahasabha but remained a loyal Congressman and an open admirer of Gandhi. To one unfamiliar with the world of nationalist politics, this may appear deeply irreconcilable, and it would be easy to be dismissive. But such is the operating mode of a 'fractured psyche'.[45] The more his 'self' got fractured into simultaneous beings—a Hindu, a Hindu nationalist, a Congressman, a Hindu Mahasabhaite, a Gandhian, a karmayogi— the more fissiparous became his nationalist identity.

Sangathan: The Construct of Unity[46]

After talking to a few knowledgeable Khasi people, I realized that conversions happen because dharm-abhimani (religiously conceited) Hindus, mutt mahantas and priests have no time to spare from their selfish lives and work for the upliftment of poor tribals.[47]

In the early years of the national movement—the 1910s and '20s—the Congress and Hindu Mahasabha were not really seen as antagonistic to each other,[48] and the boundaries between a

---

[45] See Chapter 2.

[46] Shuddhi and sangathan are terms mostly used in tandem, as shuddhi-sangathan. Sangathan literally means coming together or organization and shuddhi purification, signifying a process of re-induction of those who had converted to other religions (especially to Christianity and Islam, either by the force of Christian missionary activities or by the political rule of Islam). Shuddhi-sangathan used in tandem suggests a push for organized reconversions. In Jagat Narain Lal's writings and other available evidence, however, I found no mention of shuddhi; hence, I have preferred to use his push for sangathan as a stand-alone feature of his politics.

[47] Jagat Narain Lal, Private Papers, NMML Speeches and Writings, 2(j), p. 91.

[48] Bapu, *Hindu Mahasabha in Colonial North India*, pp. 34–35; Bayly, *Local Roots*, p. 121.

secular imagination of the nation and a more sectarian vision
of it, as constituted by religious communities, were 'blurred and
overlapping'.[49] In a political context dominated by the Hindus,
there was only a vague distinction between 'secular' political
association and involvement in religious or caste movements.[50]
Sections of the Congress leadership held dual membership
of the Hindu Mahasabha, working for the protection of
Hindu interests within the Congress. Many like Jagat Narain
performed political functions inside the Congress and social and
cultural work in the Mahasabha or other sectarian or religious
organizations. Both in UP and Bihar, it appeared that there
existed a relationship of mutual benefit between Congress and
Mahasabha till at least the late '20s, as is borne out by Jagat
Babu's writings. The Hindu Mahasabha early on was able to
mobilize people for Swaraj in tandem with shuddhi (purification)
and sangathan (organization/unity).[51] For Jagat Narain Lal,
however, it was always the idea of sangathan, and not shuddhi,
that held relevance and importance. Coupled with the agenda of
'freedom' (Swaraj), the program of sangathan became ethically
and politically more acceptable to a loyal Congressman like
Jagat Narain Lal.

The basis for sangathan lay in the unique structure and
practice of Hinduism. Not being a revealed religion, Hinduism
has had an amorphous character with a diversity of gods,
associated beliefs systems, forms of worship, sects and so on.
In addition to this diversity, the *varna* system divided Hindus
into different, hierarchical castes, ridden by mutual antipathies,
leading to the absence of any one identifiable feature or feeling
that tied everyone together. The agenda of sangathan emerged

---

[49] Bapu, see pp. 129–131.
[50] See Gordon, *Hindu Mahasabha*, p. 151.
[51] Ghosh, "The Virile and the Chaste in Community", *Social Scientist*,
Vol. 22, pp. 80–94, 81–82.

out of a need to 'unite' these varied, varying and differing affiliations. In the context of the British policy of 'Divide and Rule', the communally divisive politics of the Muslim League and religious conversions by proselytizing missionaries, several Hindu organizations and individuals felt that unity among Hindus was both necessary and possible through a revivalist thrust that would simultaneously 'reform' and 'unite'.

Sangathan therefore emerged out of an impulse for homogenization through a call for unity and reform. Any project of unity would have had to, at the very least, attempt to reform the deeply entrenched caste-ridden society with its religiously sanctioned oppression. Thus, the revivalist strain almost by necessity combined with the reformist. Savarkar's aim, for instance, as Bayly writes, 'was to unify all Hindus to compete in a social Darwinian "terrible struggle for existence".'[52] He therefore warned his higher-caste followers against 'disrespecting the sentiments of our *Sanatani* brethren'.[53] M.S. Golwalkar, a key figure in the RSS and a follower of Savarkar, claimed that they were redirecting the ancient discipline of karma yoga to prevent conversion of lower-caste Hindus and tribals to Christianity and Islam.[54]

As with most simmering propensities, there's always a trigger needed to set it off. The immediate impulse for sangathan was the Moplah rebellion (of Muslim peasants against their predominantly Hindu landlords) in Malabar in 1921, resulting in the killing of hundreds of Hindus. This, together with the conversion of Hindus in Malabar and atrocities against them in the Multan riots, triggered a 'self-conscious Hindu predicament' and revived

[52] Bayly, *Recovering Liberties*, p. 134.
[53] Savarkar's presidential address—19th session of the Akhil Bhartiya Hindu Mahasabha, Karnavati (Ahmedabad), 1937, in Savarkar, *Hindu Rashtra Darshan*, p. 1.
[54] Golwalkar, *Bunch of Thoughts* (3rd ed.). See, especially, Chapter 29, "Serving the Neglected Brethren", pp. 274–279.

the image of 'Hindus under siege'.[55] B.S. Moonje, who went
on to become one of Jagat Narain Lal's associates in the Hindu
Mahasabha, headed the Nagpur Commission on the Malabar
Riots and claimed that the 'chronic disunity and weakness of
Hindus' was exposed in the face of an 'organized Muslim unity and
violence'.[56] The need to *unite, organize and fortify* was felt widely
and vocalized openly by many members of the Congress including
Malaviya, Rajendra Prasad,[57] Jagat Narain, and Krishna Sinha.[58]
Jagat Narain writes about how the Moplah massacres and Malabar
conversions triggered 'a chill and a feeling of deep disconsolation
spread in the entire country. The Hindu community, especially,
was gripped by disquiet and anxiety.'[59] He writes admiringly about
how deeply affected B.S. Moonje was by the Moplah massacres,
and exhorted people, especially Congressmen (as Moonje himself
had done as an old Congress loyalist) to unite and organize as a
community by participating in sangathan work.[60]

Initially in Bihar, writes Papiya Ghosh, Jagat Narain, as a
member of both the Hindu Mahasabha and the Congress, pitched
the shuddhi campaign at the Christian missionaries who had,
'unnoticed' by the Hindus, covered ten out of the sixteen districts
by the mid-1920s. In his perception, 'the Christian peril' affected
the Hindus alone as 'other races were yet virile and none dare lay
their hands upon them'. 'Ultimately it was this . . . thrust that the
provincial Hindu Mahasabha settled for.'[61]

---

[55] Bapu, *Hindu Mahasabha in Colonial North India,* p. 49. Also see
Panikker, *Against Lord and State,* pp. 179–182.
[56] Bapu, *Hindu Mahasabha in Colonial North India,* note 32.
[57] See Prasad, *At the Feet of Mahatma Gandhi,* pp. 136–137.
[58] See *Searchlight,* 7 December 1924.
[59] Jagat Narain Lal, Private Papers, NMML, Speeches and Writings,
2(j), p. 32.
[60] Ibid.
[61] Ghosh, "The Virile and the Chaste", p. 81. Also see, Ghosh,
"Shuddhi, Sangathan and Swaraj", presented at NMML, New Delhi, 20

Often the terms 'shuddhi' and 'sangathan' are used interchangeably, while the truth is that they have distinct connotations. Jagat Babu's diaries bear testimony to the fact that it was not the idea of reconversion or 'purification' (shuddhi) that was the main moral impetus behind his sangathan campaign, but the idea of reform and unity. Often there may have been a chronological relation between the two campaigns but as borne by Jagat Narain Lal, not always. There is a need for this distinction because the push for shuddhi and sangathan came from two different political and ethical impulses. While sangathan aimed to strengthen and protect, shuddhi aimed to correct and restore. In the subtle variations and differences lies a richer and a more wide-ranging story of motivations and perspectives that formed the larger stream of Indian nationalism.

It is true that the idea of sangathan for Jagat Babu was closely linked to the issue of religious conversions of Hindus to Christianity. But this, from available evidence, did not translate into a pitch for reconversion. The proselytizing mission of the Christian missionaries was a source of deep anxiety to him. In a diary entry narrating events of 1922–23, he expresses this worry clearly when he is witness to large-scale conversions of tribals in Ranchi and adjoining areas of the Chhotanagpur region. He writes: 'In 1922–23, when I was sent, along with Rajendra Prasad, on deputation from Bihar Vidyaptih to Ranchi, I saw that Ranchi had become an important centre for Christian missionary activities. Many missionary centres that had come up in Ranchi and adjoining areas, had initiated large-scale propagation of Christianity among the hill tribes of Chhotanagpur region. I got a chance to visit areas adjoining

---

June 1992. Also see Political Department, Special Section, Bihar State Archives (hereafter PS) 30/1926, "Annual Report on the Hindi, Urdu and Bengali Newspapers and Periodicals published in the Province of Bihar and Orissa During 1925".

Ranchi like Chaibasa, Palamau, Gumla, etc. where thousands of tribals had converted to Christianity . . . The scenes I witnessed during my visit were a source of great agony for me. With a sorrowful heart I saw before my own eyes thousands of tribals converting to Christianity. I also saw how Christian fathers and brothers, missionaries, served the poor tribals, and through service and social work incentivized these conversions.'[62]

His second visit to Ranchi and neighbouring areas was a regional tour he undertook for the provincial Hindu Sabha. Of one incident he writes: 'One day as I was touring with a few karyakartas, I happened to see a big hall by the roadside. It was decorated with lights, had a few benches and desks were laid outside. At the desks were seated many young people and it seemed like some reading activity was going on in a school. My fellow karyakartas corrected my misconception and said this is not a school but a "training centre" of the Christian missionaries. What a deep tragedy this was both for Hindu dharma and for Hindu society. What is the fate that awaits a society that can neither reform itself nor protect itself? I see so many missionaries being prepared and routinely sent for a single mission in mind and wonder what the fate of a disorganized Hindu community and its dharma would be.'[63]

The same lament can be read in his account of conversions in Assam during his visit to the region along with Lajpat Rai, perhaps just before the special session of the Hindu Mahasabha in Gauhati in December 1926. The plan was to explore the possibilities of Hindu consolidation in the face of large-scale religious conversions of tribals to Christianity. Jagat Babu expresses his distress to find that like the Adivasis of the Chhotanagpur region, the tribals of this region too had

---

[62] Jagat Narain Lal, Private Papers, NMML. Speeches and Writings, 2(j), p. 3.

[63] Ibid., p. 5.

converted to Christianity. 'Out of an estimated population of 1,40,000', he writes, 'approximately 40,000 had converted.'[64] He adds that he saw the same situation of mushrooming churches in Shillong, Sylhet and adjoining areas, as he saw in Ranchi, and describes his deep anxiety stemming from a religion and society in crisis. He goes on to say that 'after talking to a few knowledgeable Khasi people, [he] realized that conversions happen because *dharm-abhimani* (religiously conceited) Hindus, *mutt mahantas*, and priests have no time to spare from their selfish lives and work for the upliftment of poor tribals.'[65]

On his way back from Gauhati, he records that he told Lajpat Rai that 'up till now, we have been focusing on the Hindu–Muslim question only. Not that this problem is less complex, but it appears that in a few years the Hindu Christian question will become an even more complicated problem. But Lala ji was of the opinion that, thus far, the Indian Christians had displayed an outlook that was very nationalistic in nature . . . He went on to say that many among the Indian Christians were educated and high thinking and therefore it is possible that even in due course, they will continue to be progressive and nationalistic'.[66]

Jagat Narain Lal believed that the 'missionary zeal' stemmed from the Christian order and organization—*prachar shakti* and *padhdhati*.[67] And he was deeply convinced that the lack of order and absence of systemic unity was Hindu society's biggest failing. Interestingly, while conversions may have been a source of deep anguish for Jagat Babu, his ire was directed mostly against the 'savarna Hindus'. At their doorstep, he placed the blame. 'On the other hand, I see savarna Hindus, who claim knowledge of the

---

[64] Jagat Narain Lal, Private Papers, NMML. Speeches and Writings, 2(j), p. 89.
[65] Ibid., p. 91.
[66] Ibid., 2(i), p. 16.
[67] Ibid., p. 6.

Hindu dharma but suffer from the conceit of their caste status. The savarna Hindus, instead of strengthening the Hindu dharma and working towards the prosperity of each of its followers, come to these tribal areas and loot their lands and resources, enriching no one, but their own selves. Such people are neither worried nor moved by the plight of tribals, their poverty and their simplicity, nor are they fearful that the tribals may leave their own religion and become *vidharmi* (converts). My words must surely seem bitter and unpalatable to many savarna Hindus. But the fact is, no matter how bitter, this is the truth and should pierce the conscience of each of us. For my own peace of mind, this needed to be said.'[68]

Jagat Narain writes that many proposals for strengthening the organizational network were passed at the Hindu Mahasabha meet in 1926. The special focus was the need to stem the tide of conversions. A committee was set up, he writes, empowered to undertake sangathan work in the Chhotanagpur region. The focus of the sangathan work, at least from his diaries and notes, was clearly reform and not shuddhi. For Jagat Babu, Hindu dharma's vulnerability stemmed from its own caste divisions and hierarchies. The need for addressing these was not just a matter of organizational strategy to 'unite' Hindus, but was also a matter of 'conscience'—an outcome of his philosophical orientation and belief system. As an admirer and follower of Gandhi, the reform movement against caste atrocities and untouchability was not just an instrumentalist agenda to construct a 'unified Hindu community', but also a matter of principled opposition as caste hierarchies militated against the Advaita principle of non-dualism.

This distinction is an important one, and it may be said that in this distinction lies the answer to why the reformist agenda of Hindu nationalism never really moved beyond the rhetorical precincts to gain tangible benefits. Not for Jagat Babu were the

---

[68] Ibid., p. 4.

exhortations of 'virile warrior' (as for Savarkar)[69] or the 'hyper-masculine' performativity of Hindu nationalism as an antidote to 'Hindu weakness' (Hedgewar).[70] Jagat Narain Lal's concern for Hindu unity and vulnerability may have tallied with the Hindu nationalism agenda, but the expression of it was more Gandhian than anything else. He would decry violence, cry easily, weep at the sight of suffering, lapse into long periods of introspection and anguish. The image that emerges again and again from the pages of his diary is of a man deeply moved and troubled by the 'pitiable condition' and 'plight' of the Hindu dharma. This was not a man seeking scapegoats and revenge but one urging reform from within. He thought it was possible. Sangathan may have translated into different programmes for different practitioners, but for Jagat Babu, it translated into reform work within the Hindu system, and into a demand that the Muslim community

---

[69] 'Throughout the paleolethic periods, the bronze age and the iron age man could maintain himself, multiply and master this earth chiefly through this his armed strength. Verily the Defensive Sword was the first Saviour of man! The belief in absolute non-violence condemning all armed resistance even to aggression evinces no mahatmaic saintliness but a monomaniacal senselessness!' Savarkar, *Hindu Rashtra Darshan.* p. 84. Also see, Nandy, Heildelberg Papers, 2009; Nandy, *The Intimate Enemy*, 1983.

[70] See Anderson and Damle, *The Brotherhood in Saffron,* pp. 248–249. 'The apparent failure of Gandhi's noncooperation movement, which was followed by widespread communal rioting, convinced many Hindu revivalists that a different approach was needed. Many believed that the "weakness" of the Hindu community could be overcome only if Hindus strengthened community bonds and adopted an assertive kshatriya outlook. Accordingly, communal peace, they argued, would result only if Muslims and Hindus both realized that an attack on one community would result in a devastating response by the other. When conflicts developed between members of the two communities, communal allies were often sought through appeals to the most sharply defined cleavage separating Hindus and Muslims—religion.' Anderson and Damle, *The Brotherhood in Saffron*, p. 27.

do the same. Jagat Narain Lal, therefore, can be seen here as a votary of 'empathetic' Hindu nationalism, rather than of 'vengeful Hindutva'.

Hindu Mutt Satyagraha

Had the Tarkeshwar satyagraha become a model, we would have seen nation-wide satyagrahas against corrupt temple systems and their immoral priests in various provinces . . . But the fact of the matter is that most of the savarna Hindus and prominent personalities remained apathetic and indifferent and did not display any sympathy for the cause.[71]

The pain that Jagat Babu experienced when he witnessed large-scale conversions in Ranchi and Gauhati gave way to deep frustrations with what he thought was a failure of the Hindu system to correct itself. He used the example of the reformist Akali movement in Punjab to exhort the Hindus to seek reform and revive a religion that was failing its poor and low castes. He repeatedly reiterated, even more than the need to organize politically, the need for Hinduism's religious centres to reform themselves. Unless the centres that disseminated dharma renewed themselves, there was little hope for Hindu society, he said.[72]

In the first Bihar Regional Hindu Convention in 1924–25, presided over by the Shankaracharya of Shardapith (who had also been elected as the president of Akhil Bhartiya Go Seva Mahamandal Conference of November 1922)[73], a resolution was passed to the effect that the head priest of each mutt should utilize and divert substantial temple funds for the Hindu sangathan

---

[71] Jagat Narain Lal, Private Papers, NMML, Speeches and Writings, 2(i), p. 12.
[72] Ibid., 2(j), p. 5.
[73] Patel, *Aspects of Hindu Mobilization*, Vol. 65, pp. 798–824, 803.

work.[74] Jagat Narain Lal writes that when the Shankaracharya reached the Bodh Gaya leg of his tour, Jagat Narain reminded the Shankaracharya of the need to reiterate the text of the resolution to the priests there. He writes later, after the convention, 'Jagatguru Shankaracharya ji must have spoken to the priests, but the fact of the matter is that no visible outcomes were there to be seen.'[75] What follows is an account of how Jagat Narain pioneered and made a strong pitch for a religious endowment bill to reform temple systems in Bihar. At one level, this is a story of what sangathan work had translated into for him personally, but at another level, it is yet another narrative of a Hindu seeking to reform religious associations.

What really inspired and set him on the path seeking temple reforms was a lesser-known reform movement that occurred in the important pilgrimage centre of Tarkeshwar in Hooghly district, West Bengal, in 1924. The Tarkeshwar Satyagraha, as it came to be called, was a religious reform movement that took anti-imperialist shape as the British backed the corrupt mahant (priest) of Tarkeshwar.[76] Jagat Narain Lal writes that in order to protest against the oppression and corrupt practices of the priests of the Tarkeshwar pilgrimage centre, common Hindus began a satyagraha under the leadership of Swami Viswananda. 'I knew Swami Viswananda from earlier days when he had come to Patna to participate in the regional political meets of the Congress. He sent me a telegram asking me to send *swayam sevaks* (self-help volunteers) for the Tarkeshwar satyagraha on behalf of the Hindu Mahasabha. I considered it prudent to seek the executive approval of the regional sabha before I sent volunteers. Rajendra Babu was

---

[74] Jagat Narain Lal, Private Papers, NMML, Speeches and Writings, 2(j), p. 6.
[75] Ibid.
[76] See Mandal, "Tarakeswar Satyagraha", pp. 539–546.

then a member of the executive committee. It was decided that before volunteers were sent, I should go and personally assess the situation. I set out for Calcutta, en route to Tarkeshwar, where I met newspaper reporters, participants of the satyagraha and Deshbandhu ji [C.R. Das] who had also become associated with the satyagraha. From them I got a first-hand report of the corruption and atrocities of the Tarkeshwar priests . . . Thereafter I went to Tarkeshwar where I witnessed for myself scenes of the satyagraha and heard tales of priestly tyranny and mass campaigns against moral and financial corruption.'[77]

He later writes, 'Inspired by Tarkeshwar, the air in Bihar too was changing. My intervention in Tarkeshwar soon saw me at the helm of an anti-mahant satyagraha in Bihar. It was almost as if Tarkeshwar had put the priestly heads of various pilgrimage centres and temples on notice.'[78]However, as Jagat Narain disappointedly notes, the Tarkeshwar satyagraha didn't really inspire reforms in Bihar, let alone movements against the corrupt temple systems across the nation. 'Had the Tarkeshwar satyagraha become a model, we would have seen nation-wide satyagrahas against corrupt temple systems and their immoral priests in various provinces . . . But the fact of the matter is that most of the savarna Hindus and prominent personalities remained apathetic and indifferent and did not display any sympathy for the cause.' He goes on to say that he discussed the matter with Rajendra Prasad, despite being well aware that he would not approve of satyagraha against the mutt and their priests.[79] 'Even Malaviya ji, who was by nature opposed to radical measures, would have opposed the proposal of temple satyagraha. From him too, I did not receive any clear indication of support. It was perhaps to be expected because he had never clearly

---

[77] Jagat Narain Lal, Private Papers, NMML, Speeches and Writings, 2(i).
[78] Ibid.
[79] Ibid., 2(j), pp. 12–13.

come out in support of the Tarkeshwar satyagraha. In politics too, he had never accepted nor supported Congress' politics of civil disobedience and satyagraha.'[80]

Another person Jagat Narain approached was Sir Ganesh Dutt with whom he occasionally had had the opportunity of exchanging a few ideas on Hinduism and who was an influential member of the provincial council whose social base included various communities, including, importantly, the zamindars (landlords). Since most head priests (*mutt-dheesh*) were *bhumihars* (a landowning caste), Jagat Narain believes that it was never going to be feasible for Sir Ganesh, whose power rested on zamindar patronage, to extend support for operations against the entrenched power of these temple priests (mahants). 'It would never be tolerable for bhumihar mahants to subject themselves and their *zamindari* to external control and regulation.'[81] 'Expectedly, Sir Ganesh was totally opposed to the idea of satyagraha and declared it to be harmful to the interests of the Hindus.'[82]

Jagat Babu laments and regretfully wishes that he had some support from Hindu leaders for what he calls the *Hindu Mutt Satyagraha*. 'I wanted to try and fulfil my commitment to reform Hindu temple systems . . . It was the need of the hour that the regional Hindu Sabha be kept independent of landed and caste interests. What was required was an autonomous committee to mobilize a forceful campaign for temple reforms and Hindu mutt satyagraha.'[83] As a member of the provincial Hindu Sabha and as an office-bearer of the Hindu Mahasabha, he felt that it was his calling and duty to 'work towards maintaining the sanctity and purity of the holy temples'. He writes: 'For a devout Hindu

---

[80] Jagat Narain Lal, Private Papers, NMML, Speeches and Writings, 2(i), p. 14.

[81] Ibid., p. 15.

[82] Ibid., p. 13.

[83] Ibid, p. 18.

like me, it was a matter of great concern that the wealth of the temples was being misutilized.' [84]

A regional meet of the Hindu Mahasabha was organized, which saw the participation of interested and concerned Hindus, mutt priests and heads, sadhus, sanyasis as also members of the Council such as Krishna Sinha, Rameshwar Prasad, Mahavir Singh, Shiv Shankar Jha, etc. After a lot of deliberation and debate, it was decided that an organization by the name Bihar Regional Math Mandir Raksha Committee be set up. The office bearers and members would comprise all categories of people including head priests (*mutt-dheesh*), sadhus, sanyasis and common people (grihastha).[85] The idea behind widening the membership was, Jagat Narain writes, to include common folk who not only came to the temple to gain spiritual peace and knowledge, but who also contributed to temple funds as donors. 'Mismanagement of these temple systems would harm both the priestly class and the common people as both would suffer the adverse consequences of mismanagement and misappropriation . . . It was decided that the committee would prepare a list of all the pilgrimage centres of the region and prepare a report on the status of temple holdings and problems.'[86]

Hindu Religious and Charitable Trust Endowment Bill

Like Madras, Punjab and the United Provinces, Bihar should also explore the possibility of something similar to the 'Hindu Religious Endowment Act', which would regulate and supervise the holdings and wealth of the mutts.

---

[84] Jagat Narain Lal, Private Papers, NMML, Speeches and Writings, 2(i), p. 21.
[85] Ibid., p. 17.
[86] Ibid., p. 17.

The issue of temple reforms and religious endowments was clearly very important for Jagat Narain Lal. He pursued it despite opposition and indifference of many of the frontline leaders. He realized that, unlike the Sikh community, Hindu society was not ready for satyagraha. He then considered the possibility of an alternative institutional mode of reform: 'Why not take recourse to law in initiating reforms?' he asked. 'Like Madras, Punjab and the United Provinces, Bihar should also explore the possibility of something similar to the "Hindu Religious Endowment Act" which would regulate and supervise the holdings and wealth of the mutts.'[87] He went on to study the religious endowment legislation of both Punjab and Madras, and of the United Provinces. Taking inputs from them, Jagat Narain prepared a bill along similar lines to be tabled in the Bihar Council. However, instead of introducing it himself, he asked his Hindu Sabha colleague, Rameshwar Prasad Dutt, to introduce it, he wanted to induct more people in the cause of temple reforms. 'It would only give impetus to corrupt temple mahantas who had assumed lack of leadership support.'[88]

He uses the choicest of epithets to describe the mahantas, the priests and the pujaris. They were riddled with, to use his words, *akarmanyata* (inertia), *kup mandukata* (frog-in-the-well mentality) and *vilasata* (decadence). 'These "half-literate" pandits were backed by Pandit Dharma Dutt ji. He even got himself nominated as the head of the mutt-deesh sabha and together they all vowed to oppose and destroy the bill. Property worth crores, donated by devout Hindus, lie in these temple coffers. It would have been an easy thing for them to use a few thousands for the benefit of common people. Pandit Dharma Dutt himself was a very wealthy man. He always travelled in cars and first-class compartments of trains and generally stayed in luxury. But instead of supporting

---

[87] Jagat Narain Lal, Private Papers, NMML, Speeches and Writings, 2(i), p. 18.
[88] Ibid., p. 20.

the protest campaign, he started publishing anti-reform articles in newspapers and giving us negative publicity.'[89] Jagat Babu describes these priests and mahantas as *'pragati virodhi pundit'*—anti-reformist, anti-development pundits. He also realizes that 'reformation of faith and associated practices takes time . . . and is even painful initially . . . This pain notwithstanding, once our institutions become regressive and corrupt, we as a collective are obligated to work towards their reform and transformation.'[90]

Jagat Narain Lal draws a parallel with the struggle for Swaraj. He writes that British colonialism had ensured that our mindsets had also got colonized. 'We were unable to think of freedom. But when Lokmanya and after him Gandhi ji unfurled the flag of *swaraj sangram* and acquainted people with the injustices and atrocities of the British, people became motivated and became willing martyrs for the cause of Swaraj.'[91] He goes on to say that just like the 'colonizers, the mahantas have also exploited and tricked the public. Greed and its partakers exist in every society and age. I am sure that, sooner or later, people will raise their voice against the caretakers of religion. It will be a matter of sustained effort and time, but people's eyes will open to the reality of these tricksters'.[92]

He reports, 'When the bill was presented in the Council in 1926, Sir Ganesh Dutt and Sir [Syed Mohammad] Fakruddin were the presiding ministers. The bill regulating religious charitable endowments was a very credible one and I was convinced that this government would not be able to turn it down. But how could the government ever be happy with reform? The government itself was hand-in-glove with the mahantas, and because most of them were wealthy zamindars the government was interested in keeping

---

[89] Jagat Narain Lal, Private Papers, NMML, Speeches and Writings, 2(i), p. 20–21.
[90] Ibid., pp. 21–22.
[91] Ibid., pp. 23–24
[92] Ibid., pp. 23–24

them on its side. Almost all the ministers' convenience, especially Sir Ganesh's, lay in this. That is why, when the bill was tabled, the government set up a committee to assess and submit a report on whether there was a need for a law regulating the religious and charitable trusts and mutts.

The committee comprised some members from the Council and a few members who were nominated from the outside by the government. It comprised mahants from the Imar (Puri) and Tirhut [Muzzafarpur, Bihar] mutts; Mahant Darshani Das ji from Maniyar mutt; Maharaja of Gidhaur [Bihar]; Babu Mahendra Prasad, Rai Brajraj Krishna, Babu Rameshwar Prasad Dutt, a British magistrate, along with me and a few others whose names I am forgetting. The Committee began its work by preparing a questionnaire. The questionnaire was published in the newspapers and responses were solicited from select institutions and eminent personalities. However, the work did not progress beyond that. The government was not really interested. It soon became clear that soliciting public opinion through the questionnaire was a means to stall and delay proceedings. When responses didn't come, it became an excuse and an opportunity to allow the initiative to fizzle out.'[93]

Jagat Narain Lal then very resentfully concludes that because of governmental machinations, lack of support from colleagues, at times opposition from some of the leading Hindu leaders at the forefront in Bihar, he could not go far in executing his project. With his arrest in 1928, he writes, the task of temple reforms and religious and charitable trust endowment regulation for Bihar was left unfinished.[94]

---

[93] Ibid., p. 25.

[94] In 1928, during the time Jagat Narain Lal was imprisoned, Godavari Misra made another attempt to present a bill titled 'Bihar and Orissa Hindu Religious and Charitable Endowments Bill', to the Local Legislative Council. He however later withdrew it as he considered it desirable to gauge public opinion in the matter before proceeding.

The truth is, Jagat Babu could not elicit support from those who claimed to represent the Hindu community. The Hindu Mahasabha itself did not unequivocally come out in support of either reforms or proposals for legislation. In Madras, for example, the Hindu Sabha agitated against the Madras Hindu Religious Endowments Bill, which would have allowed the Justice Party to control temple properties and endowments.[95] Jagat Narain also mentions that in August 1925, when the working committee of the Hindu Mahasabha met at Simla to plan its participation in the forthcoming central and provincial council elections, he met Narayan Swami ji of the Sanatan Dharma Pratinidhi Sabha, but found him to be evasive— 'Nothing was to be expected from those who were protecting the political interests of the orthodox.'[96]

Richard Gordon's work on Hindu Mahasabha confirms the similar outcomes in South India: 'The Mahasabha refused to become entangled in the Brahmin versus non-Brahmin controversy in the south. Since Brahmins alone opposed the Religious Endowments Bill, the Mahasabha decided to remain neutral.'[97] Although the Mahasabha attempted to represent the bitterly conflicting *Sanatan Dharm* (orthodox Hinduism) and the Arya-Samaji factions, as well as the professional elements associated with more progressive and reformist issues, 'ideologically, the Hindu Mahasabha was dominated by *Sanatan dharm*'.[98] Jagat Narain Lal's notes too reveal the bitter rivalry between the two factions in the Delhi Convention

---

Anyhow, this attempt in Bihar and Orissa proved equally abortive. *Report of the Hindu Religious and Charitable Endowments Committee, United Provinces* (The Superintendent, Government Press, United Provinces, 1931).

[95] *The Hindu*, 22 January 1925.

[96] Jagat Narain Lal, Private Papers, NMML, Writings and Speeches, 2(j), p. 19.

[97] Gordon, *Hindu Mahasabha*, p. 175.

[98] *Leader*, 16 August 1916, p. 4. Microfilm, NMML.

of the Hindu Mahasabha where, he writes, 'agitated Santanis walked out of the pandal after bitter differences with the Arya Samajis on the question of untouchability reforms'.[99] In Punjab too, the struggle between the Arya Samaj and Sanatan Dharm to control the Mahasabha platform[100] made the Hindu Mahasabha ambivalent towards the Akali gurudwara reform movement. For Jagat Babu, though, the Akali gurudwara reform movement was a reform template. As it aimed to free the gurudwaras from the control of ignorant and corrupt Udasi Sikh mahantas, it became a guiding force for the kind of temple satyagraha that he had wanted to organize.

Abductions, Music before Mosque

If our mutt-dheesh and priests are morally corrupt, let's try and reform them, or even punish them. But it doesn't mean that because they are bad, we cannot point a finger at the excesses of other religious communities?

—Jagat Narain Lal to Gandhi

As a devout Hindu, Jagat Babu felt it was his duty, and as a nationalist his mandate, to reform the Hindu community and its practices. He was fairly independent-minded and not stee red by party positions of either the Congress or the Mahasabha. He debated and disagreed with them openly if it conflicted with his own understanding. Once he even crossed paths with the Mahatma.

In one of his diaries, Jagat Babu narrates an interesting exchange with Mahatma Gandhi. During his tour of Assam (1925), apart from witnessing thousands of Khasis and Garo tribals converting

---

[99] Jagat Narain Lal, Private Papers, NMML, Writings and Speeches, 2(i), pp. 27–28.
[100] See Gordon, *Hindu Mahasabha*, 1915 to 1926, pp. 180–82.

to Christianity, he witnessed tales of abduction of Hindu women by Muslims.[101] He gave a public speech in Gauhati exhorting the people to be concerned about the safety and well-being of not just the women of their family, but of all the women of their community, as abduction was a matter that should be a matter of deep concern for all. As reported by him, so rampant was the menace of abduction, that Lajpat Rai (with whom he was touring the region) advised him to send a report to Gandhi.

As instructed, on his return to Patna, Jagat Babu wrote a letter to Gandhi, apprising him of routine abductions of Hindu women by Muslim men. Gandhi replied: 'Bhai Jagat Narain, I do not have any evidence of the events you narrate. When I find evidence, I will reflect upon the problem.' Jagat Narain writes, 'I was hurt by Gandhi ji's lack of intent. How could a *mahapurush* like him, who was so experienced and so far-sighted, fail to take cognizance of the overwhelming evidence in front of him? How was it possible that he was not aware of the serious situation in Assam? It was possible that his karyakartas form Bengal lacked the courage to narrate those gory tales that were destroying the communal peace of that region. It may have been possible that Mahatma ji was never told about these dreadful happenings.'[102] Jagat Narain went on to instruct his colleagues and ministers from the Hindu Mahasabha to meet the Mahatma and provide him with full information and details on the matter.

Soon after, Jagat Narain Lal met Gandhi at the Annual Conference of the Bihar Provincial Congress in Purulia (1925). Armed with proof of abductions in Assam, he says, he accompanied Rajendra Prasad when he went to meet Gandhi. 'I offered my humble pranam to Gandhi and then laughingly said to him: "In response to your letter, I have brought an entire library of information on

---

[101] Jagat Narain Lal, Private Papers, NMML, Writings and Speeches, 2(i), pp. 3–6.
[102] Ibid., 2(i), p. 17.

abductions". Mahatma ji ruefully replied, "What can be said when the representatives of Hindus, the mahants, acharyas, sadhus are themselves so corrupt?" I was a bit agitated by Gandhi ji's reply and logic, and said, "If our *mutt-dheesh* and priests are morally corrupt, let's try and reform them, or even punish them. But it doesn't mean that because they are bad, we cannot point a finger at the excesses of other religious communities." Our interaction was brief, but this episode remains etched in my memory.'

For Jagat Babu, the expectation of reform was not just limited to his own religion, it extended to a similar expectation of Muslim practices too. Often, this expectation would combine with his angst against what he saw as the government's partial treatment of the Muslim community. On 13 June 1926, the magazine he edited, *Mahavir*, carried an article titled 'Music before Mosque', alleging partial treatment and greater leniency to the Muslims in the matter of cow slaughter than that extended to Hindus with respect to playing music before mosques. The matter reached the political department of Bihar and Orissa where it was dismissed, saying that 'the article is hardly so offensive as to our suggesting to the Bengal government for further action. They are quite likely to reply that they are being exposed to much worse criticism in their own Press, while comments of Mahavir are not likely to do them much harm.'[103]

Jagat Narain's position with respect to cow slaughter is made more explicit in a speech at the India's National Parliament's Convention in December 1927. Commenting on a resolution Sarojini Naidu had moved—calling it the 'Magna Carta of tolerance'—asking both Muslims and Hindus to exercise restraint and consideration in matters of cow slaughter and music before mosque,[104] Jagat Narain said that the clause

---

[103] Government of Bihar and Orissa, Political Dept., File no. 210, 1926. Bihar State Archives.

[104] Resolution moved by Sarojini Naidu, 28 December, 42nd session of India's National Parliament: The Congress resolves that without prejudice

was unhappily worded and would lead to more bloodshed and riots. The ambiguity in the clause 'kill cows wherever they please' would lead to a number of interpretation and 'would lead Moslems to kill cows wherever they chose'.[105] The issue of cow slaughter was close to his heart, a matter of faith and belief, just as it was for Gandhi.

The 1920s were testing times for communal accord. An ambience of allegations and counter-allegations, distrust and suspicion fuelled communal tensions and conflict. Though the article 'Music before Mosque' was dismissed as harmless, it was soon after that Jagat Narain Lal, as the founding editor of the weekly *Mahavir*, would be charged with fanning communal tensions and sedition.

The Mahavir Sedition Case

Little did I know then that my heartfelt, honest arguments, aimed at solving the communal problems, would aggravate the masters to such an extent that they would slap a case of rajdroha (sedition) against me. It was fairly obvious that my editorial was just an excuse.

The story of the sedition charge begins in 1926, a period in which communal tensions assumed, as Jagat Narain writes, *vikral* (gargantuan) proportions. 'Calcutta, Kanpur, Bhagalpur,

---

to the rights that Hindus and Mussalmans claim, the one to play music and conduct procession wherever they please, and the other to slaughter cows for sacrifice and food wherever they please, the Mussalmans appeal to the Mussalmans to spare Hindu feelings as much as possible in the matter of the cow, and the Hindus appeal to the Hindus to spare Mussalman feelings as much as possible in the matter of music before mosque. *Indian Quarterly Register*, Vol. 2 No.3 July–Dec 1927, p. 399–401. Ideas of India—Rediscovery of India Archives, https://www.ideasofindia.org/. Last accessed on 18 August 2020.
[105] Ibid., p. 404.

Sasaram, Betia and many other places of North India were in the throes of communal tensions, rioting and killings. The distrust between Hindus and Muslims had reached such proportions that even a trivial excuse was enough to fan communal fires and start a riot.'[106]

Lord Irwin, then Viceroy of India, made, to quote Jagat Narain, 'an impassioned plea to people of the country asking them to put an end to the "barbaric communalism" that was engulfing the country. He also appealed to the leaders of the Hindu and Muslim community to use their influence to restore peace and harmony . . . In response, as the editor of *Mahavir*, I decided to write a radical editorial that expressed my own feelings in the matter . . . Little did I know then that my heartfelt, honest arguments, aimed at solving the communal problems, would aggravate the masters of the Bihar government to such an extent that they would slap a case of *rajdroha* (sedition) against me. It was fairly obvious that my editorial was just an excuse.'[107]

Jagat Narain Lal was tried and prosecuted for sedition under Section 124A of the Indian Penal Code for writing an editorial criticizing the Viceroy's address to the members of the Council and State Legislative Assembly. The prosecution stated that the 'accused who is the editor, printer and publisher of the vernacular newspaper called the "Mahabir" is charged with having brought, or attempted to bring, into hatred or contempt, or excited or attempted to excite disaffection towards, the government established by law in British India by publishing an article titled "*Viceroy ka bhashan*" on pages 3 and 4 of the issue of "Mahabir" dated 4th September 1927'. The judgment reports that 'the accused does not deny his responsibility for this article and [states] that whatever comments I have made in the

---

[106] Jagat Narain Lal, Private Papers, NMML, Writings and Speeches, 2(j), p. 26.
[107] Ibid., p. 27.

article which forms the subject matter of the complaint, I have made in perfect good faith in the discharge of my duties and responsibilities as Editor.'[108]

The 'seditious' paragraphs were translated and presented in the court. The concerned paragraph(s), the prosecution stated, 'is devoted to the consideration of the serious problem of Hindu Muslim strife which has thrown all other problems of the country into the background and that the black clouds of Hindu–Muslim have overcast the Indian firmament . . . In the 6th paragraph the writer asks—what Indian with a longing for freedom is there whose heart does not break at the sight of the bureaucracy again taking root and becoming stronger in this way? . . . The writer states that the Viceroy's heart has not yet been imprinted with the cruelty and hard-heartedness of the Indian bureaucracy . . . In para 16 [to 21] the writer says that the bureaucracy of the Viceroy's administration not only witnessed this frantic dance with great delight, but instigated it . . . they regard the domestic quarrel as the greatest supporter and helper of their own existence and achievement . . . that if today the intention of the administration becomes honest and if instead of making us fight among ourselves and instead of being mere spectators they take to establishing peace and with a true heart find out the way to effect a permanent unity between the two communities, peace would be established throughout the country even today . . . that the bureaucracy follows the policy of "divide and rule" [*bhedniti*].

[T]he writer charges the bureaucracy with having a hand in the Hindu Muslim quarrel and says that it is due to their irregular, one-sided and partial policy that this petty matter has assumed such formidable proportions . . . that in every province and in every district the administrators are adopting communal policies and

---

[108] Emperor v. Jagat Narain Lal, Section 124A IPC, File no. 260, 1927, Government of Bihar and Orissa, p. 2.

making matters more difficult and intricate.'[109] Further, '[T]he
writer says that His Excellency the Governor of Bengal adopted
a strange decision on the question of music [before mosques]
which caused Hindus and Mohammadans to fall out with each
other and be killed and says that such decisions are responsible for
augmenting this quarrel in other provinces also. In para 22, the
writer says that Behar did not catch the infection of this disease
because a few influential Mohammadans acted wisely and liberally
in the matter.'[110]

The prosecution continued: 'In para 23, the writer brings
a very grave charge against the government of this Province.
He says—but in this province too did the government leave
any stone unturned to augment the quarrel? Who set up the
quarrel of Phulwari last year? Who caused the Dinapore riots
by allowing cow sacrifice in a Mahalla where such sacrifice had
never been performed before? And who caused serious assaults
and riots to occur at Bettiah by its great carelessness? . . .
[T]he writer says that if the government enforces with the help
of military the performance of cow sacrifice at places where such
custom prevails, why does it stop forcibly music at places like
Allahabad and elsewhere where music was never stopped before
and why does it not suppress and punish those who agitate for
the stopping of the music? . . . What is the reason and what is
the secret of it? We would say it is the same policy of "Balance
of Power"' which England always adopted to control the great
powers of Europe, now helping France to overcome Germany and
now helping Germany to overcome France. In para 27 and 28,
the writer says that it would require a huge volume to relate
instances of the divide and rule policy of the government of India
and its host of administrators in the Hindu Muslim quarrel and
therefore he wishes to stop here and to impress upon Lord Irwin

---

[109] Ibid., pp. 3–5.
[110] Ibid., pp. 5–6.

that if he is really anxious to establish peace he must pull the administrators' ears and cause them to follow the right path.'[111]

'In para 29, the writer blames the two communities for dancing to the tune of the administrators and . . . says that the Muslim community is dancing gladly because the bureaucracy is a friend and it hopes, with the support of the bureaucracy, to suppress the Hindus. In para 31, the writer says that the frantic dance is never palatable to the Hindus, but that they have the power and retort under compulsion in order to protect themselves and maintain their self-respect. Lastly [...] the writer says that if the bureaucracy keeps its hands off and ceases to repeatedly incite its favourites, the Muhammadans, to fight, or if the Muhammadans themselves correct their understanding and give up acting like pawns on the chess board, peace would be established today and this frantic dance would end.'[112]

The prosecution went on to allege that '. . . the writer openly and definitely charges the government of this province with having incited riots and bloodshed at Dinapore and Bettiah and having attempted to do so at Pulwami. In para 32, which is the concluding paragraph of the article, the writer says that peace would be established immediately if the bureaucracy ceased to incite their favourites, the Muhmmadans . . . it seems to be absolutely clear and beyond question that the writer of the article has tried to impress upon his readers the unfortunate Hindu–Muslim quarrels and the subsequent riots and bloodshed are all due to the malevolent and mischievous interference of the bureaucracy and their deliberate incitement to one party to fight the other.'[113]

The prosecution argued that the words used by Jagat Narain Lal—*naukarshahi* (bureaucracy), *sasakasena* (administrative army),

---

[111] Ibid., pp. 6–7.
[112] Ibid., p. 7.
[113] Ibid., p. 8.

sasakamandal (administrative coterie) *and Bharat-sarkar* (Indian government—'these words themselves as well as the whole tenor and argument of the article indicate beyond question that the writer does not mean to criticize individual officers but the whole policy and motive of the government which according to him consists in deliberately setting one community against the other and inciting them to commit riots and bloodshed. I am equally unable to accept the defence argument that the intention of the writer is merely to appeal to the Viceroy to find a solution of the Hindu Muslim problem and that all the talk of the frantic dance to the tune of his authorities is merely flamboyant language which nobody will take seriously . . . the writer has in clearest language attributed dishonest and malevolent motives to the government . . .'[114]

The judgment went against Jagat Narain Lal: '[F]or these reasons I hold that the article in question comes within the purview of section 124A IPC and therefore the charge against the accused under that section is proved . . . It is not necessary to refer to other issues of Mahabir put in by the prosecution for the purpose of interpreting the intent of the writer. The accused is himself a lawyer and member of the Local Legislative Council, and this fact makes his offence in publishing such a rankly seditious article in his paper a very grave one.'[115]

'I accordingly find the accused Jagat Narayan guilty under Section 124A I.P.C. and sentence him to be simply imprisoned for a period of one year and also to pay a fine of Rs. 1000/- in default to be further simply imprisoned for a period of six months.'[116] In the appeal before the high court, argued by Sachchidanand Sinha, the chief justice upheld the judgement and Jagat Narain Lal spent

---

[114] Emperor v. Jagat Narain Lal, Section 124A IPC, File no. 260, 1927, Government of Bihar and Orissa, p. 7.
[115] Ibid., p. 13.
[116] Ibid.

the next one year in the Hazaribagh Central Jail. While his article, to use his words, 'was a burning plea for communal concord', the 'law of sedition, as our politicians know, is as perverse as it is all embracing'.[117]

Jagat Narain Lal appealed to the Patna High Court against his conviction, but it was rejected and the subordinate court's sentence was upheld.[118] Lala Lajpat Rai came out strongly in support, writing in the *People* that the 'Government's attitude towards the Hindus was not one of impartiality and fairness . . . the article contains statements and suggestions to the effect that the government follows a policy of "Divide and Rule". Now allegations like these have become quite hackneyed by repetition in the Indian press, both Hindu and Mussalam. Similar statements have been made by British authors and speakers also. What is the sense then of singling out a particular journalist for punishment for such statements . . . It would be hard to discover the Indian journalist who thought that Babu Jagat Narain Lal published statements which were false. Perhaps it would be safe to say that the task would be equally difficult if the whole class of educated men and women were to be searched for such a sincere believer in the impartiality and fairness of the bureaucracy. The ovation which the Bihar publicist received before going to jail, shows that thousands upon thousands in Patna think that the statements for which he has been punished are quite true; and there are reasons to think that a large number of his countrymen, who are not residents of that city, think so too.'[119]

---

[117] Lal, *LUC*, p. 57.

[118] "Babu Jagat Narain Lal's Conviction", *The Modern Review*. Vol 44, p.238. Ideas of India—Rediscovery of India Archives, https://www.ideasofindia.org/. Last accessed 18 August 2020.

[119] Ibid.

To Be or Not to Be a Hindu Mahasabha Member

The next three years of my life were full of internal and external strife . . .[120]

The business of forging identities is a complex one. Jagat Babu's own vacillations between the sacred ascetic form and its political Hindu mode, testify to a complex form of allegiance, deference and negotiation. While much of his personal conduct remained morally unambiguous, his politics often struggled to find the vocabulary of a nation-state that would not consider Hinduism to be irrelevant to its identity. Jagat Narain's fashioning of his Hindu Self may well have contributed to the prospects of Hindu identity politics, even though his own association with the Hindu Mahasabha appears to be not so much about politicizing Hinduism as much as revitalizing its core in terms of ethical organizing principles. In trying to do that, Jagat Narain—for all his emphasis on righteous conduct and dispassionate reason—made some unfortunate remarks about the Muslim leadership that were not unusual for the times. But the fact is that he remained unsparing in his indictment of Hindu priests and religious leaders too.

Jagat Babu remained deeply committed to social and religious reform, despite the fact that it remained unsupported and sometimes even opposed, as discussed earlier, by the Sanatan Dharm faction. His place in this continuum of religious beliefs and orthodoxies remained largely indeterminate. But his was not an indeterminacy that stemmed from a lack of doctrinal depth or an unhinged belief system. Jagat Babu's deepest vacillations were not while he served his terms in prison. Those were the months (cumulatively, years) when he explored and 'found his self'. His personal and political indeterminacy stemmed from a deep predicament. Out in the world, how and where could this enlightened, realized self find

---

[120] Ibid, pp. 97–98.

its political ground? His was a quest that did not align with either the religious orthodoxies of the Sanatan Dharma or the politics of Hindu nationalism. Yet he threw in his lot with the Hindu Mahasabha because he believed that the disunity of the Hindus was leading to its downfall, that unless the centres that disseminated Hinduism were reformed, unless they upheld the purest ethics of dharma, the society they led would be unhinged from its spiritual core and doomed to anarchy. The Congress, he felt, remained too squeamish, too apologetic about speaking for Hindu interests. A small but interesting anecdote narrated by Jagat Narain in his memoir, is telling of the prevailing sentiments around religion in the Congress: 'Along with my old friend, Narayan Prasad Sinha, MLA with whom I had first started the study of the Gita and the Upanishads in 1921, I wanted to form a study circle of lovers of the Gita. But, so nervous were most of the Gandhites and Congressmen of anti-religious bias of our socialist and communist fellow prisoners that they had hardly the courage to broach the matter openly,'.[121]

Jagat Narain's restless soul was always in search of spaces within which he could explore his identity, both as a Hindu and as a nationalist, often it seemed in that order of preference. He joined the Hindu Mahasabha in search of a political forum for his Hindu identity. Yet, he seldom speaks of Savarkar, which makes one think that perhaps the combination of religion and nationalism was not cast in one mould. The more the Hindu Mahasabha moved away from the Congress, the more restless Jagat Narain Lal became within the Mahasabha. The trial of becoming a nationalist had not yet been fully negotiated.

The period between 1932 and 1935, was of turmoil for Jagat Narain Lal. He writes that these three years 'were full of internal and external strife'.[122] This was the period when Bhai Parmanand assumed a more central position and control of the

---

[121] Lal, *LUC*, p. 107.
[122] Ibid., p. 95.

Hindu Mahasabha, which led to a hardening of the Mahasabha's Hindu-nationalism programme and anti-Congress agenda. Jagat Babu, self admittedly, 'always differed from the policy pursued by Bhai Parmanand in the Hindu Mahasabha'.[123] As Sinha notes, Jagat Narain Lal increasingly became disillusioned with the anti-Congress policy followed by the Hindu Mahasabha, and stopped drawing his allowance after his imprisonment in 1930,[124] a point that Jagat Narain also notes in his memoir.[125]

On his release from jail in 1932, Jagat Narain was all set to join Moonje's Servants of Hindu Society (SHS). His condition was that SHS should remain an apolitical organization focusing on constructive work. His disillusionment set in when he found that the lines between politics and seva or constructive work were not as clear as he thought them to be. In a letter to B.S. Moonje from Hazaribagh Central Jail, March 1932, he clearly states: 'The SHS should have no concern directly with politics and should remain devoted mainly to the fulfilment of constructive work and Sangathan, *Achutodhar* and Goraksha (organization, abolition of untouchability and cow protection, respectively). I consider that as the only proper policy.'[126] Jagat Babu alerts Moonje about the growing rift between the Congress and the Hindu Mahasabha. 'No one knows', he writes in the letter, 'where we would be hereafter on the political field. But the chances of being placed in different political spheres are greater in the case of those who already differ in their mentality. It is therefore that I am keeping the constructive programme of the Mahasabha alone as the objective of the SHS.'

Jagat Narain, quite naively, did not foresee that in the idea of seva and programme of seva sanghs lay the kernel of political Hinduism. He may have wanted to straddle the political boat of the Congress

---

[123] Ibid.
[124] Sinha, *Proceeding in Indian History Congress*, p. 483; See Lal, *LUC*, pp. 95–96.
[125] Lal, *LUC*, pp. 95–96
[126] Letter to B.S. Moonje. Jagat Narain Lal, Private Papers (donated to NMML).

and the seva boat of the Hindu Mahasabha, but it gradually became clear to him that this was a journey fraught with personal and political conflict. For him, the mutuality of relationship between the Congress and the Hindu Mahasabha was important and as that went down, so did his relationship with the Hindu Mahasabha. He confesses in the letter that he wrote to Moonje[127]:

> I wish to say something about the Mahasabha also. When one originally took to it and worked, we hardly knew that *it would take the shape of the Muslim League* and come into conflict with the Congress on certain points from time to time. This conflict has been the normal phase of the Sabha for the last six to seven years. And this has placed people of our type, time and again, in an awkward position in one institution or the other or in both. While it entails all necessary work and suffering, it hardly gives one mental peace. And this as a normal phase is neither bearable nor desirable and one must leave one institution or the another or reconcile both for the sake of persons of our type who would like to work if their position is not confined, i.e. either to carve out a political department of the Mahasabha and entrust it to one who may be a non-Congressman and carve out a department of constructive work of the Mahasabha and entrust it to people of our type leaving people of our type free to agree or not agree with the resolution on the political side . . .
>
> I may leave the Congress altogether as you have done and stick to the Mahasabha or as I fear knowing the irresistible inclination of my heart, I may decide against leaving an institution which has been so dear to me and for the sake of which I have borne no small suffering. I may in that case give my time to the Congress and take up social programmes of Hindu reformation individually or collectively as are dear

---

[127] Letter to B.S. Moonje. Jagat Narain Lal, Private Papers (donated to NMML), Translated.

to me. I have kept company so long with you as far as I could. Yet I consider it only fair to yourself and myself to let you know that inner struggle which has been continuing and the conclusion of which I have arrived at. If, weighing all this, you feel that I can usefully assist you in bringing the SHS into existence and building it, my full consent and the energy is at your disposal. I would in that case like to do all that is possible to draw some of the best and most influential workers to it and build it up with suitable funds, buildings, library and activity spread in all parts of the country. If this institution could be satisfactorily established, it would not only be a permanent tribute to Lalajee but a solid work achieved by you . . .

Things temporarily worked out for Jagat Narain. After his release in 1932 from Hazaribagh Central Jail in 1932, he formally joined the SHS.[128] However, things were to sour up soon when Bhai Parmanand (president elect at the Hindu Mahasabha Ajmer session, 1933) assumed control of the Hindu Mahasabha and gave it a thrust that was not what Jagat Babu had signed up for. He writes that Parmanand 'openly advocated a pro-government and anti-Congress policy, in defiance of all earlier traditions. The rift between us grew wider and wider until towards the end of the earthquake relief work in the province, I felt I could no longer associate with him . . . He had also assumed full control over the funds of the Servants of Hindu Society and contrary to all rules governing their utilization diverted them to the construction of buildings of the Hindu Sabha . . . We as trustees of the fund might have instituted legal proceedings to put a stop to this flagrant breach of regulations; but how indeed could we drag this sordid dispute in limelight?'[129]

As a mark of protest, Jagat Babu finally stopped taking his allowance from the Mahasabha. 'One thing only I could do in

---

[128] Lal, *LUC,* p. 86.
[129] Ibid.

conscience to record my resentment—to forego my allowance from the Mahasabha funds. I would not budge from my purpose: in vain did certain members of the Hindu Sabha executive try to dissuade me. That my domestic economy was thrown out of gear mattered little. *My needs must bear with all the anxiety that my decision entailed.*'[130]

* * *

On his release in 1932 from yet another term in the Hazaribagh Central Jail, Jagat Narain Lal joined Malaviya's Congress Nationalist Party in order to contest elections to the Central Assembly. His discontent with the Congress continued as the party, according to him, 'showed lamentable indecision' over the issue of Communal Award extending separate electorates to Hindus and Muslims. Though the plan had been 'condemned unequivocally from all sides as an insidious attempt at vivisecting India', the Congress had failed to officially reject the Award.[131] Jagat Babu's election campaign was not successful. He explains that 'for all my endeavours on behalf of the Hindu cause and my record service to the country, then, not only did I lose at the polls, but I forfeited my deposit as well'.[132] His only consolation was that he was able to foster the growth of the Hindusthan Seva Sangh, which he had founded in 1930.[133]

The idea of service was the one public ideal Jagat Narain Lal wouldn't let go of. It would be fair to say that politics for him always remained secondary to his commitment to social service. After successfully contesting the 1937 provincial assembly elections and becoming Parliamentary Secretary to the finance

---

[130] Lal, *LUC*, p. 96. Emphasis added.
[131] Ibid., p.97.
[132] Ibid., p. 98.
[133] Ibid., p. 104

minister,[134] and serving the ministry for twenty-seven months, he wrote: 'Office affected me very little . . . The reason was not hard to seek. I attached hardly any importance to the office I held; on the contrary, I felt I had compromised my position in public life and the high ideal I had set before me'.[135]

Jagat Babu was far too philosophically and spiritually oriented to ever be able to make politics his primary and focused pursuit. Had it not been for the freedom movement, who knows, his ascetic soul may have motivated him to renounce the world. Wrestling with the constant tug of ideals and need for contemplative space, nationalist politics was, in a sense, an undefining moment for him. Driven by disillusionment, he once said: 'Anyone else in my position would have been driven to suicide'. He contemplated giving up public life altogether as 'I had many other anxieties to wrestle with [and] even in spiritual matters . . . I was slipping downward'.[136] The more he attempted to align his religiosity with politics, the more dissonant did his outer and inner worlds become. No one was more acutely aware of his homelessness than Jagat Narain Lal. He repeatedly lamented and regretted the pitfalls and disjunctures of his chosen path.

Even when he formally signed up as a member of the Hindu Mahasabha, he never quite became one with the Hindutva proponents. He seldom, if at all, uses the word Hindutva (or even Hindu *rashtravaad* or Hindu nationalism for that matter) as a referential term for his own beliefs and decisions; an indication

---

[134]Jagat Narain Lal was the Parliamentary Secretary to the finance minister and the Labour portfolio came within the purview of his office. In his memoir, he lists the tasks he set out for himself: 'promoting the cause of labour by persuading employers to be just and generous', labour conciliation proceedings, rural reconstruction and development work, setting up of educational institutions, mass literacy and military training schemes and so on; Lal, *LUC*, pp. 104–105.

[135]Lal, *LUC*, p. 104.

[136]Ibid., p. 98.

perhaps that he remained distanced from the political thrust of Hindu nationalism that sought to merge nationalist identity with a religious identity. His letter to B.S. Moonje is unsparing in its indictment of the Hindu Mahasabha fast becoming a 'Hindu version of the Muslim League'.

Jagat Narain Lal was far too impelled by the force of his own (Hindu) identity to fathom how politically malleable identity itself is. His belief that seva and sangathan could remain tied to religious issues and identities, and remain un-politicized, or the expectation that there could be a neat separation of his 'political work with Congress' and 'social work with Hindu Mahasabha', were expectations that were both flawed and naïve. His expectation that in the shifting political allegiances, his identity would find political expression was replete with miscalculations. It only ended up endorsing a nationalist culture that would always seek the authentication of religious idiom.

An outsider to this world may well dismiss these conflictual identities as deeply irreconcilable. Perhaps they were, and maybe that is why peace eluded Jagat Narain Lal. But this conflict was not Jagat Babu's alone. Every ascetic-minded person seeking redemption in the politics of nationalism is likely to fail his own expectations. Nationalism mobilizes the sacrifice of an ascetic nationalist, but in doing so it displaces a personal quest for self-realization and submerges it in competing visions of the nation state. The more Indian nationalism mobilizes 'identity' in service of the nation, the more fractured individual identities and psyches became, eclipsing the self. Jagat Narain Lal is an exemplar: the more his self became fractured into simultaneous beings—a devout Hindu, a nationalist, a Congressman, a Hindu Mahasabhaite, a Gandhian, a karmayogi—the more he struggled to meet the requirements of a moral political life that he had set out for himself.

4

The Gathering Storm of
Anti-Colonial Nationalism

It was not as if Jagat Narain Lal became an 'anti-colonial nationalist' only from the mid-1930s onwards. His fight against imperial rule began the day he chose to give up his promising law career and join the Non-cooperation movement. And he became a 'noisy little man' for the British the day he moved the resolution for the boycott of Prince of Wales' visit to Patna in December 1921 and went to jail for it, embarking on his innings as a 'freedom fighter'. The preceding chapters testify to his fearless and selfless service as an anti-colonial nationalist.

In classifying Jagat Babu's onward journey from here on as anti-colonial, the suggestion is not that the earlier phases lacked anti-colonial content or aspiration. It is to bring to light a changing pattern in nationalist narratives in general and for Jagat Narain in particular. In the 1920s up until the mid-'30s, his struggle against imperial domination was combined with a deep quest for self-realization. If the political arena was his *karma bhumi* (domain of duty) where he served his country and its fight against colonial domination, his inner self always followed a separate, private path seeking its own freedom. Nothing came close to his yearning for contemplative spiritual solace. The mundane life of politics remained at best a duty and at worst a source of anxiety and disenchantment.[1]

His biggest disenchantment was perhaps with the failure of political Hinduism to imagine and construct a politics that was distinctly and consistently anti-colonial. For Jagat Babu, being Hindu was a self-contained, reflexive idea of defining oneself and one's deeds in relation to the cosmic whole. Attainment of vidya, as opposed to avidya, an *Isha Upanishad* teaching, remained his utmost intellectual and philosophical yearning.[2] He was initially drawn in by the idea of the political representation of the collective Hindu identity, but eventually admitted both the folly and the futility of it.

There was a distinct problem with the way Hindu nationalism fashioned itself. Its self-image was constructed largely in terms of a *religious other*—the Muslims and Christians in that order of 'othering'—and hence the primary pegs for its identity were not the principles of its own religion, Hinduism, but rather the sociological and historical reality of those it considered communal opponents and outsiders. As long as Jagat Babu remained actively associated with the Hindu Mahasabha, his primary identity lay fractured between being a Hindu, being a political Hindu and being an anti-colonial, all three in a messy, mutually conflictual mélange. He took a decade and a half to experience the full implications of these contradictions, especially between Hindu nationalism and the *Indian* national movement. Amongst the

---

[1] In one instance, he writes: 'The worries associated with Congress work and the insincerity that I sensed all [a]round me weighed heavily on my mind. I pined for mental peace. One evening I made up my mind that I could no longer endure this. I decided to leave Patna next morning in search of peace and to abstain from food until I had left the town.' Lal, *LUC*, p. 40.

[2] Ibid., pp. 21–22.

many contradictions that he was willing to live with, two that were non-negotiable for him were being a Hindu and being anti-colonial. He soon found a way to be both, without the mediating platform of political Hinduism.

In a letter dated 25 May 1934, Jagat Narain writes to B.S. Moonje again, reiterating his firm disavowal of the turn taken by the Hindu Mahasabha after Bhai Parmanand assumed control. Though this letter is much shorter than the 1932 letter (extracts of which are reproduced in the previous chapter), his exasperation and disenchantment are clear. Referring to Bhai Parmanand he writes: 'You may have read Bhaiya's statement on the Congress decisions which are entirely wide off the mark and unnecessarily offensive. It is a pity that at a time when the Mahasabha could have received utmost sympathy from Congress quarters in the rejection of the Communal Award, Bhaiya's tactics have served more and more to annoy and antagonize it . . . [W]e have our own position in relation to Hindustan which has been compromised unnecessarily by Bhaiya's speeches and statements and ought to be made clear in the eyes of the others'.[3] Jagat Narain mentions this growing rift in his memoir too. 'I had always differed from the policy pursued by Bhai Parmanand in Hindu Mahasabha . . . When Bhai Paramanand was elected president of the Hindu Mahasabha he openly advocated pro-government and anti-Congress policy, in defiance of all earlier traditions. The rift between us grew wider and wider until . . . I felt I could no longer associate with him.'[4]

By the mid-'30s, the Hindutva idea of ethno-nationalism had begun to unravel for Jagat Babu. By repeatedly following an anti-Congress policy, he felt that the Hindu Mahasabha was collaborating with the British and undermining the anti-colonial struggle of the national community. Despite his many

---

[3] Letter to B.S. Moonje. Jagat Narain Lal, Private Papers (donated to NMML).
[4] Lal, *LUC*, pp. 95–96.

disagreements with the Congress, despite his strong disapproval of its ambivalence with respect to the Communal Awards, the Congress remained for him a locus of collective nationalist aspirations and a bulwark of India's struggle for freedom. To go against it was to stand against the will of the people. By criticizing the Hindu Mahasabha as another version of the Muslim League (as he had rather brutally reminded B.S. Moonje)[5], Jagat Babu had made a choice. He chose to pitch his tent firmly in a nationalist camp that was decisively anti-colonial.

The Idea of National Community: One Electorate

The Communal Award is an insidious attempt at vivisecting India.

1932 was a year of turmoil and ferment. The thorny question of communal representation was threatening to divide the country like never before. The Simon Commission (1929) had already recommended that separate electorates be maintained for Muslims and Sikhs. In 1931, the British premier Ramsay Macdonald took this a step further at the Second Round Table Conference, where an institutional arrangement to split the Indian electorate primarily on grounds of religion through a *Communal Award* was proposed.

In a diary entry dated 18 August 1932 (while serving time in jail in the aftermath of the Civil Disobedience movement) Jagat Narain writes: 'I got a detailed report of the Communal Award from the *Statesman*. I read it carefully. The British government has, for its own self as well as the nation, sowed the seeds of poison. Let us see what poisonous tree grows out of it? Mahasabha's executive

---

[5] See Chapter 3, pp. 101–02. The Hindu Mahasabha had ideological similarities with the Muslim League in their respective beliefs of 'one religion/culture, one language' as the guiding force of nationhood, borrowing from the parochial nationalism of western Europe. The Mahasabha saw the national movement as a movement for civilizational assertion, primarily against others who were claiming Hindustan as their own land.

session is being convened, and rightly so, to decide on policy matters relating to the Award. I am apprehensive though that they might take decisions and positions which might make my future cooperation with them difficult. It is possible that I might face this dilemma and I look to god to show me the way forward'.[6]

The Hindu Mahasabha, as expected, had rejected the Communal Award in keeping with its general opposition to any legislative safeguards or reservation of seats for Muslims.[7] The Congress on the other hand faced one of its biggest political and moral quandaries as the Communal Award was threatening to drive a further wedge between Hindus and Muslims. At Bombay session held in October 1934, the INC resolution declared: ' . . . the Congress claims to represent equally all the communities composing the Indian Nation and therefore, in view of the division of opinion, can neither accept nor reject the communal award as long as the division of opinion lasts . . .'[8]

The Congress may not have accepted the Award in principle but had practically accepted all its real effects. 'The Hindu Mahasabha bombarded the Congress with its criticism,' and the Communal Award not only divided the communities but threatened to split the Congress itself.[9] Jagat Narain reports that top-ranking Congress officials had frankly voiced their disapproval, but this had failed to translate into an official rejection. He adds that the 'Congress in neither accepting the award nor rejecting it outright,

---

[6] Jagat Narain Lal, Private Papers, Speeches and Writings, 2(1), p. 5.

[7] See B.S. Moonje's letter to Raja Narendra Nath, dated 25 June 1929, Jaykar Papers, File no. 436, NMML.

[8] *Indian National Congress, Resolutions 1934–36*, pp. 19–20.

[9] Sharma, "Communal Award and the Indian National Congress", *Proceedings of the Indian History Congress*, Vol. 33, pp. 566–570, 568–569. For an interpretation of how the Hindu Mahasabha rejection of reservations and any legislative safeguards for Muslims made negotiations difficult for the Congress, see Bapu, *Hindu Mahasabha in Colonial India*, pp. 149–50.

showed lamentable indecision, for the plan had been condemned unequivocally on all sides as an insidious attempt at vivisecting India'.[10] Distressed by the Congress resolution on the Communal Award, one of its stalwarts, Madan Mohan Malaviya, even tendered his resignation and set up his own party, the Congress Nationalist Party, that Jagat Narain Lal went on to join.

The discord over the Communal Award and Congress' stand continued in the form of agitations and counter resolutions by many local affiliates and provincial Congress units. Then Congress President Nehru, while admitting how hard Bengal had been hit by the communal decision, asked for a ban on agitation against the Award by Congress organizations.[11] Jagat Narain in the meantime had been fairly vocal in his opposition to what he thought would threaten the communal fabric of the country. In a letter, Nehru writes to him in 1936, in the countdown to the 1937 provincial assembly elections (the Congress was also attempting to strike a rapprochement with Malaviya's Congress Nationalist Party of which Jagat Narain Lal was a member), he explains the reasons for 'ban on agitations':

Firstly, the primary consideration for us should always be the issue of independence. Everything should be judged from that point of view . . . Congress wishes to avoid any activity which diverts attention from the main to the other matters. Such other matters which fit in with the larger issue, then, should be pressed with all vigour. When owing to various factors, it does not fit in, a special agitation based on it will injure the larger cause by making it appear that we are really thinking in terms of changes within the framework [of the] New Act, that is British imperialism. Secondly, the agitation would depend on [the] internal situation. It may be that an agitation, say carried in the main by Hindus, leads to a rival agitation in favour of the "Award" carried in the

---

[10] Lal, *LUC*, p. 97.
[11] AICC, 24/1936, Congress Election Manifesto.

main by the Muslims. This results in creating a situation in favour of the retention of the "Award", for such a conflict is inevitably exploited by the British Government against us. Therefore, the idea of one-sided agitation is not favoured by the Congress.[12]

In response to Nehru's letter, Jagat Babu relented. He wrote: 'It was about time that an amicable settlement was arrived at between Pandit Malaviya ji, representing the Congress Nationalist Party, and the Congress President, Pandit Jawaharlal Nehru, in respect to the elections to the Provincial Legislatures . . . I agreed to stand for the Provincial Legislature, in obedience of the wishes of my friends, though in view of my health, it might have been prudent to keep away from active politics.'[13] Jagat Babu contested elections for the Bihar Provincial Congress Legislature on a Congress ticket. 'The election', he writes, 'was almost a walk-over for me. The Hindu Sabha candidate forfeited his deposit.'[14] His rift with the Hindu Mahasabha by now was fairly wide open.

Jagat Narain Lal went on to become a member of the Bihar Congress Ministry as Parliamentary Secretary to the finance minister. The labour portfolio, he writes, 'came within the purview of [his] office and [he] had to deal with all the mills and factories in this capacity.'[15] He goes on to write that '[i]t is no small satisfaction to think that the Congress ministry was able to cope with the pressing problems with [no formal] labour department or labour machinery equipped for the purpose and was able to keep things going as well as possible.'[16] For him, issues of labour were not just a 'side portfolio' his ministry was saddled with. In his view, the finance ministry that was also concerned with labour, among

---

[12] AICC, 24/1936, Nehru to Jagat Narain Lal, 30 September 1936.
[13] Lal, *LUC*, p. 99.
[14] Ibid., p. 102.
[15] Ibid., p. 103.
[16] Jagat Narain Lal, Private Papers, NMML, Speeches and Writings, 1(c), p. 3.

so many other subjects, had to play as effective a part as possible.[17]
In the conduct of his portfolio, he even wrote a short treatise on
labour and capital, which I discuss in the next chapter. An oft
ignored and sidelined project of nation-building is the ironing out
of class contradictions between labour and capital. Jagat Babu was
astute enough to understand the significance of a workable unity
between labour and capital, a concern that was usually the preserve
of socialist national liberation movements.

Right Action as a Nationalist's Duty

Gandhiji's lesson in this regard seems right: Adherence to your siddhant
[principles] *is the only rule that should be followed while choosing one's*
path of action.

Jagat Narain Lal was arrested in December 1940 again for
participating in the campaign against the British and offering
'Individual Satyagraha'. The world was in the grip of World War
II. The Congress withheld its cooperation in the war effort and
made its support to Britain conditional to the British laying out
clearly what was there in it for India. The British government did
not clearly declare its war aims, the Congress remained unsatisfied
and in response several Congress provincial ministries resigned
in 1939 and Governor's rule began. The announcement of the
'August Offer',[18] too, was rejected by the Congress (under the

---

[17] Ibid.

[18] The August Offer was a proposal made by Viceroy Linlithgow in
1940 promising the expansion of the executive council of the Viceroy
of India to include more Indians, the establishment of an advisory war
council, giving full weight to minority opinion, and the recognition
of Indians' right to frame their own constitution. He committed the
British government to the revision of the Act of 1935 after the war. In
any such revision, however, 'full weight should be given to the views of
the minorities'. For more details, see, Mishra, "India's Response to the

presidentship of Maulana Azad with full support from Gandhi), which felt that the offer 'was ridiculously out of place' in a country demanding complete independence.[19]

'Differences broke out between the Congress and the British', recounted Jagat Narain, 'on the issue of war aims. All Congress ministries resigned in Nov 1939. As no settlement was in sight, the Congress launched its programme of individual civil disobedience under the leadership of Mahatma Gandhi.' He writes: '"Individual satyagrahas" began in 1940. We were all under the impression that Gandhi ji would choose from among Rajendra Parsad, Sardar Patel, Rajagopalchari, or Nehru as the *pratham* [first] satyagarhi. All four, at that time, were close aides of Gandhi ji. But the whole country was taken by a huge surprise when the news came that he chose Vinoba Bhave as the pratham satyagrahi.'[20]

Jagat Babu was one of those who signed up as an individual satyagrahi. 'Satyagraha camps were started for the training of individual satyagrahis,' He writes, 'and for a week, we all had to join the provincial training camp conducted at Sonepur. I took leave of a dear companion of mine on his deathbed in a hospital at Patna to join-up . . . We all courted imprisonment by shouting slogans prescribed by Gandhiji on dates selected by us. We were promptly arrested and taken to jail.'[21]

As individual satyagrahas gathered a following, the government of Bihar in the middle of October came up with a policy that stated: *Speeches or propaganda which are prejudicial acts will be prosecuted promptly under the Defence of India Rules where the*

British Offer of August 1940", 1979, pp. 717–719. Also see, Sitaramayya, *History of the Congress.* Vol. 2, pp. 234–238.

[19] Mishra, "India's Response to the British Offer of August 1940", 1979, pp. 717–719, 719.

[20] Jagat Narain Lal, Private Papers. Published as a translation: Jagat Narain Lal, "Why Jagat Narain Lal, Once a Hindu Mahasabha Member, Saw Nehru as a Fellow Patriot", Wire, 9 April 2019.

[21] Jagat Narain, *LUC*, p. 106.

evidence warrants it. Cases of persistent propaganda which cannot be dealt with by prosecution may be referred to Government for action under the Defence of India Rule 26.[22]

The government of Bihar responded with zeal and alacrity and proceeded to arrest those who offered satyagraha. Apart from Shrikrishna Sinha and Anugraha Narayan Sinha who were leading the movement, many others were arrested and convicted under the Defence of India Rules and each sentenced to one year's rigorous imprisonment. Those arrested included included 'Shri Sarangdhar Sinha, M.L.A., Shri Punyadeo Sharma, M.L.C, Shri Jagat Narayan Lal, M.L.A., who offered Satyagraha at Patna . . .'[23] According to a report of the Congress, 907 people had been arrested till 3 March 1941 and the total amount of fines imposed in Bihar alone was Rs 33,699. There were many more who offered satyagraha but were not arrested.[24]

Jagat Babu once again chronicles his time in the jail. 'Prison life this time proved to be highly beneficial to those who had been in office', he writes. 'The Ministers, dragged down from their positions of power and influence, now, in prison, rubbed shoulders with many whom they had either not had the time to meet and talk while in office, or had offended in the discharge of their normal duties. Here was an opportunity for remonstrances – polite or bitter. Efforts were made, on the one hand, to remove causes of friction among party groups within the Congress and, on the other to found and strengthen such groups.'[25]

He adds: 'My jail term began on 10 December 1940. Eight years after my last visit, I again got a chance to enter into those walls and see for myself, how much "dirt" had accumulated over

---

[22] Datta, *History of the freedom Movement in Bihar*, Vol. 2, p. 287.

[23] Ibid., p. 390.

[24] Indian National Congress, Report of the General Secretaries, March–October 1940, p. 20 (released by the AICC in March 1941).

[25] Lal, *LUC*, p. 108.

the years.'[26] From what he goes on to say, it is fairly obvious that he refers here metaphorically to 'dirt' within his own self. Each of his jail terms was an outcome of his political activities but once inside the prison, he became almost schizophrenically detached from the outside world, spending his days in meditative contemplation on the deeper quests of his existence. This time he toys with the idea of adopting brahmacharya. Taking inspiration from the teachings of Gandhi and Tolstoy, he asks: 'Could it be true that in the absence of Brahmacharya, spiritual existence is not possible?'[27] He refers to Tolstoy's *The First Step* and *The Relations of the Sexes* (Hindi translation *Stree aur Purush*), and to Gandhi's *Mangal Prabhat*. Perhaps he is mustering the resolve to climb, as he says, 'the third step of the ladder', referring to the Gandhian ideal of brahmacharya.

The tussle between his political participation and his deep need for spiritual exploration was constant. Still in jail, on 5 July 1941 he writes: 'It has been my experience that a person cannot remain steadfast amidst competing calls of duty. The turmoil of politics and society make it difficult for me to remain steady. Gandhi ji's lesson in this regard seems right: Adherence to your principles (siddhant) is the only rule that should be followed while choosing one's path of action. This is all that is there in the hands of a mortal being and this alone can be a guide to contentment'.[28] This is not a belated realization of what was a fairly obvious code for moral conduct, but more of an acknowledgement and a resolution within Jagat Babu. He finally comes to realize that this simple guideline is as good as it gets.

He set up a Gita study circle and economics classes in the prison. 'The study of Gita became very popular and a large number

---

[26] Jagat Narain, Private Papers, Speeches and Writings, 2(f), p. 3. Translated.

[27] Ibid., p. 5.

[28] Ibid., p. 15.

of Gandhites and other Congressmen joined our group . . . We got hold of five or six of the most authoritative commentaries on Gita—those of Shankara, Ramanuja, Jnaneshwar Maharaj, Lokmanya Tilak and Mahatma Gandhi—and discussed the interpretation of every sloka. Our progress was slow, but it was a truly elevating experience.'[29]

Jagat Babu was released in August 1941,[30] around the same time as Shrikrishna Sinha and Anugraha Narayan Sinha. Together they began touring Bihar, explaining the significance of satyagraha and the need for observance of non-violence. Bihar in those days was in the throes of communal violence, once again fuelled by the Muslim League observing a Pakistan day (23 March) and the Hindu Mahasabha an Anti-Pakistan day (27 April), exacerbating the climate of suspicion and mistrust.[31] On 23 September, Jagat Narain Lal along with Shrikrishna Sinha, Anugraha Narayan Sinha and Jagjiwan Ram visited Arrah and spoke at length on the policy of the Congress in a public meeting attended by a large number of people.[32]

Individual satyagraha was a campaign that had been conducted on a small scale with a limited objective. It had continued for over fourteen months before it was suspended by the Congress in the wake of successive Japanese air raids in Assam, Bengal and Visakhapatnam. Most of the frontline leaders were behind bars, and fears about the campaign becoming leaderless and therefore unmonitored forced the Congress' hand. But individual satyagraha had registered 'moral protest against an imperialist policy of the British Government, which had dragged India into the war effort without making due concession to her legitimate

---

[29] Lal, *LUC*, p. 108.

[30] Jagat Narain Lal, Private Papers, NMML, Speeches and Writing, 2(f), p. 18.

[31] Datta, *History of the freedom Movement in Bihar*, Vol. 2, p. 394.

[32] Ibid., p. 398.

aspirations'.[33] From this point of view it was a fairly successful national experiment, conducted with discipline and dignity. It was, as B. Pattabhi Sitaramayya, member and historian of the INC, chronicles, orderly and even effective.[34]

By December 1941, most satyagrahis and political prisoners had been released, including Jawaharlal Nehru and Maulana Azad. In less than three months of their release, they had to face the British Commission headed by Sir Stafford Cripps.

Undivided India: The Jagat Narain Lal Resolution

With unequivocal support from Jawaharlal ji, I tabled a resolution for 'undivided India'.

Sir Stafford Cripps visited India in March 1942 to discuss the British government's Draft Declaration on the Constitution of India.[35] The Cripps proposals for granting Dominion status to the Indian Union was accompanied by an exit option—any province not willing to accept the constitution would be given 'the same full status as the Indian Union'. These proposals were rejected by the Congress on largely two grounds: one, because they were designed to appease the Muslim League's call for Pakistan; and two because they fell short of India's demand for complete independence. The Congress Working Committee rejected the Declaration on 7 April 1942. The Muslim League too rejected the proposal because its demand for a separate Union of Muslim majority provinces was not recognized. The Mission failed and

---

[33] Ibid., p. 400.

[34] Sitaramyya, *History of Indian National Congress*, Vol. II, p. 336.

[35] The British government was keen to secure the full cooperation of India in the effort against the Japanese. The mounting threat of Japanese invasion, as well as pressure from allies, led Prime Minister Winston Churchill to send Stafford Cripps to India to discuss the Draft Declaration containing proposals for a new Constitution and self-government for India.

the issue of India's Constitution was postponed until the end of the war.

It was following this that C. Rajagopalachari, or Rajaji as he was called, brought the 'Madras Resolution' to the AICC meeting in Allahabad on 7 May 1942. The resolution recommended that the All India Muslim League's demand for separation from a united India ought to be acknowledged and that the League might be invited for consultations for arriving at an agreement for securing the 'installation of a national government to meet the present national emergency'.

Rajaji's assessment ended up generating resentment throughout Congress circles, embittering leaders like Nehru, Azad, Patel and many others, including Jagat Babu. His first resolution was defeated by an overwhelming majority (120 to 15) while the second was withdrawn. It was then that a positive statement of the Congress position, known as the Jagat Narain Lal resolution, was passed by a substantial majority (92 for and 17 against). It stated that '[A]ny proposal to disintegrate India by giving liberty to any state or territorial unit to secede from the Indian Union or Federation would be highly detrimental to the best interests of the people of the different States and Provinces and the country as a whole, and the Congress cannot agree to any such proposal.'[36]

Expressing his unequivocal stand for an undivided India, Jagat Narain wrote, 'In May 1942, an AICC meeting was convened under the presidentship of Maulana Azad. With unequivocal support from Jawaharlal ji, I tabled a resolution for "undivided India". It was pitted against C. Rajagopalachari's resolution favouring the partition of India in accordance with the Stafford Cripps proposals. My resolution was backed by many Congressmen in the hope that the partition-talk would quieten down, and was passed by an overwhelming majority vote. This proposal received a

---

[36] AICC File No. G22/1942, NMML

lot of attention in the newspapers and was greeted wholeheartedly by the nation.'[37]

Across India, Congressmen were outraged by the suggestion that India should concede 'separation', writes Rajmohan Gandhi, Rajaji's biographer.[38] Azad was 'astonished'; Nehru termed C.R.'s move 'undesirable' and 'extraordinary'; Patel was furious. The Mahatma was critical but also understanding.[39] Rajaji tendered his resignation and for the moment at least, Jagat Narain Lal's resolution, asserting the geographical and political integrity of India as a territorial single unit, seemed the way forward.[40]

In August 1942, Gandhi, with CWC and AICC endorsement launched the Quit India movement. By dawn on 9 August, Gandhi and many other leaders were arrested and the Congress was banned. Jagat Babu was at the forefront of the Quit India movement in Bihar, with much of his activity having gone underground. On 12 September 1942, 'he addressed a secret meeting at Baman Bigha near Harnaut and was constantly moving around in Nalanda and Bakhtiyarpur districts to evade arrest . . .'[41] During one such movement from Birgu Milkhi village in Bakhtiyarpur district, while crossing the river Punpun in a boat,

---

[37] Jagat Narain Lal, Private Papers, Speeches and Writings, 1(d), p. 2.

[38] Gandhi, *Rajaji: A Life*, p. 235.

[39] Ibid.

[40] Pattabhi Sitaramyya however suggests that there may have been parallel and conflicting considerations at play. He says that 'the President of the Congress still confirmed in a letter to Dr. Abdul Latif, who was working on the Scheme of Pakistan, that Jagat Narain Lal's resolution did not affect the position contained in the Delhi resolution recognizing the right of territorial units to self-determination, which remained intact and was not disturbed or discounted by the Allahabad resolution opposing Pakistan,' (Sitaramyya, *History of Indian National Congress*, Vol. II, p. 346).

[41] Jagat Narain Lal, *Light unto a Cell* (2019 edition), Sinha (ed.), p. xvi.

Jagat Babu was surrounded, arrested, tried and sentenced to three years' rigorous imprisonment.[42]

On Partition and Pakistan

. . . the past of the Hindus and Muslims is a past of mutual animosities and destruction . . . the prospects might perhaps be different if the past of the two communities can be forgotten by both. Hence, the importance of forgetfulness as a factor in building a nation.

This time Jagat Babu spent close to three years in confinement. As someone who had tabled the resolution for an undivided India, the creation of Pakistan remained an issue on which he continued to reflect and write about in the Hazaribagh Central Jail, which by now had become a familiar abode for him. His Pakistan diaries (which resemble an untitled manuscript, divided into seven chapters) continue to grapple with issues of self-determination, of both India and Pakistan. In one instance, he summarizes Ambedkar's response from his book *Pakistan or the Partition of India* and then adds, 'The politicians who are anxious to concede to the Muslims the right to separate state and secede should note the warning given here by Dr. Ambedkar. The doctor says that it should be borne clearly in mind that once the secession has taken place, it would be futile to entertain the hope that it would be

---

[42] Ibid. The fact of his arrest was also attested by Pattabhi Sitaramyya—he states that a government pamphlet titled, 'Congress Responsibility for the disturbances, 1942–43', published by Sir Richard Tottenham, contained a passage stating that Jagat Narain Lal was personally responsible for instigating a mob that committed arson and looting in the Patna area on August 12 and that he had been sentenced to three years' rigorous imprisonment on that charge. Sitaramayya, *History of the Congress*, Vol. II, p. vii.

possible to win back the seceding provinces as was done in USA after the civil war.'[43]

But what is more interesting are Jagat Babu's reasons for favouring a united India. Reflecting on what makes and hold a nation together, he says 'nationalism is a matter of historical experience. Neither race, nor lineage, nor country has sufficed to mould a people into a nation. In the words of Renan: "Racial facts, important as they are in the beginning, have a constant tendency to lose their importance . . . language invites reunion; it does not force it. United States and England, Spanish America and Spain, speak the same language and do not form single nations. On the contrary, Switzerland owes her stability to the fact that she was founded by the assents of her several parts who speak three or four different languages. In reality, there is something superior to language—Will. The Will of Switzerland to be united. This Will is much more important fact than a similarity of language often obtained by persecution."'

Drawing from Ernest Renan's *Essay on Nationality*, he writes: 'it is no more the land than the race that makes a nation. The land provides a sub-stratum, the field of battle and work; man provides the soul.' Discarding both race and language, Jagat Narain goes on to argue that even historical antecedents are not reliable attributes of nationhood. He gives the example of Hindus and Muslims in India. 'Instead of being united by common historical antecedents, the past of the Hindus and Muslims is a past of mutual animosities and destruction, both in the political as well as in the religious fields . . . the prospects might perhaps be different if the past of the two communities can be forgotten by both. Hence, the importance of forgetfulness as a factor in building a nation. Thus "forgetfulness" and, I shall say even historical error, form an essential factor in the creation of a nation.'[44]

---

[43] Jagat Narain Lal, Private Papers, Speeches and Writings, 17(II), p. 15.
[44] Ibid., p. 16.

According to him, the two communities may never really 'forget or obliterate their past because their past is embedded in their religion. For each to give up its past is to give up its religion'. But then he says that in spite of this divergent 'genealogical system', 'it must be admitted that there do exist cases where people are aware of their nationality, but this awareness does not produce in them that possession which is called nationalism. In other words, there may be nations conscious of themselves but without being charged with nationalism'.

He continues, 'On the basis of such reasoning, it may be urged that the Mussalmans may hold that they are a nation; but they need not on that account demand a separate national existence. Why can they not be content with the position which the French occupy in Canada and the English occupy in South Africa?'[45] This, Jagat Narain Lal says, 'is quite a sound position', clearly making a pitch against the Partition of India and imagining the formation of a united India on the basis of shared affinities and a *will* to live together.

The question is, he asks, 'what should be considered to be the true expression of that Will? For the past sixty years the Indian National Congress has worked to evolve one united nation and has put forward a united demand for the establishment of a free government of the people in this country. Hindus, Muslims, Christians, Parsis, Sikhs have upheld this demand, and Madrasis, Punjabis, Bengalis, Biharis, Marathas and others have all stood on one platform and put forward a united demand for it. Should not that be treated as the Will on the part of all sections of the people to live as one nation in this country? Why should the morbid will prevail, which but a section of Muslims have been encouraged to develop for separation or partition of this country?'

Jagat Babu's passionate advocacy for a united India was soon to meet a disappointing end. It was while in jail that he received the

---

[45] Ibid., pp. 20–21.

news of a rapprochement between Gandhi and Rajagopalachari with respect to the 'much-reviled and prophetic Rajaji formula' for a Congress-League agreement.[46] As Rajmohan Gandhi notes in Rajaji's biography: 'Calling on Linlithgow in November [1942], C.R. had suggested that Gandhi was likely now to be readier for a compromise . . .'[47] Gandhi was in the Pune jail in the aftermath of the Quit India movement, which is when Rajaji approached him, hoping to get him on board.[48] The Rajaji formula required the League to cooperate with Congress in the formation of a provisional national government—if, on its part, Congress agreed to abide by a plebiscite on the question of Pakistan.[49]

The Rajaji formula received Gandhi's approval, for in April 1943, after his meeting with Gandhi, C.R. met with Jinnah and indicated to him that Gandhi was flexible about Pakistan.[50] The news of these parleys reached Jagat Babu in jail and, needless to say, he was deeply anguished. 'As the mover of the Anti-Pakistan resolution at the AICC in Allahabad, who is still lodged in Hazaribagh Central jail . . . [I] adhere to that resolution in its letter and spirit and am watching with deepest pain and anguish the unfortunate course of events which have developed by the offer of Rajaji to Mr. Jinnah of Pakistan, and Mahatma Gandhi's approval of the same. Rajaji's views on the question are too well known. They were repudiated by an overwhelming majority by the AICC at its Allahabad meeting and practically by the whole country. That Gandhiji should have reviewed the same and given his private consent to it and should now be publically endorsing it in the face of a positive resolution of the AICC, and in repudiation of his own strong and definite views expressed on the question,

---

[46] Gandhi, *Rajaji*, p. 235.
[47] Ibid.
[48] Ibid.; Guha, *Gandhi*, 2018, p. 701.
[49] Gandhi, *Rajaji*. For details, see, Guha, *Gandhi*, pp. 734–735.
[50] Gandhi, *Rajaji*.

and in the teeth of opposition of all the parties and interests to be affected, at a time so inopportune and uncalled for, is the deepest tragedy of the hour. I hope God will give the nation the courage and the strength to speak out freely and convince Gandhiji of the futility and inadvisability of this idea and to turn down this proposal which is calculated to bring everlasting ruin and misery to this country.'[51]

Jagat Babu, disappointed, wrote: 'There was no way for Gandhiji to speak on behalf of all political prisoners, particularly at a time when he had had no opportunity to ascertain the views of all of them nor did he actually do so . . . While political prisoners have full faith in Gandhiji's leadership in the fight for Swaraj, opinion is sharply divided among them on the Pakistan question and the Rajaji formula and the offer that has been made on that basis to Mr. Jinnah by Gandhi's approval. There is an influential section which feels that Rajaji's formula endorsing the same is prejudicial to the interests of the country.'[52]

Much later, Jagat Babu would reminisce on the event: 'Gandhi ji had already begun his talks with Jinnah on his Pakistan proposal in 1944. Partition was becoming imminent. I realized that my 1942 resolution—which the AICC had passed with a resounding majority and which ruled out "liberty to any component State or territorial unit to secede"—was becoming a road-block in the talks between Gandhi ji and Jinnah saheb. Hence, my proposal for an undivided India was dropped and Congress accepted Jinnah saheb's proposal for the partition of India. Gandhi ji till the end was opposed to the partition proposal. But seeing the growing consensus among senior leaders like Sardar Patel,

---

[51] Jagat Narain Lal, Private Papers, Notebook 9, NMML, pp. 36–38. This note has been written by Jagat Narain Lal in the third person, indicating that he was authorizing someone to move a resolution on his behalf.

[52] Ibid., pp. 35–36.

C. Rajagopalachari, and Jawaharlal Nehru, Gandhi ji acquiesced and did not offer any constructive opposition to the partition proposal. As a result, the British government drew up a proposal for both Partition and the complete independence of India. India was declared as a free nation on 15th August 1947 and Nehru was elected the first Prime Minister of a *free* India.'[53]

* * *

Anti-colonial nationalism is not an ideal with fixed attributes, but a concept with trajectories and content that may vary vastly between different historical settings. Here, it has been conceptualized in terms of two key features. First, quite simply, in terms of having India's Independence as its telos, with attributes that were by and large rational rather than emotional; second, in terms of taking a political stand against religious nationalism as developed by Hindutva ideologues such as Savarkar, Golwalkar, Moonje and others. This meant that anti-colonial nationalism pitted itself not only against the colonizing power, but also against Hindu nationalism and its idea that India belonged more to people of particular religious descent. In effect, it delinked the idea of citizenship from religious or cultural identity.

Jagat Narain Babu's diaries and letters attest to the fact that there was a growing distance between anti-colonial nationalism and Hindu nationalism at that juncture of history. More than ever before, the national question had become fused with the colonial question, and, in a sense, it became impossible to think of 'Freedom' without thinking of India's liberation from colonial rule. It may be the case that the national question had been historically fused with the colonial question from the early 20th century. However, equally true is the fact that in the decades that followed, assertions of national identity flourished alongside cultural assertions and

---

[53] Jagat Narain Lal, *Speeches and Writings*, 1(d), p. 5. Emphasis mine.

mobilizations, both collaboratively and conflictually—the Shuddhi and Sangathan movements, the campaign for Hindi as the official language, temple reform movements, seva sangathans, the Khilafat movement, issues of cow protection and music before mosques, the Dravidian movement, campaign for communal representation and so on. Issues of cultural assertion and identity politics proliferated alongside, if not at loggerheads with, the dominant strand of the anti-colonial 'freedom movement'.

From the late '30s–early '40s onwards, however, with the nation being *imagined* materially and its nuts and bolts being worked out—in legislations (Government of India Act 1935), elections (first provincial assembly elections 1973), legislative councils and ministries, proposals (Cripps), plans (Cabinet Mission), etc.—the idea of a meta-*national community* began to coalesce and gradually supersede cultural coalitions on religious, linguistic or caste lines. The gathering force of nationalism in the 1940s overwhelmed, and went beyond, the psychological, cultural or micro-sociological perceptions of the self and social identification. In the collective aspiration to 'have a nation' they could call their own, nationalism became almost a mystic phrase that promised the people freedom and the semblance of cosmopolitan oneness.

It is quite likely that some cultural identities may have felt smothered and marginalized. They remained, though, for the time being, silent and buried in the euphoric womb of a nation-in-the-making. Most of these 'sub-identities'—linguistic, religious or ethnic—were not numerically or ideologically dominant enough to become a sufficient force against the British. So anti-colonial nationalism became a discourse during the 1940s.[54]

---

[54] In any case, language-based identities, were not in a position to wrest power from the colonial authority, which as Tharakeshwar proposes, was a 'supra-language power'. Tharakeshwar, "Competing Imaginations", in *Interrogating Reorganisation of States*, pp. 190–191.

Of course, there were competing strands, especially of religion-based nationalism, that eventually led to the formation of the two nation-states, but that was not influential enough to dent the more cosmopolitan idea that came to be designated and identified as 'Indian' nationalism. The nation-state became the norm that seemed to overwhelm all other cultural identities. As Anderson argues, 'In a world in which the nation state is the overwhelming norm, all of this means that nations can now be imagined without linguistic [and cultural] commonality . . . out of a general awareness of what modern history has demonstrated to be possible.'[55]

Driven by the imperative of a 'united India', the anti-colonial nationalist discourse had its task cut out for it—to soothe, subsume and simultaneously represent cultural identities within the singularity of nationhood. Nationalist talk, coupled with the promise of modernity and development, pacified and promised these historically novel, structurally contingent and variously distinct identities a 'separate but equal' status in a politically free India. The promise of citizenship as uniform equal status for all, the assurance of empirical differentiation to make space for the minorities and the marginalized, laid the foundations of, to borrow a phrase from Daniel Carpenter, 'democratic singularity and democratic virtue'.[56]

However, there was an anomalous feature. The *cosmopolitanism* mandated by nationhood was alien to a people with communitarian standards. The inherited cultures of the nation lacked the vocabulary of modern nationhood and democracy. Indian nationalism therefore had to be re-equipped, mostly by drawing from Western standards of liberal-democratic nationalism. But as Partha Chatterjee says, 'it could not do so simply by imitating

---

[55] Anderson, *Imagined Communities*, p.123.
[56] Carpenter, "Representation at a Visual Interface", in *Anxieties of Democracy*, p. 77.

the alien culture, for then the nation would lose its distinctive identity. The search was therefore for a regeneration of a national culture that adapted to the requirements of progress, but retaining at the same time its distinctiveness.'[57] Given India's vastness and variedness, the ambition was deeply contradictory. Anti-colonialism rejected the alien intruder but accepted 'the value of the standard set by alien culture'.[58] Herein lay the liberal-rationalist dilemma of Indian nationalism. While its posturing was anti-colonial, it aspired for Western values of democratic nationhood. Hostility to the substantive content it imitated lent Indian nationalism and the emergent nation an incongruity and ambivalence that marked not just this phase of anti-colonial nationalism, but also the post-colonial India that emerged from its throes.

---

[57] Chatterjee, *Nationalist Thought and the Colonial World*, p. 2.
[58] Ibid.

5

The Promise of Civic Nationalism

Thus far, a national community had been defined largely in terms of its opposition to colonialism. Independent India needed a new identity as a nation, its modern nationalist consciousness had to find new moorings. Partition and the communal bloodbath in its aftermath, the clamour for linguistic reorganization of provinces, peasant rebellions (Tebhaga and Telangana to name two of the most significant), the impossibly entrenched economic backwardness and caste hierarchies, had already served notice on the aspirational similitude of nationhood. We are not really *one*, we are not all the *same*, they seemed to say. With our fragmented past living in the present, with our present struggling with its disjointedness, the task before the Constituent Assembly (CA) was doubly difficult. It had to fashion a nationalist consciousness and an anti-colonial modernity while being mindful of India's civilizational inheritances and contradictions. Loaded in this single sentence was a burden so extensive, a task so paradoxical, that the only way forward was perhaps to wrap the provisions of the Constitution up into a *gathari* (bundle, bale) and hope that each time this was opened, each of these carefully laid out

'provisions' had not been displaced or forced another out of its
assigned place.

Jagat Narain Lal was by now firmly in the Congress camp,
but like many others, toggling between its Centre and its Right.
But in pitching his tent outside of the Hindu Mahasabha, he
had made at least one clear departure. Rather than take a leaf out
of Savarkar's Hindutva thesis that shaped much of the Hindu
nationalist vision—of citizenship being conferred on those for
whom this country was both fatherland (*pitribhumi*) and holy
land (*punyabhumi*)—Jagat Narain chose principles akin to *jus soli*[1]
(by birth), *jus sanguinis* (by descent) and naturalization, the most
common means of conferring citizenship in modern times. Not that
his writings had ever endorsed the Savarkarite vision, but having
once been a member of the Hindu Mahasabha made the burden
his to carry, *unless* of course he made an explicit departure from it.
In April 1947, amidst the CA debates on citizenship, Jagat Narain
Lal proposed the model of Irish Citizenship for India. His idea
of citizenship would include '[e]very person, without distinction
of sex, domiciled in the area of the jurisdiction of the . . . State at
the time of the coming into operation of this Constitution . . .'[2]
By pitching for a model of shared and equal citizenship, Jagat
Narain threw his weight behind the principles of civic nationalism
that guided much of the liberal democratic world. He had come
to understand that in the absence of a settled idea of common
religious and ethnic genealogy (that was the basis of the "Hindu-
Rashtra" ideology)[3], the only thing that could bind this plural
nation was a set of political values and practices, shared by equal
and rights-bearing citizens. Between the ethno-nationalistic route

---

[1] See, Jayal, "Citizenship" in *Oxford Handbook of the Indian Constitution*,
pp. 164–165.
[2] Constituent Assembly Debates (henceforth CAD)—3.18.169
[3] For an exposition of this idea, see for instance, Savarkar, *Hindutva*
(7th ed.); Golwalkar, *We or Our Nation Redefined* (4th ed.).

of assuming a religio-cultural continuity and unity, and the civic-nationalist route of creating a unity of equal and rights-bearing citizens, Jagat Babu chose the latter.

A word about my choice of the term *civic nationalism*.[4] One of the most hotly debated principles in the CA (second only to the language issue) was the word 'secular'. Given (a) the Western origin and genealogy of the term; (b) the centrality of religion and religious morality in the conduct of public life of India; (c) Gandhi's steadfast espousal of the need for politics to be guided by ethics of dharma; (d) the consciousness of a need to decolonize the conceptual and ideational content of nationhood— given this reality, independent India did not really imagine itself as a secular nation. This is not to say that we chose to be non-secular—many constitutional provisions, as also our constitutional morality, embody a distinctly secular ethos. Just that we chose to *not* describe ourselves as secular. And that choice was telling.

The idea that we could be secular in a different sort of way— by the state being equidistant from all religions, rather than neutral and separate from religion—was a noble idea but made for messy political choices. How could the state not intervene and liberate individuals from oppressive religious hierarchies? How could the state be equidistant and yet protect minority rights and institutions? How could the state be neutral and yet be able to check majoritarian encroachments? Thus, even as descriptor of state's 'equidistant' interaction with religions, it fell short of being accurate. Hence, my preference for the term civic nationalism in place of secular nationalism[5]—but with the caveat that even

---

[4] For recent definitions of 'civic' nationalism, see Ignatieff, *Blood and Belonging*, pp. 5–9; Barry, *Culture and Equality*, pp. 79–109; Mason, *Community, Solidarity, and Belonging*, pp. 115–47.

[5] See for instance, Bilgrami, *Secularism, Identity, and Enchantment*; "Two Concepts of Secularism", *EPW* Vol. 29, republished in *Secularism and Its Critics;* and Bilgrami, "Secularism and the Moral Psychology of Identity," *EPW*, pp. 2527–2540; Bhargava, "What Is Indian

civic nationalism was not a terminological choice made by the Constitution makers. I choose it because it comes closest to describing both the intent and the content of choices made by our founding fathers.

The civic idea of nationalism has a lesser ambition, and a lighter burden to bear than its loftier cousin: secular nationalism. Perhaps its greatest merit lies in the fact that it shifts focus (and institutional agenda) from a stance on religion to that on rights. In a multi-religious, multi-ethnic society, the civic idea allows for a latitude—to function maximally through recognition, appreciation and *respect* for diversity and difference, or minimally through *toleration*, which may entail negative judgments and may even denigrate the other.[6] It may even, in the presence of a large religious majority, allow for retention of a majoritarian ethic. As an ethical and political site, the idea of civic nationalism does not have a well-defined secular content that stands in sharp contrast with ethno-nationalism. In its minimalist avatar, the idea of civic nationalism retains a potential for a hierarchical and majoritarian core, rather than the full and equal recognition of difference that secularism demands. From it stems the burden of toleration rather than the fraternal bonds of sympathy and appreciation.[7] India chose this path, retaining a majoritarian propensity that's latent in the best of times, but actively manifest in the worst. And Jagat

---

Secularism and What Is It For?" *India Review* Vol. 1, pp. 1–32; Bhargava, "Respect, Domination and Principled Distance", *EPW*, Vol. 48.

[6] For discussions, see, Taylor, "The Collapse of Toleration", *The Guardian*, 17 May 2007; Taylor, "How to Define Secularism", Taylor and Stepan (eds), *Boundaries of Toleration*, pp. 59–78.

[7] See generally, Bilgrami, *Secularism, Identity, and Enchantment*, pp. 10–18; Devji, "An Indian History of Toleration", *Open Magazine*, 7 January 2018. For a discussion of the different degrees and spectrum of toleration, see, Bhargava, "Beyond Toleration", in Stepan and Taylor (eds), *Boundaries of Toleration* (Also in the same volume, Kaviraj, "Modernity, State, and Toleration in Indian History", pp. 233–266).

Babu walked this path, attempting to combine the goal of unity with the principles of liberty and equality, without being religion-neutral. How this was to be achieved was as much Jagat Narain Lal's as India's task to figure out.

The Imperative of Unity

. . . the one crying need of the hour is the maintenance of solidarity and unity in this country.

It's probably fair to say that the neatest vision of a national community was articulated by ethno-nationalists. For them, the national community was pre-political, underwritten by commonality of descent and religion. The liberal democratic camp, on the other hand, had to deal with messier formulations. It was divided between those who tacitly or overtly, partly or completely, agreed with the ethno-nationalists about the value of shared religious ties, and those who countered this idea with the political idea of the 'civic'. For the latter, the idea of a national community derived not from a commonality of 'original' and 'righteous' descent, but from a charter of rights and institutions that would authorize and organize the national community into a republic. With perspectives spanning a very wide spectrum of ideologies and agendas, many issues, particularly those relating to citizenship, religious rights, secularism, linguistic reorganization, became vexed and keenly contested in the Constituent Assembly. Where did Jagat Narain Lal stand amidst the vortex of these contestations? Expectedly, he had moved away from the Sarvarkarite 'holyland' proviso and endorsed a more modern and liberal democratic conception.

Citizenship is seldom just about demarcating a valid citizen, and Jagat Narain Lal understood that. It is substantively about what rights the citizen ought to be endowed with. Jagat Narain reflects on the right to religious freedom, linguistic autonomy, freedom of speech, parliamentary privileges, property rights, relations between labour and capital and so on. Throughout these reflections there is an espousal of the 'civic' principles of liberty and equality. What is interesting is that for Jagat Babu, like for many others, each of these claims is mediated by his concern for the unity and solidarity of newly independent India.

On 24 November 1949, Jagat Narain Lal made an unequivocal statement in the CA: '. . . I want to add a few words about this Constitution. It has been attacked and criticized by various friends and supported by various others. I consider this Constitution to be both Federal and Unitary. It is a Federal Constitution, yet it is Unitary. It is a Unitary Constitution, yet it is Federal. Neither is it based entirely on the American model, nor on the British model. It combines both these models and has added something of its own to suit our Indian conditions. The powers of control which have been given to the Centre, are, I consider, very necessary. The one crying need of our country has been the maintenance of solidarity. Time after time in its history, we have found this solidarity being broken and India falling at the feet of foreign Conquerors. Therefore, Sir, at a time when all foreign rule has been eliminated, the one crying need of the hour is the maintenance of solidarity and unity in this country.'[8]

The two terms 'civic' and 'nationalism' of the conjoined terminology—civic nationalism— may end up with conflicting mandates, particularly in a culturally diverse country like India. *Civic* may imply even those individual freedoms that include freedom to privilege your cultural, religious or linguistic identity above that of nationalist identity. In contrast, *nationalism* thrives on the idiom of similitude, of unity and oneness. The contrasting mandates posed (and have continued to pose) an enormous challenge. The challenge

---

[8] Jagat Narain Lal, CAD, September 1949, Vol. 11, Document 165, Para 195 Henceforth, expressed as a numerical value, for example, (11.165.195).

was negotiated variously, encompassing a diverse range of semantic, conceptual and political reasoning. For Jagat Narain Lal, this negotiation meant that as far as religious and linguistic identities and rights were concerned, he advocated their subordination to the goals of unity and solidarity of the Nation. But as far as individual rights (like free speech) were concerned, he stood firmly in support of them. Interestingly, to this mix of cultural and individual rights, Jagat Narain Lal (recall that he was an economist) added his views on a third set of rights—the rights of labour and the impoverished masses. Jagat Narain Lal does not dwell in detail on a wide array of rights, but what we get from him is a sampling of all three— Individual (free speech), Cultural (religious and language rights) and Social (labour entitlements).

Freedom of Press—Free Speech

. . . at this stage and in this century, it is becoming for us, as an advanced country, to guarantee full freedom of speech and expression.

On 1 September 1949, Article 13—freedom of speech and expression—of the Draft Constitution was under consideration. Specifically, the matter of freedom of the press and its taxation was being discussed. Was the power to tax a power to destroy? Would taxing the press muzzle its freedom to express its views? Voices like Deshbandhu Gupta and Das Bhargava were of the opinion that it 'offends Article 13 and therefore is out of order'— it will lead to 'material curtailment and abridgement,' said Das Bhargava.[9] Others like Alladi Krishnaswamy Ayyar, B.R. Ambedkar, R.K. Sidhva were of the view that the press should not be immune from 'ordinary liabilities incidental to citizenship'?[10] R.K. Sidhva, for example, said that *freedom of speech and expression*

---

[9] Das Bhargava, CAD, September 1949 (9.129.212).
[10] Alladi Krishanswami Ayyar, CAD, September 1949 (9.129.210).

did not mean that newspapers should be exempt from paying taxes on their profits.[11]

Free speech debates in the modern world have seldom questioned its principle. Free speech and its normative and consequential values are taken as an *a priori* assumption for a democracy. The debates and tussles are nearly always about 'reasonable restrictions', given that free speech cannot be an absolute right. Even those who call themselves 'free speech absolutists' agree upon this. So also did the Constituent Assembly. Their debates were informed by a consciousness that there's a thin line between the autonomy of a person or the press to speak freely, and their duty and obligation to the collective interest. Jagat Babu was mindful of this, which is why, in two separate instances, he reached two divergent conclusions about 'restrictions'.

The first instance was the aforementioned matter of taxation of the press. He was of the view that taxation was a measure that would give the state a handle with which to curb the autonomy of the press. As someone who ran a printing press—the Sri Krishna Press that published the journal *Mahavir* of which he was the editor till 1928—and who had served a jail term on charges of sedition for publishing material critical of the government in 1928,[12] Jagat Narain Lal had a personal understanding of the political value of press freedom. Speaking about the individual's inalienable right to free speech and expression, he wrote: 'The law of sedition, as our politicians know, is as perverse as it is all embracing.'

---

[11] R.K. Sidhva, CAD, September 1949 (9.129.171).

[12] He was also charged under IPC Section 292 and 124A on two different occasions—the first on 21 June 1927, 'for the publication of obscence advertisement' of *Kok Shastra* (a book dealing with matters of sexual pleasure) in *Mahavir* magazine (Bihar State Archives. File no 176/1926); and under Section 124A on charges of sedition for publishing an article in the *Searchlight* (16 April 1931) about the Kanpur communal riots in 1931 (Bihar State Archives File 260/1927). For more details see, pp. 92–98 of Chapter 3 of this book.

Addressing the CA in September 1949, he made an impassioned speech citing curbs on the press as one of the factors that spurred resistance movements in both England and America.

'As representing the Press, some of us claim to be heard by this House. Sir, freedom of speech and expression are terms which we have imported from the English and American Constitutions and we are trying to forge a Constitution at present which shall be ahead of these Constitutions. If we are forging a constitution which instead of being ahead of these constitutions goes backward, I should say that we cannot be proud of such a constitution. I have heard Mr. Sidhva. His interpretation seems to be too narrow. Dr. Ambedkar shuddered at the idea of the whole judgement of the Supreme Court being read. I do not propose to read the entire judgement. I will confine myself only to a few passages. I would like him as an eminent jurist to go through them. It is not simply a judgment to be merely casually read but it embodies the public opinion both from England and American constitutions; and I should say that at this stage and in this century, it is becoming for us, as an advanced country, to guarantee full freedom of speech and expression.

'I will read only a few passages:

'"In 1712, in response to a message from Queen Anne (Hansard's *Parliamentary History of England*, Vol. 6. p. 1063), Parliament imposed a tax upon all newspapers and upon advertisements. That the main purpose of these taxes was to suppress the publication of comments and criticisms objectionable to the Crown does not admit of doubt. There followed more than a century of resistance to, and evasion of, the taxes, and of agitation for their repeal. It was pointed out that these taxes constituted one of the factors that aroused the American Colonists to protest against taxation for the purposes of the home government; and that the Revolution really began when, in 1765, that government sent stamps for newspaper duties to the American colonists."[13]

---

[13] Jagat Narain Lal, CAD, September 1949 (9.129.172).

He added, '*It is idle to suppose that so many of the best men of England would for a century of time have waged, as they did, stubborn and often precarious warfare against these taxes if a mere matter of taxation had been involved*'.[14]

The matter of taxation was a finer point' in the larger debate on the parameters of free speech. Ambedkar stated in the Constituent Assembly, 'The press is merely another way of stating an individual or a citizen. The press has no special rights which are not to be given to or which are not to be exercised by the citizen in his individual capacity'. However, Jagat Narain was of the view that in matters that had the potential to curtail its freedom and autonomy, the press ought to be treated as a category with special privileges. That taxes could be used as a weapon to muzzle the press had been borne out by both American and English history. 'The aim of [their] struggle was not simply to relieve the Press of the burden of taxation but to establish and preserve the right of . . . people to full information in respect of the doings or misdoings of their Government. If words so telling as this could be interpreted as an intention to evade taxation, it is very unfortunate indeed.'[15]

Jagat Narain Lal however makes a very interesting distinction in the matter of privileges. For him, the rationale of granting parliamentarians immunity from the restrictions of ordinary law (arrest and/or judicial review) was to prevent legislators from unwelcome scrutiny (by courts, public, private individuals, police), the threat of which could fetter deliberations inside the house of parliament.[16] This rationale would be defeated, according to him, if under the garb of free

---

[14] Jagat Narain Lal, CAD, September 1949 (9.129.173).
[15] Ibid. (9.129.174).
[16] For a discussion on the various aspects of legislative immunities, see, Chauhan, "Legislature: Privileges and Process", *Oxford Handbook of the Indian Constitution*, pp. 290–296.

speech, parliamentary privileges were to be over-extended to include the right to publish parliamentary speeches and debates without parliament's scrutiny.

The matter being discussed in the CA was Article 85 of the Draft Constitution that dealt with privileges and immunities. Pointing out a 'lacuna', Naziruddin questioned the limitations on the right of legislators to freely publish their speeches. Why should this need to be authorized by parliament, he asked? 'Freedom of the Press is a very important item among the rights of the people. If anything could be published by or under the authority of the House, the Press should have freedom to publish it . . . It is somewhat anomalous that the Press could not publish what can be published by the authority of the House.'[17]

One would have expected that as a forceful votary of a free press, Jagat Babu would have been on the same page as Ahmad. Surprisingly, he disagreed. According to him, the members of parliament already had the privilege (under Clause 2) to publish a speech delivered in parliament; only it required *the authorization by parliament*. Disapprovingly he says, 'My friends want . . . that the member who has delivered a speech in the parliament should have a further immunity, should have the right and privilege of publishing their speech outside in the Press. That may relate to the freedom of the Press, but that does not pertain to the freedom of the member so far as his speech or his vote in the parliament is concerned. I think that is stretching a point too far and it is neither fair nor proper'.

He goes on to cite his reasons. 'If a member, for example, wants to deliver a speech in the parliament, not for the purpose simply of making an honest speech, but for the purpose of maligning somebody or some institution and he starts straightaway by delivering a speech and publishing the same in so many other papers outside, I should say, that is not an honest expression of

---

[17] Naziruddin Ahmad, CAD, 19 May 1949 (8.87. 284).

opinion and that is not a bona fide expression of opinion either. Therefore, I would like honourable Members to confine the privileges which are given and the immunity which is sought to be given to members of parliament . . .'[18]

The point Jagat Narain Lal raised is worthy of consideration. Parliamentary privileges ensure that a parliamentarian's speech-acts enjoy 'immunity' from the scrutiny of ordinary laws and their 'reasonable restrictions' (that ordinarily apply to cases of defamation and libel, etc.). His argument was that since a person's speech-act (in the course of parliamentary proceedings) is exempt from review by the courts and from presumptive legal injury, it would follow that a published parliamentary speech would enjoy the same immunity, regardless of whether it is slanderous or libellous. This extrapolation of the privilege, exceeded the bounds of fairness in Jagat Narain Lal's view. The very objective of unfettered deliberation inside parliament would be defeated, if libel, slander and falsehoods, published outside, were to enjoy immunity from prosecution. Jagat Narain concedes that while this could be seen as a matter of the freedom of the press (freedom to report parliamentary proceedings and thereby serve the public interest), the absence of restraint on speech-acts of parliamentarians would be detrimental to the conduct of parliament. For him, this was not a liberty-limiting provision, as much an issue of reasonable restrictions on a reedom.

---

[18] Jagat Narain Lal, CAD, 19 May 1949 (8.87.300).

Religious Rights

The words 'Secular State' should not have come into the Constitution. It would have been enough if it had been said that the State should not interfere with any religion.

In November 1949, amidst the Constituent Assembly seeking the fourth amendment to Government of India Act, 1935, several matters pertaining to alteration of names of provinces, to the Directive Principles, to the issue of cow slaughter, to issues relating to minority reservations and so on were being discussed and debated, when Jagat Narain Lal expressed his reservations on the use of the term 'secular'. He said:

'I am sorry, Sir, that there has been an undue anxiety in our minds about the avoidance of the name of God. Looking to the foreign constitutions, constitutions of other countries, I find that there is at least one constitution, the Constitution of South Africa which in its very first article says: "The people of the Union acknowledge the sovereignty and guidance of Almighty God." In our country, Sir, which has always remained religious and has retained its spiritual character and which has produced one of them greatest spiritual personalities in the world in modern times too, I would have liked that the name of God should have been introduced.'

Jagat Babu belonged to a fairly vocal strand of scholarly and political opinion at the time, which held that the idiom of secularity was alien to India and contrary to its civilizational values. Many members of the Constituent Assembly vocally articulated this belief. Loknath Mishra from Orissa for example said: 'Gradually it seems to me that our "secular State" is a slippery phrase, a device to by-pass the ancient culture of the land . . . Do we really believe that religion can be divorced from life , . . . ?'[19]

---

[19] Mishra, CAD, Vol. 7, 6 December 1948 (7.67.7).

Secularism, as Akeel Bilgrami notes, '*is a stance taken about religion*'.[20] Tracing its origins to the Enlightenment, as a *political doctrine*, it mandated a separation of religion and politics, private and public morality. In that sense, secularism defines itself against religion.[21] For a country like India, where its civilizational heritage sanctified and codified ethical conduct as both personal and *raj dharma*, the idea that political and personal doctrines would be governed by two different norms was abhorrent. For most, it represented a stance against religion.

Jagat Narain Lal, echoed what Gandhi had repeatedly said— that the word 'secular' did not represent a religious-minded country where almost all conduct of ethics is mediated by religious precepts and teachings. Religion, for many like Jagat babu, was a guide to ethical conduct and should guide the conduct of the polity and the private individual alike.[22]

In recognition and cognizance of these views, the CA attempted variant of a secularism where the state was not *separate* but instead *neutral* and *equidistant*[23] from all religions. But Jagat Narain Lal, along with many others like T.K. Shah, K.M. Munshi, Purushottam Das Tandon, pointed out in the CA debates that if the Indian variant of 'secularism' did not really connote antipathy to religion, and only meant a state that treated all religions equally, why use such a word which had a tendency to cast a pejorative shadow on matters of 'faith'.[24] As Jagat Narain said on the floor of

---

[20] Bilgrami, *Secularism, Identity, and Enchantment*, p. 4.

[21] Ibid., p. 4.

[22] In a notebook, where Jagat Narain Lal is writing about 'National Education in India', he expresses the view that: 'Religion in the widest sense should inspire education and a curriculum devoid of an ethical basis would prove barren in the end.' Jagat Narain Lal, Private Papers, NMML, Notebook 13, p. 21.

[23] Ibid., p. 10.

[24] For a detailed discussion, see, Jha, "Secularism in the Constituent Assembly Debates", *EPW*, Vol. 37, No.30. pp. 3175–3180.

the Constituent Assembly, '[t]he words "Secular State" should not have come into the Constitution. It would have been enough if it had been said that the State should not interfere with any religion. Or, we could have said that the State should have a spiritual and moral outlook, instead of saying that it should be secular. The introduction of [this] word has created a lot of misunderstanding.'[25] Many like Jagat Narain were sceptical of the word 'secular' not because they found the principle itself abhorrent, as a recent article seemed to suggest,[26] but because they considered it an un-Indian, deculturalized import form the Western liberal tradition. Why should one be squeamish about admitting that we are a religious society, Jagat Babu would often ask?

One of the misunderstandings that he was likely referring to was with respect to the content of the right to religious freedom. Should the right to religion imply, other than to practise and profess, also a right to propagate? And second, if propagation led to conversions, as it would, what would be the status of children? Would they automatically also adopt the religion of their converted parents? Should they be given the agency to choose their own religion once they attained adulthood?

The right to religious propagation was granted despite reservations expressed,[27] and despite the deep misgivings many like Jagat Babu had periodically shared about widespread conversions to Christianity in the Chotanagpur and North-eastern regions.[28]

---

[25] Jagat Narain Lal, CAD, 29 April 1947 (11.165.198).

[26] Chakravarty, "How India's founding fathers saw the nauseating principle of secularity of the State", Scroll, 2 December 2015.

[27] Purushottam Das Tandon for example said: 'I know Congressmen more than my friend over there. I know their feelings more intimately than probably he has ever had an opportunity of doing, and I know that most Congressmen are opposed to this idea of "propagation". But we agreed to keep the word "propagate" out of regard for our Christian friends.' CAD, 1 May 1947 (3.20.162).

[28] See Chapter 3 on Hindu Nationalism.

Speaking in the Constituent Assembly, Jagat Narain Lal argued that Clause 13 (moved by Vallabhbhai Patel) which granted 'the right freely to profess, practice and propagate religion subject to public order, morality or health', went to the 'farthest limit'.[29] In response to an amendment moved by K.M. Munshi,[30] he went on to cite examples:

'If you look to any of the best of modern world Constitutions, you will find that nowhere has this right to propagate been conceded. If you look at Article 50 of the Swiss Confederation, it lays down that "the free exercise of religion is guaranteed within limits compatible with public order and morality." It ends there. If you, look at Article 44 sub-clause (2) 1 of the Irish Free State, you will find there, "Freedom of conscience and the free profession and practice of religion are subject to public order and morality, guaranteed to every citizen".[31]

'If you refer to Article 124 of the Constitution of the Union of the Soviet Socialist Republics you will find: "In order to ensure citizens' freedom of conscience, the Church in the U.S.S.R. is separated from the State and the school from the Church. Freedom of religious worship and freedom of anti-religious propaganda is recognised for all citizens."[32]

'My submission is that this House has gone to the farthest limit possible with regard to the minorities, knowing well the fact that there are a few minorities in this country whose right to carry on propaganda extends to the point of creating various difficulties. I do not want to go into its details. The previous speaker had referred to certain things in this connection.

---

[29] Jagat Narain Lal, CAD, 1 May 1947 (3.20.203).
[30] K.M. Munshi's proposed amendment to Clause 13 stated: 'Any conversion from one religion to another of any person brought about by fraud, coercion or undue influence or of a minor under the age of 18 shall not be recognised by law.'
[31] Jagat Narain Lal, CAD, 1 May 1947 (3.20.203).
[32] Ibid. (3.20.204)

I submit that that should be sufficient. Hon'ble Tandonji by his observation that on reading the mind of most of the Congress members of this House, he did not want to keep "right to do propaganda" (on the statute), has rightly interpreted the mind of most of us. The fact is that we desire to make the minorities feel that the rights which they had been enjoying till now shall be allowed to continue within reasonable limits by the majority. We have no desire to curtail them in any way. But we do not concede the right to do propaganda.'

The reality of a proselytizing and organized religion like Christianity placed the disorganized, hierarchized Hinduism at a disadvantage. Democracy's first mandate is equality before law. But Jagat Narain Lal's argument was that the jurisprudence around both 'reasonable restrictions' and 'public morality' yielded enough ground to make case for qualifying the right to religion and restricting the right to propagate.

'I want to appeal to those who profess to speak for the minorities not to press for too much. They must be satisfied with this much. It will be too much to press for more. That would be taking undue advantage of the generosity of the majority. That will be very regrettable. It is difficult, rather impossible, for us to go to that limit. I think that the amendment tabled by Mr. Munshi becomes essential if the right to propagate is conceded. The House should, therefore, accept it.'

The point about the 'generosity of the majority' is an interesting one. There's an an implicit suggestion that attitudes of toleration and generosity towards other faiths derive from the very nature of the Hindu religion and from its unique capacity for openness and accommodation of diversity. As Rochana Bajpai says, '[s]ecularism as toleration of minorities was redolent of the superiority of Hindu religion and self-congratulation on the forbearance and self-restraint of Hindus . . .'[33]

---

[33] Bajpai, *Debating Difference*, pp. 106.

The question was, where to draw the line? Jagat Narain seems to be suggesting that a 'formal equality' of religious rights—the freedom to practise, profess and propagate religion—would imperil Hinduism, which is not a proselytizing religion. In other words, he seems to be asking for a distinction to be made between the private practice of religion and its public mission, between freedom of conscience and the conduct of organized religion. The right to practise and profess religion was consistent with the principles of liberty and hence 'rightable' but the right to propagate was 'other-regarding'—in the sense that it affected the Hindu practice (through religious conversions), and therefore was not a valid claim. The free exercise of any religion should be stopped when it becomes inconsistent with the ideals and conduct of another religion, is what Jagat Babu believed.

If indeed secularism is about acknowledging and respecting wider forms of religious and cultural diversity, Jagat Babu seems to be asking through his support to Munshi's amendment, why not acknowledge the evangelizing practice of Christianity and desist from granting the right to propagate? In citing examples from other constitutions, he also seems to be suggesting that the *right to propagate is not a necessary stick in the bundle of religious rights.*

Linguistic Identities

. . . any distribution of provinces on a linguistic basis must be completely avoided . . . if a redistribution of provinces is to take place, it should be carried out on an administrative basis.

If there was one thing that global history of nationalism taught Jagat Babu, it was that language played a definitive role in formation of nationalities. It acted both as a unifying feature as in the case of Germany and as a fissiparous tendency as in the disintegration of the Austro-Hungarian Empire, but mostly certifying what Fichte had famously stated: 'Wherever a separate language is found, there is also a separate nation which has the right to manage its affairs independently and to rule itself.'[34] It was probably his interest in and knowledge of the nationalist histories of the world that led to Jagat Narain Lal's appointment as one of the four members of the Linguistic Provinces Commission (better known as the Dar Commission, named after the chairman of the Commission, S.K. Dar, a retired judge of the Allahabad High Court) on 17 June 1948.[35] This was independent India's first exploration of language becoming a plausible basis for the reorganization of states. The more immediate question before the Commission was to assess the 'administrative, financial and other consequences' of formation of new provinces of Andhra, Karnataka, Kerala and Maharashtra. But there were larger implications extending beyond these four states. Whatever the Commission decided, if accepted, would set a precedent for future linguistic reorganization of states.

What followed was the circulation of a detailed questionnaire, not just for the four aforementioned states but also their parent provinces of Madras, Bombay and the Hindi Central Provinces.[36] The Commission submitted its report on 10 December 1948, asking the question: 'Given the "infancy of Indian nationalism", is it a good time "to redeem this pledge"?' The report stated:

'India has in the words of its Prime Minister, just survived a major operation. It is in the midst of an undeclared war with Pakistan. It has still to settle its refugee problem and the problem of feeding its teeming millions and as a result of British

---

[34] Roy, 'The Growth of Linguistic States in the Indian Federation', in *Essays on Indian Federalism*, p. 220.
[35] *Report of the Linguistic Provinces Commission* (henceforth DCR), p. 36.
[36] Ibid., pp. 38–40. The Central Provinces contained two distinct linguistic regions: Mahakoshal, consisting mainly of Hindi-speaking districts, and Vidarbha, chiefly, but not exclusively, a Marathi-speaking area.

withdrawal, it is working and must work for some time to come with a depleted and overstrained administration. And if these anxieties were not sufficient, India is about to experiment under the new Constitution with autonomous states and adult franchise without the cementing force of a national language to take the place of English.'[37]

The task was an onerous one for Jagat Narain Lal and Chairman Dar. They interacted with stakeholders of Madras, Bombay and CP, and multiple contested districts of the proposed states of Andhra, Kerala, Maharashtra and Karnataka. 'This inquiry', the Dar Commission eloquently reports, 'in some ways has been an eye opener for us. The work of 60 years of INC was standing before us face to face with centuries-old India of narrow loyalties, petty jealousies, and ignorant prejudices engaged in a moral conflict, and we are simply horrified to see how thin was the ice upon which we were skating. Some of the ablest men [of] the country came before us and confidentially and emphatically stated that language in this country stood for and represented culture, tradition, race, history, individuality, and, finally, a sub-nation; that the government of a linguistic group could not be safely left in the hands of a multi-lingual group; and that each linguistic group must have a territory of its own and that its territory was inviolate and could not be shared by any other linguistic group . . . the bitter dispute which rages between Tamils and Telugus . . . and in greater degree between Marathas and Gujaratis . . . reveals a mentality which to our mind will be the death-knell of Indian nationalism.'[38]

'India can only live by the strength of its nationalism; Indian nationalism must find its expression in democracy and not in a kind of fascism: that democracy in this country can only function through a Federation, as an absolute unitary government for

---

[37] DCR, para 8. p.1–2.
[38] Ibid., para 143, p. 32–33

such a vast country is neither desirable nor practicable; and a federation requires contended and happy units and some measure of autonomy for these units.'[39]

'The first and the last need of India at the present moment is that it should be made a nation . . . Everything which helps the growth of nationalism, has to go forward, and everything, which throws obstacles in its way, has to be rejected or should stand over. We have applied this test to linguistic provinces also, and judged by this test, in our opinion, they fail and cannot be supported.'[40]

'Our conclusions, therefore, are:

(1) The formation of provinces on exclusively or even mainly linguistic considerations is not in the larger interest of the Indian nation and should not be taken in hand;
(2) The existing provinces of Madras, Bombay, C.P. and Berar present serious administrative problems for which an administrative solution is urgently necessary, and it is for the Centre to find a satisfactory solution to these problems.
(3) The aforesaid problems do not call for an immediate re-formation of provinces. As soon as the Indian states have been integrated and the country has stabilized itself and other conditions are favourable, they may be reformed and convenient administrative provinces set up.'

The commission was also cognizant of the fact that provincial boundaries fixed along linguistic lines would entail a huge financial and administrative cost at a time when India could ill afford it, given the enormous task of mitigating poverty and consolidating a post-Partition, post-colonial state. Two full chapters—III and IV—were dedicated to assessing the financial, economic and administrative costs and consequences.

---

[39] Ibid, para 144, p. 33.
[40] DCR, para 147, p. 33.

What we get from the Dar Commission is not an outright rejection of the principle of linguistic reorganization but a postponement of the vexed issue. The postponement can be read as more than just that, given the Commission's unequivocal stance that sub-identities foster sub-nationalisms and may run counter to the sentiment of nationalism. There is little, though, in the report that suggests that the Dar Commission rejected language as a *principle* of organization.

Perusing through Jagat Narain Lal's notes of nation-states' histories, there are two related thought processes that get reflected in the Dar Commission Report. First, the standard expectation emerging out of European experiences is that linguistic homogeneity augurs well for the core strength and stability of a new nation state. As a corollary, therefore, linguistic diversity is likely to present its own challenges of fostering sub-identities that may compete or erode nationalist identities. In a linguistically diverse country like India, therefore, measures to fix boundaries on the basis of language affinities would only exacerbate the play of sub-identities and disunity. On the other hand, given India's linguistic diversity, a complete disregard for linguistic considerations would echo the biases and inconsideration of its erstwhile imperial masters. It would be hard to expect that citizens would remain bound together by nothing more than a shared experience of colonial domination. A nation and its nationalist impulses may be indissociable from language, but that does not imply a foregone conclusion about what language 'we speak' in a multi-lingual society.

The Dar Commission Report stated that 'whenever such a work [of linguistic reorganization of provinces] is taken in hand, oneness of language may be one of the factors taken into consideration along with others; but it should not be decisive or the main factor. Generally speaking, bilingual districts in border areas, which have developed an economic and organic life of their own, should not be broken up and should be disposed of on consideration of their own special needs . . . subject to the above and other relevant and paramount considerations, if some new provinces come into being and produce more or less linguistic homogeneity, they need not be objected to.'

There is no doubt a reluctance, even on the matter of principle, to accord linguistic affinities as the sole arbiter in the redrawing of state boundaries. But this reluctance stems from an understanding of the complex and layered ties that hold a region together. In the interstitial spaces between linguistic identities—where territory, language and ethnicity did *not* coalesce into neat divisible blocks— the task presented its own specific set of demands. It gave the Commission a sense that linguistic reorganization of provinces at this stage might open up a pandora's box. Instead of settling reorganization claims for good, it might actually unleash newer mobilizations along ethno-linguistic lines, a possibility a fledgling state could ill afford. It may be therefore said that in principle, the Dar Commission seemed neither opposed nor in favour. The only thing that could be confidently asserted was firstly, the relationship between the language and its region, and between the individual and the language community; and secondly, the priority of national identity over the linguistic-cultural one. *Cultural issues could and should wait* was what S.K Dar, Panna Lall and Jagat Narain Lal adjudicated. Without discarding the principle of linguistic self-definition, the policy matter was postponed. The times being as they were, nationalist affinities trumped the normative claim of linguistic and ethnic affinities.

The Dar Commission stated that it was unanimous in its opinion as regards both the issue of national language and linguistic reorganization of provinces. Both the language of the report and the voice reflected, quite accurately, Jagat Narain's own position on the two matters. In November 1949, months after the Dar Commission had submitted its report, he stood up in the CA and repeated the primary consideration behind the Commission's report. 'Time after time in its history, we have found this solidarity being broken and India falling at the feet of foreign conquerors. Therefore, Sir, at a time when all foreign rule has been eliminated, the one crying need of the hour is the maintenance of solidarity and unity in this country. Following upon that, I would further add that any distribution of provinces on a linguistic basis must be completely avoided. We have strongly held the view that if a redistribution of provinces is to take place, it should be carried out on an administrative basis. Sir, the formation of an Andhra province is to be welcomed from that point of view. In our deliberations and enquiries, we found that if there was a strong case, there could not be a stronger and a riper case than for the formation of an Andhra province on administrative grounds. We also came to the conclusion that there was necessity of a redistribution of provinces on administrative grounds in the case of certain other provinces too. If and when the necessary conditions are there, and an opportune time comes, that redistribution may also take place.'[41]

While assessing the views of both Jagat Narain Lal and the Dar Commission, it is necessary to come to grips with India's political situation then. It is necessary to be mindful of how precarious India's political and socio-economic realities were and what associated anxieties were. In the drive to adopt Hindi as the official language of the central government and to resist (even if by deferring) linguistic reorganization, lay Dar Commission's strategy to give primacy to models of integration and principles of common national citizenship "that would sustain the unity of the world's largest democracy in the face of staggering diversity and in the aftermath of Partition . . .'[42]

As stated above, the nation, and as a consequence nationalism, are indissociable from 'language'. As Benedict Anderson famously

---

[41] Jagat Narain Lal, CAD, 25 November 1949 (11.165.195).
[42] Choudhry, "Language" in *Oxford Handbook of the Indian Constitution*, p. 181.

said: 'What an eye is to the lover . . . language is to the Patriot.'[43]
Propelled by the idea of unity, oneness and the umbrella of an
overarching single identity, the idea of multiple language and
diversity would always run counter to the idea of similitude and
nationalism. Given the hundreds of languages spoken in India,
how could the CA debates not be confronted with the question of
a *national language*?

Purushottam Das Tandon emerged as one of Hindi's
votaries and Jagat Narain Lal as one of his supporters. Tandon's
proposed amendments may have begun from a standpoint of
making Hindi the official language and for the use of numerals
in Devanagari (for him dropping Devanagari numerals for their
international form was a 'monstrosity') but he came around most
respectfully and democratically. In response to Gopalaswami
Ayyangar's provisions which asked for continued use of English
as an official language for at least fifteen years, Tandon said: 'it is
for our brethren in the South to say as to what time they require
and I entirely agree with the view that it is not for us to force
their hands in the matter . . ." He agreed to a fifteen-year period
of use of English but opposed the 'hard provision' of 'Hindi not
being used at all except in addition to English for five years and
more, till a commission makes a recommendation'.[44] Again in
the matter of the form of numerals, his stand was similar. He
was not in favour of the continued usage of international form of
numerals. He said: 'Many of us do not like the introduction or
the acceptance of international forms of numerals. But, I have all
along held the view that we should not force our views on others
and whatever has been achieved by unanimity is welcome. I hope
that when the time comes, we shall be able to see one another's
point of view.'[45]

---

[43] Anderson, *Imagined Communities,* p. 154.
[44] Jagat Narain Lal, CAD, Vol. 9, 14 September 1949 (9.140.133-135).
[45] Ibid., Vol. 11, 25 November 1949 (11.165.199).

What were the imperatives driving Jagat Narain Lal's language standpoint? Since he had contributed to the framing of Tandon's amendment, it would be fair to assume (and extrapolate from his earlier stance on linguistic reorganization) that they were consistent with the imperatives of civic nationalism. The first imperative of the 'civic' principle is of non-coercion: thus no language would be imposed upon any state against their will.[46] The myriad contestations in the CA, leading to compromise and consensus, were an admission that a 'civic nation' did not need to be unified by commonalities of language (or culture or religion). It simply required a disposition on the part of lawmakers to uphold the principle of non-coercion and non-discrimination. The protection or promotion of one national culture thus did not emerge as a feasible and/or desirable goal of the state.

The second imperative of civic nationalism is that of the 'national' mandate: the Dar Commission's resistance to linguistic reorganization was, to use Sujit Choudhry's words, 'part of an integrated strategy to build a common national citizenship that would sustain the unity of the world's largest democracy in the face of staggering diversity and in the aftermath of Partition . . .'[47] The report stated that 'in order to secure stability and integration, India should have a strong Centre and a national language . . . Till nationalism has acquired sufficient strength to permit formation of autonomous provinces . . .'[48] And, 'As soon as India has been physically and emotionally integrated, the Indian state problem solved, the national

---

[46] For a kernel of this idea, see Mehta, "Babble of Babel", *Indian Express*, 2 November 2006; For useful discussions of 'nation' and 'culture', see Kymlicka, *Multicultural Citizenship*, p. 18; Miller, *On Nationality*, pp. 21–27; Tamir, *Liberal Nationalism*, p. 69; DCR, para.133, p. 80.

[47] Choudhry, "Language", in *Oxford Handbook*.

[48] DCR, Para 34, p. 80.

sentiment strengthened, the scientific planning of the existing provinces of India can be taken in hand . . ."[49]

Labour Rights

From the spirit of narrow and selfish exclusion to much higher and enlightened vision, where the interest of the employer need not be at variance with that of the labourer, and the interest of both need not be at variance with that of the state and the consumer . . .

Apart from individual freedoms and cultural identities, the idea of civic nationalism is underlined by a third idea—that of equity. The principle of equity goes beyond the mandate of formal equality (equality before law) and is usually provisioned through socio-economic rights like the right to work, food, livelihood, education, health and so on. One of the primary reasons why this triad of rights (Individual, Cultural and Social) finds instantiation in constitutional provisions is because each of these clusters represents a need in a post-colonial state. Though not in equal measure, each of these has been given space in the Indian Constitution. No matter how imperfectly, Jagat Babu too straddles this field.

In November 1949, Jagat Narain Lal speaking in the Constituent Assembly in defence of the Directive Principles of State Policy (Chapter IV the Indian Constitution that contains the socio-economic provisions) said: 'I have found that even the incorporation of directive principles in our Constitution has been attacked by some people inside and outside too. But, these directive principles are very necessary. They contain the principles on which our State has to act and those principles are both Gandhian and socialistic, a mixture of both in their character. Article 45 of the Irish Constitution also contains those directive principles.'

---

[49] DCR, Para 138, p. 81.

Recall that after the 1937 elections, Jagat Narain Lal was assigned the labour and finance portfolio (as Secretary, Finance, in the Bihar government). It may have been his training in economics and his reputation as a professor of economics at the Bihar Vidyapith that led to his appointment. Over a decade later, he made extensive notes and interventions in the CAD on matters of the relationship between labour and capital, property rights, federal division of financial powers, issues of the Consolidated Fund of India. But most interesting and revealing of his economic ideology is an incomplete manuscript titled 'Labour and Capital' from the 1930s. In a nutshell, it tells us two things: one, how pervasive the idea of a socialistic economy was; and two, how influential Gandhian ideas against capitalism and materialism were. The eclectic nationalist in Jagat Babu combined these ideas and presented his own thesis on the entitlement of labour in India.

Before beginning what he calls a 'small brochure' on labour and capital, he says that his attempt is not to produce a 'comprehensive study of the subject in all its aspects but to draw attention of all who are interested in labour . . . to certain aspects of the question which have appealed to me.'[50] Jagat Narain Lal begins by asking two rhetorical questions: First, why should attention be paid only to industrial labour which, after all, is but a fraction of the vastness of labour lying neglected and scattered in the villages of this country. 'As if', he adds, 'we had finished our part of the duty towards labour thinking about them (industrial labour) and working and agitating for them alone.'[51] He further subdivided labour in villages into two categories—agricultural and landless—adding a caveat that 'no hard and fast line can be drawn between the two, except that the former owns a little land and ekes out his existence partially by the produce of his land and partially or

---

[50] Jagat Narain Lal, Private Papers, NMML, Speeches and Writings, 1(c), p. 3.
[51] Ibid.

mostly by wages in cash or kind earned by working in the fields or cottages of other agriculturalists. The latter has no land and lives entirely through work in others' fields and cottages.'[52] He adds that, unlike in the West, 'it is therefore difficult to draw a hard and fast line of distinction between classes of people who constitute village labour.'[53] The only distinction that can be made, he writes, is between village labour who tend to remain routed to their villages, and industrial labour who are 'often migrants'.[54] He adds that, in contrast to industrial labour, 'village labour leads a life more healthy, more moral and more happy in so far as happiness can be felt and achieved in living with the members of one's own family'.[55]

Second, he asks, 'Why should we slavishly imitate the West and borrow all our ideas . . . without reference to the conditions and the circumstances prevailing in our country and the traditions and the culture peculiar to it?'[56] 'The entire world is watching with wonder and amazement, this colossal socialistic experiment on the one hand and the play of Fascism, Nazism and Imperialism on the other —which are engaged in a war of mutual destruction the like of which the world has hardly ever seen.'[57]

Jagat Narain continues: 'These questions naturally come up and confront a nationalist anxious to seek indigenous solutions of the problems that arise here.' But hastily adds, 'not that there is no desire to profit from whatever may be found to be good and useful in any country, in an age when the old barriers of time and space have been swept away and the entire world seems to be interconnected as a family as it were. But the consciousness that

---

[52] Ibid., p. 11.
[53] Jagat Narain Lal, Private Papers, NMML, Speeches and Writings, 1(c), p. 12.
[54] Ibid., pp. 13–14.
[55] Ibid., p. 15.
[56] Ibid., p. 6.
[57] Ibid., p. 18.

every country has that something peculiarly its own which it might contribute for its own welfare, and for the progress and welfare of the world as well, compels the Indian nationalist to stand firm as it were and refuse to be swept away by the strong currents which come rushing from the outside world. Like the rushing water of the floods, they will disappear after a while wreaking havoc behind and silt and sediments also here and there, which may prove a source of fertility as well.'[58]

Jagat Babu's own ideas emerge as a combination of Gandhian and socialistic (both self-admittedly) ideas. Speaking in the Constituent Assembly, he as much as said it in so many words: 'I have found that even the incorporation of directive principles in our Constitution has been attacked by some people inside and outside too. But, these directive principles are very necessary. They contain the principles on which our State has to act and those principles are both Gandhian and socialistic, a mixture of both in their character.'[59]

In Jagat Narain's view, a testimony to Gandhi's influence, the roots of labour-capital conflict lay in the following according: 'Influx of cheap Western imports into towns and villages— from the cloth to the toys, the needle, the lantern, the kerosene oil, lamps, tools, razors—has completely upset the old village economy entirely . . .'[60] Almost all traditional cottage industries— the rice mills, the flour mills, the oil mills, the ironsmith, the handlooms—all face the threat of extinction in the face of cheap imports, he writes. This along with 'increase of population and the consequent pressure of population upon soil, has replaced plenty with scarcity and busy life with unemployment and starvation in

---

[58] Jagat Narain Lal, Private Papers, NMML, Speeches and Writings, 1(c), pp. 6-7.
[59] Jagat Narain Lal, CAD, 25 November 1949 (11.165.196).
[60] Ibid., p. 9.

the villages'.[61] He cites this as one of the root causes of migration of labour to towns in search of 'living wages'.

Combining Gandhian and socialistic thought, Jagat Narain offers a critique of machinery and materialism. 'The machinery in its train has brought from the West, the conflict of labour and capital, the system of factory production and large-scale manufacture, the huddling together and overcrowding of large masses of labour, both male and female, in industrial areas, and all the evil incidental threats of drinking, loosening of sexual morality, gambling, insanitation, decay of health and the growth of a band of reckless people, defiant of social and moral laws.'[62]

While Gandhi was somewhat obvious as a source of influence, Karl Marx was less so. 'Marx', Jagat Narain writes, 'has gone into the very root of the "Conception of Capital" and examined the history of its growth and accumulation. His celebrated *Theory of Surplus Value* is meant to show how, when society outgrows the elementary stage of the individual producer, all capital accumulates by exploitation of labour. It means that the income of the Capitalist is drawn from only one source i.e. by depriving the labourer of a material portion of what he has produced.'[63] He notes that Marx's theory of surplus value is keenly contested, but despite the many critiques, there is no denying that the Capitalistic system of production results in conflict between labour and capital.

'The real conflict', Jagat Narain argues, 'arises out of the keen contrast felt between the conditions of life shared by the Capitalist and those shared by the labourers . . . Leaving out land & machinery, the only human agency visible at the two ends are—on the one end, the Capitalist; on the other, the large

---

[61] Ibid., p. 10.
[62] Jagat Narain Lal, Private Papers, NMML, Speeches and Writings, 1(c), p. 9.
[63] Ibid., pp. 21–23.

body of labourers. But the Capitalist rolls in wealth and has all the pleasures and comforts of life which wealth can purchase, and all this wealth comes out of the same enterprise. The labourers, on the other hand, live in poverty and squalor, conditions most unsanitary and unenviable and have to see their wife & children condemned to life of eternal misery, although they work hard physically for the same enterprise. The contrast is telling and obvious and it has only to be fully painted in order to awaken the sense of bitterness, wrath and indignation against those who are responsible for bringing it about.'[64]

He continues: 'The revolt of the human spirit against this subservience is typified in the overthrow of those systems wherever possible and the establishment of the principles of democracy wherein power emanates not from the king—but people whose will alone is the final arbiter. The king, if he continues is only a symbol and a majestic expression of that will but nothing more'.

Jagat Babu then asks, 'The question is how this conflict is to be avoided? How is the condition of the masses to be sufficiently improved economically, socially and morally as to raise them up to the level of human beings capable of exercising their rights and duties in the society and of contributing the very best in them to it'.[65]

Conflict was inevitable, he argued, but even in conflict, labour was an unequal partner. 'Being less resourceful, as compared with the Capitalist, Labour started to organise itself—to pool together the intelligence, the ability and the resources of all who comprised it for the purpose of being able to bargain with the Capitalist on equal terms.' At first they were suppressed in capitalist countries, but as they rallied together and grew from strength to strength, trade and labour unions came to be 'declared not only perfectly legitimate and

---

[64] Jagat Narain Lal, Private Papers, NMML, Speeches and Writings, 1(c), p. 24.
[65] Ibid., p. 25.

legal but . . . recognised . . . as the authorised spokesman of the labour in the different industries'.[66]

He also adds that 'labour is also most efficiently organised in the leading industrialised countries of the West like England, America, France, Germany, Austria, Italy etc. In the latter three countries though it has received a tremendous setback on account of present actions of Nazism & Fascism. These conditions are becoming more & more visible in India too. Where labour organisations are not yet fully developed & organised as in many of the small industries and some of the large-sized factories situated in remote corners, state regulations have not yet been able to give labour the much-needed relief either in the matter of wages or in conditions of living and work. They have still to drag on more or less the same miserable existence which they have been doing in the past.'[67]

Jagat Narain Lal goes on to contend that while hartals and slow-downs, coupled with the machinery of conciliation and arbitration, tended to improve the lot of the labourer and smoothen relations between labour and capital, while these did bring about uniform improvement in conditions of living, work and wages through the world (as reported by the International Labour Bureau, of which almost all governments of the world were members), they did not do much to address the real source of conflict—'gross inequality of economic relations'.[68]

He refers to the 'long and chequered history' of Socialist and Marxist thought 'culminating in the Bolshevik revolution' and suggests that those methods of addressing inequality only led to conflict and strife in society and were 'terrible in their import'.[69] One of Jagat Babu's abiding concerns was the vulnerability of a

---

[66] Ibid., p. 26.
[67] Jagat Narain Lal, Private Papers, NMML, Speeches and Writings, 1(c), p. 33.
[68] Ibid., p. 27.
[69] Ibid., p. 22.

'new India', with identities and ideologies threatening to tear it apart, one of them being the revolutionary ideology of Marxism. 'Workers fired by various ideologies are . . . impatient to see these ideologies translated into action even before the shackles that bind the entire nation have had time to break or to be broken. The question can no longer be shelved and the country must make up its mind and choose its own path, before it's too late and, before a medley of ideologies only makes confusion more confounded.'[70] Jagat Babu's clear insight into what he regarded as the fundamental principles of a rational development economics makes it possible for him to understand that the political economy of independent India could not have as its starting point the axiomatic inequality of exchange relations.

Jagat Narain Lal's keen and perceptive understanding of the hierarchies of exchange relations and chains of exploitation made him realize that national interest could not be conceptualized or realized independent of labour reforms and legislation. There had to be a way to combine the two. He proposes a fourfold path, taking lessons from the long (albeit 'chequered', he says) history of 'cooperative effort' in countries like Germany, Sweden and Denmark: '(a) Cooperation in the domain of production and sale or exchange; (b) profit sharing and bonuses, etc. between Capital and labour i.e. between manufacturers (representing companies & Capitalistic employers) & labourers; (c) raising standards of wages, improving conditions of work and living through voluntary agreements between Capitalists and labourers, and through legislations initiated by Governments to standardise wages, regulate hours of work, conditions of living, etc.; (d) arbitration and conciliation, voluntary or compulsory, preceding or following a strike, partial or complete.'[71]

---

[70] Jagat Narain Lal, Private Papers, NMML, Speeches and Writings, 1(c), p. 28.
[71] Ibid., p. 30.

In line with the social democratic models of 'welfare' in the aforementioned countries, and keeping in mind Indian conditions, Jagat Narain proposes a 'cooperative system'. The following summary from John Gunther's *Inside Europe*, in Jagat Babu's notebook reveals his ideological bent: 'Approximately one third of all retail trade and more than ten percent of the wholesale trade & manufacture for domestic consumption are carried on by cooperatives without profit in Sweden, writes Marquis Childs, the author of *Sweden: The Middle Way*. The cooperatives have opened the way to cheap housing (there are no slums in Sweden— or Denmark—any more than there are any aged poor) and a comprehensive raising of living standards. Denmark & Sweden have the highest standards of living in Europe. Yet the essential privileges of capitalism are not abrogated. People may possess private property, they may trade at a profit, they may own production. Sweden, as Mr. Childs says, "is the country where capitalism is controlled, but the individual remains free".'[72]

For Jagat Narain Lal, the capitalistic system had its merits, but it led to exploitative conditions for labour and to permanent strife and conflict between labour and capital. The socialist way too had its merits but its prescription for labour revolt was antithetical to the goals of national integration and conflict management. The social democratic prescription of a cooperative system of production and distribution seemed a possible way forward despite, as he says, its 'unimpressive' trial in India and despite the fact that as a system, it has not 'been able to capture the imagination of the world to the extent of replacing either the Capitalistic or the individualistic system of production'.[73]

He goes on to say: 'Whatever, the efforts made and results achieved in the other countries, I venture to say that those methods

---

[72] Jagat Narain Lal, Private Papers, NMML, Speeches and Writings, 1(c), p. 32.
[73] Ibid.

have not yet been given a fair trial in our own. There is much that is good in them, much that is calculated to lift the employer and the Capitalist on the one hand and the labourers and labour organization on the other. From the spirit of narrow and selfish exclusion to much higher and enlightened vision, where the interest of the employer need not be at variance with that of the labourer, and the interest of both need not be variance with that of the state and the consumer; where the employer and the labourer can take a much longer view of things . . .'

* * *

In the account of Jagat Babu's reconciliation and identification with the principles of civic nationhood, is a larger story of what India chose to *be*. Much like the trajectory of Indian nationalism, the assertions of ascriptive identities were subsumed under the larger similitude of national identity. The idea of a free India was so heady, its force so propelling, that identitarian questions of Self and Community, for the time being at least, seemed to retreat.

What emerged from the many debates and contestations of the Constituent Assembly was an idea of India that was premised on an ideological commitment to a common destiny, a shared set of principles, citizenship and civic institutions in a liberal-democratic state. Its basis included a commitment to procedures for the legitimate enactment of laws and exercise of power, and a creation of a common political identity rather than an ethnic or a cultural one.[74] As Will Kymlicka states, '[t]his non-cultural conception of national membership is often said to be what distinguishes the

---

[74] For a discussion on the civic, constitutional state, see Habermas, "Struggles for Recognition in the Democratic Constitutional State" in *Multiculturalism*, p. 135.

"civic" or "constitutional" nationalism . . . from illiberal "ethnic" nationalism."[75]

Civic nationhood, though, seldom adheres to the 'ideal type' model. In societies that are culturally more homogeneous and less unequal, liberal principles of liberty and equality are widely regarded as sufficient bases for rights and entitlements. However, in countries that are diverse and more unequal, these foundational liberal principles are often bolstered with principles of *Recognition*—recognition of cultural differences, of linguistic particularities, religious differences, tribal ethnicities, community geographies and economic disparities. One could say that in using recognition as the bases for many constitutional entitlements, India has evolved its own unique and perhaps even a fuller idea of 'civic nationhood', encompassing a broader range of rights, entitlements and claims than what may have been envisaged at the point and place of the concept's origin in Western democracies. It was in pursuit of this broader idea of democracy that a more comprehensive range of rights was adopted by our founding fathers, Jagat Narain Lal included.

In multi-ethnic, multi-religious, multi-cultural societies like India, however, there is at the core of civic nationalism, a tension between its civic imperatives of liberty, equality and recognition, and the nationalistic imperative of unity. *Liberty* entails a practice of freedom, which includes the freedom to be different. And *Unity* demands a subsumption of these differences. India's hope to coalesce and unify as a nation, despite all her diversities, was a hope that was not really mindful of the contradictions between its two foundational imperatives.

Let me use Jagat Babu as a lens to explain this. His hesitation to grant linguistic autonomy to provinces in the wake of post-partition, post-independence turmoil, his support for Purushottam Das Tandon's amendment seeking Hindi as a

---

[75] Kymlicka, *Multicultural Citizenship*, p. 24.

national language (which he too had had a hand in framing), his opposition to the right to *propagate* religion, his lifelong angst against conversion as corollary of religious freedom, were all governed primarily by a nationalist impulse for unity. But simultaneously, he was also very easily able to walk the 'civic talk' by becoming a vocal votary of free press and free speech, labour rights and of framing citizenship in non-ethnic terms. The straddling of the two boats was not just a symptom of Jagat Babu's ideological ambivalence. He was not the only such voice in the Constituent Assembly. There were many in the CA who endorsed civic/liberal principles while also harbouring the majoritarian impulse of unity. I call it majoritarian because the receptacle of 'unity' is not an empty one. In terms of which values do we unify and cohere? The easy and obvious answer always has been, the set of values that ensures what philosopher Jeremy Bentham famously termed as the 'greatest happiness of greatest numbers'.

A logic of *assimilation* clearly underpins the project of civic nationalism. Cultural assimilation is the price that must be paid for integration into the political community. To the extent that diversity and personal freedoms do not run counter to or threaten the nationalist impulse, they are accommodated, tolerated or even celebrated. But when such a threat is perceived, the dormant majoritarian impulse becomes an active one, slipping into majoritarian modes of adjudication. The distance between principles of civic nationalism and ethno-nationalism becomes narrower, the demarcating lines fuzzier.

While civic nationalism certainly has a larger and more inclusive heart than ethno-nationalism, and while there is a distinction to be made between 'good nationalism' and 'bad nationalism',[76] there is an often unacknowledged contradiction

---

[76] For a discussion, see, Spencer and Wollman, *Nationalism*, pp. 94–154. According to them, '. . . at the heart of nationalism as a political project,

between its civic impulse for freedom and its nationalist impulse that sees 'too much' difference as antithetical to the national interest. At this level, there is perhaps, as Bauman has argued, an 'essential incompatibility between nationalism and the idea of free choice'.[77]

---

whatever form it takes, is a logic that tends towards exclusion. There must after all always be people who are not part of the nation; the nation is always framed with the presumption of the existence of the outsider, the other, against which the nation is itself defined and constructed. The problem of the other is common to all forms of nationalism, constantly creating and recreating the conditions in which supposedly "good" forms of nationalism turn "bad". The problem of dualism is that it obscures and cannot explain this continual slippage, and creates the illusion that somehow or other it can be avoided, when so much of the evidence points the other way.' (p. 96)

[77] Quoted from Spencer and Wollman, *Nationalism*, p.153.

6

An Inheritance of Contradictions

Sometimes it is in the hidden recesses of history that we find an inheritance whose value may lie primarily in how it is beheld. The fact that Jagat Narain Lal traverses almost the entire spectrum of Indian nationalism—its *ascetic*, *Hindu nationalist*, *anti-colonial*, and *civic* modes (categories mine)—gives his biography a retrospective and analytical meaning that goes beyond his personal contribution or his ideas. There are bigger contributors, taller nationalists, more valiant fighters of freedom, but none I know as intimately or who so tortuously embodied the many possibilities and contradictions of nationalism. In leafing through my grandfather's life, page by yellowed page, I realized that I had more than just his political biography, the project that I had initially begun with. In a manner of speaking, this was also a personal biography of nationalism. In this saga of nationalism lies not just my personal inheritance as a granddaughter, but a collective inheritance of a nation that continues to grapple with its legacy of both its possibilities and contradictions.

I do not really have a story of nationalism that is vastly different or that counters the prevailing view of nationalist history. What I have is a ringside view of Indian nationalism, intimate enough to lend me an experience of nationalism, yet distant enough (in more senses than one) for it to be neither apologetic nor adulatory. My grandfather's diaries helped me understand that within each of the nationalist idioms that I have outlined, there are important distinctions and details that have been rendered invisible by telescopic readings of nationalist history. For instance, the ascetic consciousness of a Mahatma Gandhi differed from a Jagat Narain Lal's, which in turn differed from the code of self-cultivation or *anushilan* that influenced 20th-century Hindu nationalist activity (and its 'construction of a "Hindu" male subject, poised in a stance of permanent provocation towards the 'Muslim' male other').[1] As with Jagat Narain Lal, often the search for an ascetic self had far deeper roots and motivations than the instrumentalities of the national movement. In fact, one of Jagat Babu's deepest disenchantments stemmed from the gaping gap he discovered between the promise of political Hinduism and spiritual Hinduism. It helped me understand that not all Hindu nationalist subjects were constructed in terms of an 'other'. Some were constructed as a representation of Hindu sensibilities and were more sentimental than political, the former having a proclivity to spill into the latter in times of heightened communal tensions, but yet with a distinction that is worth noting and preserving. Unpacking sub-categories of ideology, such as of nationalism, into their conceptual and experiential histories offers not only a deeper understanding of nationalism's varied ideological architecture, but also a more accurate assessment of continuities and changes in their contemporary articulations.

As an areligious and deeply secular person, I could not have been ideologically more distant from my very religious, very Hindu grandfather. But as I got to know him better,

---

[1] Wakankar, "Body, Crowd, Identity", *Social Text*, No. 45, pp. 45–73; see p. 47.

I realized that rather than me 'bestowing' a tolerant gaze on him, it was he who was demonstrating what it was to be a devout Hindu who chose the path of civic values and rules of civic nationhood. The burden of toleration is made lighter when one critical component of one's identity is not forsaken for another. Jagat Babu's life was riddled with tortuous ambivalence, but he fashioned it into one that sought its multiple resolutions in an idea of civic nationhood and its ethos and structure of democracy.

In 1952, Jagat Narain Lal debated on the floor of the Bihar Assembly, lauding the makers of India's sovereign democratic republic:

> We have to congratulate ourselves for conducting successfully this mammoth exercise of voting. In a country where there is such paucity of education, this is nothing short of a miraculous feat . . . Our honourable Governor has touched upon two things that I wish to bring to notice. He has expressed his deep satisfaction that the citizens of this country have conducted themselves with a laudable sense of maturity . . . When the issue of adult suffrage was being discussed in the house, there was apprehension and nervousness as regards the risks of this enterprise and our ability to undertake it. It was an unchartered territory and we really didn't know how it was going to pan out . . . we were apprehensive and were in the dark about the outcomes of adult suffrage—whether communism would be ushered in or whether we'll sink into disorder was not known. But I will laud the public— moulded by Bapu, this country demonstrated that it has truly imbibed his values. It is a matter of great pride that we were able to conduct ourselves with so much order and calm. I wish to congratulate the officials and election authorities that they have been able to conduct a peaceful and successful election. There have been mistakes . . . Some of which I have

personally experienced. Yet, I want to express my gratitude that such a critical exercise of our democratic nationhood has been completed successfully . . .[2]

In another Assembly debate, he said:

> . . . I met the food minister of Government of India and he appreciated the work done to avert the food crisis in our area. Despite continuing food crisis in the last three years, we had managed to bring enough food stocks to deal with the crisis. Our Prime Minister, Pandit Jawaharlal had said that it doesn't matter where we get food from—we will procure it at any cost but we will not let the people of this country die. We should congratulate the government for such a commitment. [Referring to criticism from the opposition parties, Jagat Narain says] There is a *shloka* in Sanskrit according to which *gaali* (criticism) from friends is akin to appreciation . . . I shall pray to God that soon a day will dawn on us when we become *atma-nirbhar* (self-sufficient) and will not have to go around with a beggar's bowl. I want to tell this house and through it convey to the public that this country will make every effort to move towards that . . . Yes, we have made mistakes. Pandit ji has also admitted to that using strong words, but it is our intention to rectify them.[3]

Ordinary as these two speeches may seem, they speak of a resolve to tread the democratic path. Jagat Narain Lal may have been a devout Hindu, but this was not the language of someone that sought the religious supremacy of Hinduism or a Hindu nation. There are numerous more interventions in both his two terms as an MLA, as

---

[2] Bihar Legislative Assembly Debates. Vol. 5, No. 2, 26–27, January 1952. Translated.

[3] Ibid., Vol. 5, No. 7, 17 March 1952. Translated.

a Deputy Speaker from 1951 to 1956 and as a minister who held the dual portfolio of Law along with Cooperatives and Animal Husbandry from 1956–1961. Many of his interventions related to holding individual ministers accountable for expenditure and revenue receipts, relief measures, foodgrain disbursement, irrigation status, employment generation and so on. He carried the mandate of civic nationhood on his democratic, not his Hindu, shoulders.

It is clear that despite imbibing the ethos of civic nationhood and becoming its vocal practitioner, Jagat Narain Lal's civic consciousness was not the same as a Nehru's or an Ambedkar's. Nehru's embrace of liberal democracy and Ambedkar's of social justice, had less ambivalent, deeper and strongly liberal roots. Yet Jagat Babu's conception of citizenship transcending community is closer to Nehru and Ambedkar than his politics would suggest. He chose to uphold the key principles of liberal citizenship, notwithstanding his 'Hinduness'.

It was almost as if he said, all right, we have a bunch of conflicting tendencies threatening to pull us apart, but let's decide on bases for shared principles of common citizenship and civic rules. Let's choose to abide by three sets of principles. One, that we as a nation are defined by our political attachment to it, regardless of ethnicity, religion, race, colour and language. Second, that the nation is in principle a community of equal rights bearing citizens with a patriotic attachment to a shared set of principles and values (Even when he disputed, in the Constituent Assembly, that the right to religious freedom should not mean the freedom to propagate religion, it was arguably his way of treating a non-proselytizing Hinduism at par with, or *equal* to, proselytizing religions like Christianity or Islam). And third, that we abide by the rules and norms of a democratic republic that vests sovereignty in its people.[4]

---

[4] For recent definitions of civic nationalism, see Ignatieff, *Blood and Belonging*, p. 5–9; Barry, *Culture and Equality*, pp. 79–109; Barry,

The importance of a legacy like Jagat Narain Lal's lies, not in its defence or exaltation, but in a reconnaissance of the *nationalist journey* that this inheritance takes. What makes Jagat Babu's legacy especially worth returning to in our present circumstances is the relevance of his approach to questions of nationalism, particularly from his standpoint as a devout Hindu.

There were at least two distinctive features of his approach. The first was to make a clear distinction between Hinduism and Hindutva. Every word of Jagat Babu's memoir, *Light unto a Cell* is a striving for a higher consciousness, a spiritual self that drew its guiding light from the upanishads and the Gita. Every moment spent in the dark recesses of the prison presented itself as an opportunity for meditation and contemplation on the philosophical and spiritual truths revealed in plural traditions of Hindu philosophy. At times it almost seemed that he was living the Advaita philosophy of non-dualism where he was but a representation of the Divine Being in whose pursuit he wished to abandon and immerse himself. Politics was at best a duty; nationalism, a call for solidarity.

Perhaps the whole idea of religious consciousness permeating the being is fraught in politics as it becomes an essentialized identity. This, as Jagat Babu realized, was never an accurate representation of what he was and felt like as a Hindu. The sublimation of his quest for higher meaning at the altar of nationalist politics always made him feel that he was sinking into an abyss of complete loss of his private and spiritual self.

For him, Hinduism could not form the kernel of a nation. He may have flirted with the idea of Hindu representation, advocated cow protection and set up Hindu *seva sanghs*,[5] it always seemed that he was trying to balance what other religions

---

"Statism and Cosmopolitanism", *Nomos*. Vol. 41; Mason, *Community, Solidarity, and Belonging*, pp. 115–47.

[5] Refer to Chapter 3 on Hindu Nationalism.

were doing for their people—just like there were organizations like the Theosophical Society, Arya Samaj and Muslim Jamaats.[6] Hindus too, particularly the underprivileged, needed their sentiments to be respected and welfare to be looked after—so he believed. Sometimes his responses would stem from the exigencies of competing communal interests, but never from a conviction in a Hindu Rashtra.

It is indeed puzzling why a devout Hindu like him, a committed member of the Hindu Mahasabha for more than a decade, mentions Hindutva and Savarkar only once in his writings. And even that one time, it is about recommending the book *Hindutva* for wider readership.[7] He never uses the term Hindutva to describe the aims and objectives of the nation they are trying to free from foreign rule. Once it becomes clear to him that Hindutva is not about Hinduism, or about seva (the idea of social service that was central to his idea of Hinduism's objectives), he parts ways with the Hindu Mahasabha (roughly around the mid-1930s). In this parting of ways is an important distinction that's worth noting— between his personal religious, spiritual, philosophical journey and his political one in pursuit of a free nation.

In choosing sides between an anti-colonial, inclusive Congress and a sectarian, colonial-collaborator Hindu Mahasabha, Jagat Narain Lal admits to another realization that marks his second approach: that a civic—not a religious or ethnic—consciousness is needed to give shape to an Indian nation with a shared past. The idea of civic consciousness is an interesting one, and one that can be read both as dispassionate political agreement on shared principles of nationhood, and as a shared sensibility, a culture of civility that emerged out of varied practices of living and struggling

---

[6] Tabliq-e-Jamaat (1911), Jamaat-e-Ulma-e-Hind (1919), Jamaat-e-Islami (1941), to name a few prominent ones.

[7] Jagat Narain Lal, Private Papers (donated to NMML). Diary with unclear date, but seems to be around 1925; p. 54.

together. 'Civility here conveys a shared aesthetic of training one's Self and others—"in rhetoric, ritual, and jurisprudence"—to foster co-living.'[8]

Jagat Babu also realized that the future of India lay not in a neat resolution of the conflicts, for they were built-in and part of India's psychosomatic nature—a genetic combination of its civilizational and colonial history that bequeathed to it the multiple religions, caste, ethnicities and cultures. The future lay in making the best possible compromises between the extremes. Choosing sides between liberal individualism and socialism, Hindu nationalism and secularity, federal and unitary features, diversity and unity, was perhaps not an option. The future *could not* lie in making stark choices without breaking one of those legacies apart. The only way forward, as my grandfather realized, was to move on with these inheritances, contradictory as they might have been, making the canopy of civic consciousness large and inclusive enough to allow the fate of the nation, as imagined, to unfold.

But destiny's child is often a wayward one. The recognition of a truncated freedom, Partition's violence, feudal mentalities, social unfreedoms and caste hierarchies besieged the new nation and its modernist imagination. The spectre of these continued to haunt India even as she embarked on a massive nation-building exercise based on a state-led planned economy, heavy industries, large-scale public works. The headiness of freedom and the anti-colonial sentiment lent spirit to and bound the nation emotionally. It was too early to realize that once the lore of nationalist valour became a distant memory and a tired recollection, there would be a lacuna that would needed to be filled. And that the cold, dispassionate civic identity would make way for the more passionate attachments of inherited identities—religious, linguistic and ethnic.

---

[8] For a discussion see, Khan, "Politics and Piety in India", *TWAILR*, Reflections No.21.

The First Rupture

Despite all its promises, all its inclusiveness, the canopy it afforded to differences, the civic nation that was founded in 1950 was not an outcome of any resolution of contradictions— between colonial and post-colonial,[9] between liberal and communitarian impulses,[10] between modernity, secularism and tradition.[11] Paradoxes were pushed under the carpet in the hope that they would over time somehow resolve themselves and disappear. If the Constitution was an embodiment of that hope, the unfolding of conflicts between the imperative of liberty and that of equality, between equality and the need for protective discrimination, between the language of rights and the proclivity towards majoritarianism, all got bared as claims of social justice and identity politics peeled off the layers that concealed them. And there came a point when the founding values of civic nationhood themselves were forsaken, first in 1975 with the declaration of national Emergency and then in 2014 with the inscription of Hindutva into our nationalist consciousness.

It is true that the Emergency should be remembered as a rupture in Indian democracy. And as Prime Minister Modi reminded the nation in 2016 at the Ramnath Goenka Awards ceremony: 'Every generation must keep reflecting on the Emergency period in an unbiased manner so that no future political leader can even wish to commit the same sin'.[12] Yes, no one should minimize the lethal blow the Emergency dealt to our freedoms and democratic values. It suspended the rule of law, turned the judiciary into a mute spectator of injustice,

---

[9] Chatterjee, *Nationalist Thought and the Colonial World*, pp. 14–34.

[10] Mehta, "The Real Contest for India", *Indian Express*, 22 May 2014.

[11] Nandy, *The Intimate Enemy*, pp. 1–63.

[12] "RNG Awards: Need to reflect on Emergency so that no leader dares to repeat it, says PM Narendra Modi", *Indian Express*, 3 November 2016.

and unleashed violence on those who stood up against it. It was a frontal attack on the very edifice of our democracy, revealing just how fragile our freedoms are and how predatory a state can get in pursuit of power. But the truth is that the Emergency was revoked and elections were held, in which Indians punished their rulers for the abuses the Emergency had sanctioned. Indira Gandhi lost her seat (So did her son Sanjay Gandhi, the architect of some of the Emergency's worst excesses). Today, the Emergency is remembered as a distant blot, and an aberration, with a deep mix of revulsion and relief.

Speculations aside, no one knows why Indira Gandhi decided to hold elections and re-install democracy in 1977. One of the lesser acknowledged reasons, however, is the enduring strength of the civic consensus in 1950 to uphold the value of democracy and civic republicanism—that people are sovereign and that the buck of democracy stops with them. True, Indira Gandhi may have expected to win, but even in that expectation lay the reiteration of the norm called democracy. It is for this reason I call 2014 a watershed year. Because this time the norm was inverted.

In 1977, the principles of democracy prevailed over its aberrant 'Emergency' form because the virtue of civic consciousness made a comeback. In the years that followed, despite all the contradictions and compromises, despite the entrenched caste hierarchies and majoritarian impulses, there always remained a negotiating space for identities—caste, religious, regional, ethnic—to dissent and demand more equitable resources and representation. For example, even in the face of deeply entrenched structures of caste hierarchies, there remained space for Dalit mobilization and lower-caste resurgence. The decision to implement the Mandal Commission by the V.P. Singh government in 1990, and the tumult in its aftermath, stand testimony to the existence of both an institutional and a civic space for dissension. The rise of regional parties, representing regional, linguistic, class and ethnic interests in the 1980s–90s is another example of, as Myron Weiner puts it, a strategy of 'accommodation and absorption'.[13]

The norm of civic consciousness held up in 1977 because its umbrella made room for the varied idioms of nationalism. As in the pre-independence period, and as exemplified by my grandfather, the post-independence civic canopy allowed for each of these to find a representation. One could be a Vinoba Bhave or a Jayaprakash Narayan as a practitioner of the 'ascetic idiom', embodying the qualities of sacrifice, philanthropy, service and denial of political power. One could be an Atal Bihari Vajpayee, combining in oneself the virtues of civic consciousness and the ideology of Hindtuva. One could be a communist comrade like E.M.S. Namboodripad and resist liberalization as a form of 'economic colonialism' (whose effect, he said, would be the same as a 'thirsty man taking a cup of poison'). One could be a Nehru, a Patel, a Rajendra Prasad, and uphold the virtues, in varied manner, of secular, civic consciousness. And one could even be a combination of several idioms of nationalism, and be pragmatically protean like Indira Gandhi was.

Herein lay the success of a tragedy. The civic space always remained capacious and conflictual enough to be malleable. Meant to be accommodative of conflictual interests, as its political story unfolded, these accommodations turned into corrosive compromises, at times irreversibly so, making a return to the 'original' value impossible. A glaring example of this is the withering of the secular ethos of India. Politically cashable forms of secularism came to be used increasingly as a weapon to do one of the following: To neutralize rising religio-identitarian aspirations of the Akali Dal in the late '70s/'80s, for instance, by patronizing a more virulent counterforce—Bhindranwale; or, taking another example, to pander to 'Muslim vote bank' as in the infamous legislation that followed the Shah Bano Case

---

[13] Weiner, *The Politics of Scarcity*, p. 9.

Supreme Court judgment in 1985;[14] or for the Supreme Court to rule in the *Manohar Joshi Case* (1995) judgement that seeking votes in the name of Hinduism was not a 'corrupt practice', according to the Representation of People Act (RPA). All these happened under the watch of secular principles, indicting forever not just their perverse deployment, but also, sadly, the principles themselves. In politics, norm and deviation do not have equal weight. Deviations punch far above their numerical weight, setting precedents, making history and serving notice on the future.

The principled accommodations and compromises in 1950 were one thing; the political compromises in blatant pursuit of power in later decades were quite another. The former held the principles together even when political choices faltered. The latter forsook the principles of democratic consciousness till a point when it accommodated so much capaciousness, and so much 'bad faith', that India bit by bit lost its civic identity and the culture of civility that had allowed its plurality to breathe. Once the century turned, the unravelling of the edges began. The frayed civic canopy no longer afforded us the pride or reassurance of a nationalist identity.

What we choose to be, is different from what we eventually become, which is a longer evolutionary project. Could we become a civic nation in the truly liberal sense of the term and be culture and ethno-neutral? Perhaps not, and perhaps we were never meant to be so. The very distinction between civic nationalism and ethno-nationalism is overstated since it has always been infused with a spatial geography that is decidedly Eurocentric.[15]

---

[14] The Muslim Women (Protection of Rights on Divorce) Act, 1986, was brought in to overturn the judgment of the Supreme Court following pressure from Muslim groups, including Ulamas, who said that the judgement was in conflict with Sharia.
[15] Fozdar and Low, "'They Have to Abide by Our Laws and Stuff': Ethnonationalism Masquerading as Civic Nationalism", *Nations and*

Affirmations of civic values are a potent means to signify moral and developmental superiority and to relegate culture, religion and other ethnic attributes to the un-modern and primordial. This is not to say that all nationalisms are equal, or to ignore the vituperative effects of the ethno-nationalist project. Some of the most violent mobilizations against religious and ethnic minorities (in Pakistan, India, Bangladesh, Myanmar, Sri Lanka, etc.) have happened in the name of ethno-nationalism. It is also to not say that there is no distinction to be made between *good nationalism* and *bad nationalism*.[16] It is rather to draw attention to an almost oxymoronic tension within the term 'civic nationalism', which renders its distinction from ethno-nationalism fuzzy enough to invite a collapse.

My close reading of Jagat Narain Lal's life and politics alerted me to the tension between these two sub-terminologies—*civic* and *national*. The functional imperative of nationalism is always to tame the cultural profusion of hundreds of languages, ethnicities, religions and other cultural markers. The civic imperative on the other hand seeks to entitle differences and protect citizens' liberty to live those differences. Both propensities remain embedded in the project of civic nationhood, with no reliable way of knowing which of the two would be the dominant and governing imperative for futures to come. While the two projects of ethno-nationalism and civic nationalism, differ in their imagination and vision of nation and the place of diversities in the operative field of politics and policymaking, there may be slippages that narrow the gap between the two. It was the repeated, almost easy, slippages that led to their collapse into each other, sporadically at first, but systemically from 2014 onwards when Hindutva nationalism announced itself as the new 'civic'.

Nationalism 21 (3), pp. 524–543, p. 525.
[16] Spencer and Wollman, *Nationalism*, pp.153–154.

The Second Re-Public

In the preface to his book, *Capitalism and Freedom* (1982), Milton Friedman wrote the famous words: 'Only a crisis – actual or perceived – produces real change. When that crisis occurs, the actions that are taken depend on the ideas that are lying around.'[17] Well, one could say that in 2014, Hindutva was the idea that was 'lying around' to be picked up and fashioned into an altered and politically viable conception of nationhood.

From the early years of the 1920s, the Hindu Mahasabha, the Rashtriya Swayamsevak Sangh (RSS) and the affiliate organizations of the Sangh had worked on an idea of nationhood that was contrary to the founding values of the Indian national movement (or what we understand as its dominant strand), as well as of the Constitution in the post-independence period. Over the years, the Hindu Mahasabha, the RSS, the Jan Sangh, the BJP and its many affiliate organizations kept the idea of Hindutva alive and available until the political impossible became the politically inevitable in 2014. This is not to suggest that Hindutva nationalism was always inevitable. What made it inevitable was the non-availability of alternative ideas. Civic nationalism by now was a spent force struggling to abide by a set of principles it could consistently call its own.

Hindutva nationalism arrived quietly in 2014, in fact so softly that many did not hear its footsteps. It came riding on the back of civic democracy, talking welfare schemes, equal opportunity, minority rights, *even* empowerment of the Waqf Board 'in consultation with religious leaders'.[18] Many of its key agendas, like building the Ram temple, Article 370, Uniform Civil Code, sat quietly in the 2014 election manifesto and were strategically

---

[17] Friedman, *Capitalism and Freedom*, p. xiv.
[18] BJP Manifesto, 2014. Highlights: http://cdn.narendramodi.in/wp-content/uploads/2014/04/Manifesto2014highlights.pdf

missing from election rhetoric. It led many to believe that the democratic institutional framework and developmental realities would be able to tame the agenda of Hindutva,[19] or indeed that there might be a conception of 'developmental Hindutva'.[20] It arrived as a promise of development, of '*achhe din*' and '*sabka saath, sabka vikas*', as a better functioning civic democracy. It did not posture itself as its replacement.

I have often wondered about the phenomenal reach of Hindutva's appeal. What ingrains this political dispensation so deeply in Indian minds, beyond reproach and fact-check? How is it that it has enticed some of the biggest beneficiaries of post-independence democracy, some of them even with memories of the national movement? A plausible explanation is that Hindutva postures itself as a reminder of that passion and recreates the promise of nationalist regeneration.[21] For a nation that's more a 'federation of communities',[22] the dispassionate, rule-bound civic promise was never going to be enough. India had already seen the dynamic of identity politics play out with beneficial effect for lower-caste mobilization and democratic upsurge from the late 1980s onwards. 'For those who longed for some elite revenge and the restoration of some social conservative status quo, national [Hindutva] populism was a very useful instrument: it conveyed

---

[19] See for instance, Varshney, "Modi on Balance", *Indian Express*, 29 April 2014; also my response, Chandra, "Against Complacency", *Indian Express*, 6 May 2014.

[20] Baru, "Developmental Hindutva", *Indian Express*, 14 April 2017; and my response, Chandra, "Saffron Blind", *Indian Express*, 25 April 2017.

[21] For example, Modi is known to tell his aides that he wants to create a *jan andolan* in spirit of the freedom movement. Swacch Bharat and Ram temple are framed as Hindutva's version of the Salt March and 1942 (except that this is top-down, not bottom up, and exclusive, not inclusive).

[22] A term I borrow from Pratap Bhanu Mehta. See, "Being Free to be Free", *Open Magazine*, 12 August 2015.

the idea that the relevant unit of society was neither caste nor class, but the ethnic nation.'[23]

So conscious was its posturing as a 'national movement' that Hindutva appropriated not just nationalist mascots like Mahatma Gandhi and Sardar Patel, but also the varied nationalist idioms of the freedom movement. It packed the appeal of *ascetic* service with *Hindutva/Hindu consciousness*; it redirected the uniting force of *anti-colonial* sentiment into a divisive vengeance towards 'internal enemies'; and finally, it used the idiom of *civic nationhood* minimally to subvert the norms of democracy itself. So closely does it mimic the idioms of the Indian national movement, it renders the machinations of its own power games invisible. It's interesting to unpack just how the emulation and the subversion works.

While conducting an election rally in Jhansi in 2013, Narendra Modi hailed the BJP for choosing a *samaanya vyakti* (ordinary man) who had been born in a *pichhda parivar* (poor/ backward family), as the party's prime ministerial candidate. He went on to tell his audience, 'Don't make me a Prime Minister; make me a *chowkidar* (guard). I will go to Delhi and occupy my post just like a chowkidar who will not let anyone lay their *panja* (hand/palm; also Congress symbol) on it.'[24] In December 2016, when Modi addressed BJP volunteers at a 'Parivartan Rally', he described himself as a fakir, fighting on behalf of the nation against corruption. Casting himself in the ascetic mould, he became a self-described chowkidar who would protect the nation, a *pradhan sevak* in service of the people, and a fakir, unattached to family and material possessions, who would lead India not just politically, but also socially, morally and

---

[23] Chatterjee, Hanson and Jaffrelot, *Majoritarian State,* p. 9.

[24] A hand held up palm-forward is the Congress party symbol. *Panja* though is used as word to describe a predatory animal's paw; See "I don't want to become PM, want to be a Chowkidar, says Narendra Modi", IndiaToday.in, video, 25 October 2013.

spiritually. He portrayed himself as ordinary but blessed with extra-ordinary will to rise above his ordinariness in the interest of the nation. The *shehzada* (the entitled, dynastic prince) didn't stand a chance in front of the ascetic *vikaspurush* for whom this nation was the only family he had. It didn't matter that Modi didn't mingle with ordinary people, didn't face questions, or that he wore monogrammed suits, had the nattiest designer wardrobe amongst all his political contemporaries, or that he unapologetically embraced the glint and the glamour of power and wealth. He still represented what political scientist Morris Jones referred to as the 'saintly idiom' of Indian politics, albeit one that had little or no connection with aspiration for a higher existential order.

The second idiom of *Hindu nationalism* is also continually being tweaked to fit modern requirements of India's global image as the world's largest democracy. Hindutva as it stands today is an improvement over Savarkar's foundational idea (first envisaged in 1923 in his book *Hindutva*) that India, that is Bharat, belongs to Hindus alone. For the Hindus alone is India both *pitri bhumi* (fatherland) and *punya bhumi* (holyland).[25] Hindus, Savarkar said, had to be 'masters in their own house'.[26] The RSS's revered guru, Golwalkar, furthered this idea of a Hindu Rashtra which believed that 'in this land of ours, Bharat, the national life is of the Hindu People. In short, this is the Hindu nation.'[27]

Modern-day Hindtuva takes this foundational thesis and fine-tunes it to function within the larger framework of civic democracy. It converts itself into a high-modernist ideology that

---

[25] Savarkar went on to say that 'some of our Mohammedan or Christian . . . cannot be recognized as [this land] is not to them a Holyland. Consequently, their names and their outlook smack of a foreign origin. Their love is divided.' Savarkar, *Hindutva*, p. 113.

[26] Savarkar, *Hindu Rashtra Darshan*, p. 13.

[27] Golwalkar, *Bunch of Thoughts*, p. 85.

takes the potent mix of nationalism, techno-development, formal democracy and combines it with a singular idea of Hinduism into one fused entity called Hindutva.[28] In the end, it becomes a vast faith-creating exercise that employs multiple rationalizations for its reproduction and continued exercise.

The new rhetoric of Hindutva takes care that at least their key ideologues present an inclusive vision that is consistent with the tenets of democracy. Mohan Bhagwat, the RSS chief (19 September 2018), responding to a Golwalkar reference (to a Muslim being '*shatru*' in his *Bunch of Thoughts*) used his democratic voice to state that Hindutva is an evolving and inclusive project and that Indian Muslims are people of this country.[29] However, in the same speech, Bhagwat went on to say: 'Everyone living in India is a Hindu'.

Bhagwat's is not a casual, one-off statement meant to convey the normalcy of communal cohabitation.[30] The rhetoric is a well-rehearsed one and pervasive.'[31] The rhetoric begins with

---

[28] Savarkar, its founding father, too, was of the opinion that Hindutva is 'not to be confused with the other conjugate term Hinduism. Hinduism is only a derivate, a fraction, a part of Hindutva.' Savarkar, *Hindutva: Who Is a Hindu*, p.3.

[29] Tiwari, "Mohan Bhagwat's silence on Golwalkar telling", *Indian Express*, 20 September 2018.

[30] "Hindutva unifying factor: RSS leader Krishna Gopal", *Economic Times*, 3 January 2020; "Mohan Bhagwat, 130 Crore Indians Are Hindu Society", *The Hindu*, 26 December 2019; "Hinduism not a Religion but a Way of Life", *The Hindu*, 2 April 2016.

[31] The Supreme Court for instance stated in a 1996 judgment that 'it cannot be held that in the abstract the mere word 'Hindutva' by itself invariably must mean Hindu religion. The so-called plank of the political party [is not relevant] for the purpose of pleading corrupt practice in the election petition against a particular candidate.' Manohar Joshi Case (996 AIR 796, 1996 SCC (1) 169). This judgement penned by then Chief Justice J.S. Verma had turned into a milestone. Since then there have been seven court verdicts examining Hindutva or Hinduism. The apex court held that seeking votes in the name of Hinduism was not a

the idea that Hinduism/Hindutva—uttered interchangeably to suggest that they are one and the same—is a way of life; that it is a set of cultural practices shared between different communities; that to be a Hindu is to be part of the land called Hindustan; what else do we call people from Hindustan but 'Hindus'? In one smooth, congenial shot Bhagwat's statement delivers the two key ideological tenets of Hindutva.

First, 'for everyone to be Hindu' there has to be 'one Hinduism', represented in the form of an essentialized conception of a *singular* Hindu religion. For it to reach here, Hindutva has to surmount a challenge Hinduism posed for its nationalist project. Hinduism is just too diverse and plural. For every belief and practice that exists, there seems to be a validity of its exact opposite. You could be a Hindu and believe in one omnipotent being or worship many gods; you could be a part of a sect or you could be a devout Hindu and shun the deification of mortal humans; you could be a vegetarian or a non-vegetarian; you could believe in animal sacrifice or be its fiercest critic; you could be a practitioner of ahimsa or not be its strict advocate; you could believe in the caste system or call for its annihilation; you could believe in *one* Ramayana or in hundreds of its retellings in different languages that, as A.K. Ramanujan reminds us, don't always carry Valmiki's narrative.[32] This multiplicity of belief systems poses an enormous challenge for projects of nationalism that seek a united, coherent imagination of one nation, one people, one faith.

'corrupt practice' according to the Representation of People Act (RPA). In 2016, a seven-judge Bench of the apex court led by Chief Justice of India, T.S. Thakur, dismissed a petition filed by social activist Teesta Setalvad, author Shamsul Islam and senior journalist Dilip Mandal, who argued that the interpretation of the 1995 judgement has supposedly led to 'Hindutva becoming a mark of nationalism and citizenship.'

[32] Ramanujan, "Three Hundred Ramayans", *Open Magazine*, 28 October 2011.

With so many different 'ways of life', in what terms does Hindutva fashion its 'singular' Hinduism? The quest for singularity seeks prescription of norms and practices that can form the basis of this uniformity. Hindutva first seeks an end to the caste system, for the divisiveness of the caste system is a bane for the unity and uniformity it sought.[33] However, despite its consistent advocacy against the caste system, Hindutva as a practice has not really challenged Brahmanical orthodoxy. Brahmanical conservatism still rules our social psyche in many visible and invisible ways, and often serves as the adjudicator of what this singular, homogeneous culture should comprise. Even today it prescribes what is sacred, pure, natural and *sanskari*, and proscribes what is profane, impure, unnatural and alien. For instance, consuming beef is an act of untold travesty (despite this meat being food for many Dalit Hindus), a sin that deserves severest of punishments; Durga is deemed sacred, while Mahishasur (the demon-god of the Adivasis and Dalits) is regarded profane; gay sex is considered unnatural and allowing women of menstruating age entry into Sabarimala temple is offensive to the idea of purity and godly celibacy.[34] These and the myriad other examples from our own everyday lives suggest that our social relationships continue to be disciplined through the conservative lens of Brahmanical social values and that the ruling idea of Hindutva does nothing consistent to oppose it.

The well-aired rhetoric of 'everyone living in Hindustan is a Hindu' and 'Hindutva is a way of life', is meant to convey not just the universalized idea of One Hinduism but also that being Hindu (whatever that indeterminate, capacious category is taken to mean) is the only legitimate and rightful way to be in this

---

[33] Savarkar, a strong critic of the caste system even drew up a seven-point reform agenda. Savarkar, *Hindutva*, pp. 85–90.
[34] Excerpted from, Chandra, "In Service of Politics", *Indian Express*, 4 January 2019.

Hindu land. It renders 'other' ways of being as alien and seldom an authentic part of this country to begin with. Underlying Hindutva, therefore, is its second bread-and-butter idea; of the illegitimacy of other religio-cultural ways of being in India. The idea that India is a land of Hindus, is a Hindu Rashtra, is conveyed, circulated and repeated variously and vituperatively.[35]

If there was any room left for a gap between intent and rhetoric, or for a reassurance that at least the institutional structure abides by the norms of equal citizenship, the BJP regime launched its Citizenship Amendment Act (CAA) 2019 in conjunction with the National Citizenship Register. [36] For the first time in the history of India, the idea of citizenship has been constitutionally linked to religion, carrying forward Hindutva mandate that rests quite unambiguously on the Savarkarite idea of India being the 'natural' home of the Hindus. More importantly, the India that is Bharat can never be an equal home to Muslims. [37] By welcoming only

---

[35] For instance, BJP MP from Gorakhpur, Ravi Kishan, termed India a Hindu Rashtra as the majority of the population belongs to this religious community; "India is a Hindu Rashtra", News18.com, 4 December 2019.

[36] The CAA 2019 seeks to make foreign illegal migrants of certain religious communities—Hindus, Sikhs, Jains, Buddhists, Parsis, Christians—coming from Afghanistan, Bangladesh and Pakistan, eligible for Indian citizenship. The Act allows a person to apply for citizenship by naturalization, if the person meets certain qualifications. One of the qualifications is that the person must have resided in India or been in central government service for the last twelve months and at least eleven years of the preceding fourteen years. For the specified class of illegal migrants, belonging only to the specified religious denominations (that excludes Muslims), the number of years of residency has been relaxed from eleven years to five years.

[37] There are three levels at which religion has been linked to citizenship. First, the qualifying criterion for an illegal migrant to apply for Indian citizenship is religious. The exclusion of Muslims from citizenship qualification is glaring, given many categories of Muslims (Hazaras, Ahmadiyyas, Mujahirs and so on) who suffer equal if not more

non-Muslim migrants, the ruling regime signals to India's own minorities which religious minority community it devalues and delegitimizes. Ambarien Alqadar poignantly captures her sense of loss, as she writes: 'Looking at the barren trees through my study window, I'm haunted by the specter of detention centres being built in far-flung corners of India. On my Facebook feed, viral videos of Muslim men being openly lynched make my stomach turn. I don't have a language to articulate that fear except that I can hear its heavy steps draw near.'[38]

The intent of the Constitution was never this. Even a devout Hindu like my grandfather upheld the principle of citizenship based on birth on the soil of a country (of *jus soli*), along with a concurrent provision for citizenship based on descent (*jus sanguinis*) as a more modern and valid principle of citizenship.[39] What the 2019 amendment does is to ignore the constitutional intent and consolidate a shift towards citizenship based on descent. By introducing an explicitly religious criterion into a hitherto religion-neutral law, the Hindutva regime has installed what Christophe Jaffrelot terms an 'ethnic democracy'.[40]

The rising receptiveness towards the use of religion in constitutional and political governance is accompanied by the

---

persecution in their home states. Second, these migrants have to be from only three countries—Pakistan, Afghanistan and Bangladesh—all of which are Muslim majority countries, perpetrating a racist idea that 'religious persecution' happens only in Islamic countries. And third, read along with the NRC (introduced in the Parliament first in 2003), the CAA seeks to exclude Muslim 'illegal' migrants from claims to Indian citizenship.

[38] Alqadar, "What does it mean to live under the constant fear of being declared a foreigner in your own country?", ThePolisProject.com, 22 July 2020.

[39] Jagat Narain Lal, CAD, Vol. 3, Para 169 (3. 18. 169).

[40] For details, see, Jaffrelot, A "De Facto Ethnic Democracy? Obliterating and Targeting the Other, Hindu Vigilantes, and the Ethno-State", in *Majoritarian State*, p. 42-67.

ascendancy of illiberal politics. Nationalism can be fashioned or conceptualized either in terms of its own aspirational values of nationhood or in terms of a majoritarian consolidation against one traitorous 'enemy' or the other. As the Hindutva ideology fuses the national identity with a religious one, it simultaneously marks those dissenting against the inscription of religion in politics as anti-national, enemies of the state. Here Hindutva can be seen as innovating and subverting the anti-colonial idiom of nationalism. In the absence of an external colonizing power, the idea of 'enemy of the nation' morphs into a nationalism seeking to weed out 'internal', seditious, 'anti-national' enemies of the state. Sample the statements below from elected representatives of the BJP.

BJP MLA Surendra Singh from Bairia, UP, in January 2018:

> '. . . there are a very few Muslims who are patriotic. Once India becomes a Hindu rashtra, Muslims who assimilate into our culture will stay in India. Those who will not are free to take asylum in any other country . . . As the RSS completes 100 years in 2025, by 2024, India will become a Hindu rashtra.'[41]

BJP MLA Basanagouda Patil Yatnal from Karnataka, in a speech to mark the victory in the Kargil War, 26 July 2018:[42]

> '[Intellectuals] enjoy the food, air and water of this country . . .
> They give statements against the army and the country . . .

---

[41] "India will become 'Hindu Rashtra' by 2024, says Uttar Pradesh's BJP MLA Surendra Singh", Firstpost, 14 January 2018.
[42] "Would have lined intellectuals up and shot them if I was Home minister: Karnataka BJP MLA", *Hindustan Times*, 27 July 2018.

if I become the Home Minister, I will order them to be lined up and shot.'

Amit Shah, Home Minister, on the floor of the Parliament, 11 April 2019:[43]

'We will ensure implementation of NRC in the entire country. We will remove every single infiltrator from the country, except Buddha [sic], Hindus and Sikhs.'

Union Minister of Social Justice and Empowerment, Thawar Chand Gehlot, in support of the CAA, Mandsaur, MP, January 2020:

'Many people question that when Pakistan was formed on religious lines as an Islamic nation, then why were Muslims allowed to live here, they should have been sent to Pakistan and all Hindus, Sikhs, Christians and other religious minorities from there should have been allowed to settle here.'[44]

BJP and RSS leader Rajeshwar Singh in January 2020:

'Muslims and Christians will be wiped out of India by December 31, 2021 . . . "we" have decided that Islam and Christianity will be finished in India by 2021 . . . this is the pledge taken by my colleagues. This is our pledge.'[45]

---

[43] "Will remove every single infiltrator", *Indian Express*, 11 April 2019.

[44] "Union minister makes controversial statements at pro-CAA program", *New Indian Express*, 12 January 2020.

[45] "Muslims and Christians will be wiped out of India by December 31, 2021: BJP leader Rajeshwar Singh", SabrangIndia.com, 14 December 2014.

Language is a bearer of politics and always a mirror of its times. If we listen to these speeches by elected representatives of the state carefully, we'll hear an evolving narrative. This narrative fuses national identity with a religious one. It then marks out the 'others'—the anti-nationals, the liberals, the secular democrats, the independent Press, the worshippers of other gods, the eaters of other food and the lovers of other loves. National pride, religious affiliation and a deep, visceral hatred for the presumed anti-nationals become interlinked.

Who are these anti-national traitors and what seditious ploys do they engineer? Where do I begin? It could be 'the disloyal Kashmiri ingrate, the insidious Bengali infiltrator, the beef-eating cattle thief, the preying Romeo, the ghettos crowded with burqas and beards',[46] or it could be the traitorous 'urban naxal', the liberal anti-national or the westernized secularist.[47] At times they look like elected representatives of Kashmir, at times like a young pregnant girl or a paraplegic university professor, an ailing poet, or like human rights lawyers, activists, professors, and occasionally even like a young girl who says *Pakistan Zindabad, Hindustan Zindabad* in that damning, seditious order. Wherever Hindutva turns—back to history, forward to the future, or to the present times—it finds its most dangerous enemy. So despised are these 'anti-nationals' that it is routinely proposed that this enemy be subjugated to the power of 'social death'.[48] Threats and use of violence, street violence, state

---

[46] Kesavan, "Experiments in the politics of sadomasochism", *Telegraph*, 20 July 2020.

[47] As I write, there are sixteen academics, scholars, lawyers, civil rights activists, poets, professors of English and law, who have been incarcerated under the draconian anti-terror law, the Unlawful Activity Prevention Act (UAPA), in jail for the last three years, without bail, without a chargesheet. For details see, Chandra, "'Extraordinary' Laws are becoming Central to the Politics of Repression in India", Wire, 28 August 2018; also Chandra, "'Activists' Arrests", Wire, 1 November 2018.

[48] 'Social death' used by sociologists such as Orlando Patterson and Zygmut Bauman to describe the ways in which someone is treated as

violence become the many technologies of control, inseparably entangled with the assertion of Hindutva nationalism and the purge of the traitorous anti-national.[49]

The fourth idiom of nationalism, and one of the most enduring of our founding constitutional legacies is that of civic nationhood—the idea that the nation comprises of 'equal citizens' who share 'equal rights'. The idea of equality is the bedrock of the civic conception, implying that in the eyes of law and governance, one is as equal as another. Provisioned in Articles 14–18 of the Indian Constitution, the right to equality means that the identities we are born with, or acquire, ought to have little or no bearing in the eyes of law and state policy.

Hindutva abides by this rule of equality and doesn't replace civic modalities. However, what it does is to invert the idiom to make equality itself a pliant majoritarian tool. If religious minorities are equal in the eyes of law, why should they be accorded special funding and privileges by the state? The rationale of equality becomes the rationale for stripping away of protective rights of minorities and underprivileged. 'Protective discrimination' is repackaged as an idea that militates against equality of citizens. In a manner of speaking, Hindutva nationalism uses the master's tools to dismantle the master's house.

There are several cases in point: The Hindutva regime's agenda of a *uniform* civil code and its legislation criminalizing the Indian Muslim practice of Triple Talaq (even after it was outlawed by the Supreme Court on a petition by Muslim women and organizations)[50] as an exemplar of gender justice; its questioning of the legality and legitimacy of state-funded

---

if they were non-existent or dead. Rendered irrelevant, Kralova three characteristics of social death—loss of identity, loss of connectedness and losses associated with disintegration of the body. Králová, "What is social death?", pp. 235–248.

[49] Ibid.

[50] Shayara Banu vs. Union of India; https://indiankanoon.org/doc/115701246/

'minority institutions' like the Aligarh Muslim University;[51] its citation of Article 14's criterion of 'reasonable classification' to table a discriminatory citizenship legislation;[52] its repetitious circulation of the need to purge the word 'secularism' from the Preamble to the Constitution; its rhetoric that diminishes what had all along been practised as 'secular' as 'sickular' or 'pseudo'— are all narratives that allege that Equality was just a façade to appease the minorities.

On the idea of protective discrimination and caste-based 'reservations', Hindutva had to tread more carefully. Instead of denouncing it (and possibly committing political hara-kiri) it chose a more elliptical route to uphold the principle of equality. First, like in the past, it periodically stressed on the need to transcend caste identities in the name of Hindu unity. Secondly, it has chosen to not openly defend the idea of reservations. For example, as Modi presented himself as a self-made man, a former

---

[51] In the year 1981, the Parliament of India made an amendment to the Aligarh Muslim University Act 1920, which restored the minority character of the university, but the controversy did not end there. The amendment was challenged in the Allahabad High Court in the year 2005 and the court read down this amendment restoring the Azeez Basha ruling. In 2019, a three-judge bench, led by CJI Ranjan Gogoi, decided to refer the issue to a larger bench after hearing preliminary arguments from the varsity, which has said its minority status cannot be changed every time government changes or the political party in power changes. Mukul Rohtagi, representing the challenge against the minority institution argued before the SC stating that 'As the executive government at the Centre, we can't be seen as setting up a minority institution in a secular state'. The challenge and Rohtagi's statement come despite Article 30 of the Indian Constitution. Article 30 of the Indian Constitution gives the minorities the right to 'establish and administer educational institutions of their choice'. There are three terms in the sentence—'establish', 'administer', and 'of their choice'.

[52] 'Article 14 of the Constitution does not bar Parliament to frame laws that are based on reasonable classification. And reasonable classification is there in this Bill,' Shah told the Upper House.

chaiwallah, he did not defend positive discrimination. He presents himself as 'the perfect antidote to Mandal for the middle-class upper castes.'[53] The result was a fragmentation of the lower and OBC votes, and a steady decline in the share of their seats in the Parliament. In 2014, the percentage of MPs from the upper castes rose to 44.5 per cent, on a par with its representation in the 1980s, whereas the share of OBC MPs dropped to 20 per cent, a trend that continued (with minor variations) in 2019 too.[54] The BJP, as Christophe Jaffrelot puts it, became the vanguard for 'elite revenge' who demand an 'equal' and level playing field for all, notwithstanding the history of their own privileges.

What is interesting, however, is that at all points the democratic framework is kept functionally intact. Majoritarian appeal in fact relies on the legitimizing force of popular support. Chatterjee, Hanson and Jaffrelot argue that populist appeal is a trait of ethnic democracies—they seek 'open public spaces' to articulate themselves[55] and seek the legitimacy of institutional framework to universalize themselves. The 'democratic' dimension relies on institutions legally sanctioned by the Constitution, but the 'ethnic' dimension relies on the subversion of institutions such as the Election Commission,[56]

---

[53] Jaffrelot, "30 years on: Is it 'game over' for Mandal Politics", *Indian Express,* 22 August 2020.

[54] Caste and Community representation in the Hindi belt (1962–2019); Source: SPINPER (Social Profile of India's National and Provincial Elected Representatives), Ashoka University/ CNRS-Sciences Po-Trivedi Center for Political Data/ CERI-CDSP.

[55] Chatterji, Hansen, Jaffrelot (eds), *Majoritarian State,* p. 4–5.

[56] Be it the scheduling of the 2019 elections in seven long phases, allegedly to favour certain parties, taking timely action against violations of the Model Code of Conduct (MCC), stopping campaign keeping in view a certain party's campaign schedules, cancelling candidatures, transfers, posting and suspending election observers on ambiguous grounds, allowing surrogate campaigns by giving the nod for leaders to visit religious shrines when the MCC was still in force, denying counting

the Judiciary[57] and the Police[58] that have come increasingly to serve majoritarian democratic interests in India.[59]

Formal, informal and stealthy steps towards the inscription of religion in state conduct and the Constitution tend to manifest in societies divided over the state's religious or secular character, where constitutional arrangements on religion are often a product

---

of VVPAT and so on; Bhatnagar, "EC Hands out Fourth 'Clean Chit' to Modi", Wire, 4 May 2019.

[57] The refusal of the Supreme Court to stay the CAA in January 2020 despite 144 petitions challenging the constitutionality of the law; its restraining order to all High Courts from hearing any CAA-related petition; its further postponement of its own CAA hearing after the 'Sabarimala case' and other pending pleas, despite the failure of the state to file a reply within the mandated four weeks (from 22 January 2020); the refusal of the Supreme Court to reconsider a 1995 (three bench headed by Justice Verma) judgment states that Hindutva by itself does not mean Hindu religion, in effect legitimizing Hindutva based electoral campaigns; the 2019 amendments to the UAPA (which shifts the burden of proving one's innocence on the terror accused); the Supreme Court's Ayodhya–Babri Masjid judgment, amidst chants of *Jai Shri Ram* by lawyers, assigning the entire disputed land to Hindu litigants; the exoneration of all six accused in a lynching case of a Muslim cattle trader.

Roy, "Supreme Court issues notice in fresh petitions challenging Citizenship Amendment Act", Bar and Bench, 20 May 2020.

[58] Not registering FIRs against perpetrators of murderous hate crimes; instead, charge-sheeting victims of communal lynchings; sending the meat, and not the body of murdered Akhlaq, for forensic analysis; arresting the pregnant anti-CAA protestor and Pinjra Tod activist but not registering an FIR against BJP MLA Kapil Mishra who openly incited violence, or against the man who, in open view of the police, fired a gun at the anti-CAA protestors; and a myriad more examples where the shadowy arm of the law insidiously backs the impunity of Hindutva and assists the self-proclaimed caretakers of the Hindu rashtra.

[59] The Unalwful Activities (Prevention) Act, 2019. The Gazette of India. Available at http://egazette.nic.in/WriteReadData/2019/210355.pdf

Aditi, "Rajasthan Court acquits all accused", Bar and Bench, 15 August 2019.

of a compromise at the time of constitution-making. One of the reasons why the Constituent Assembly agonized over the term 'secular' was a degree of widespread discomfort about regarding and declaring religion as an undesirable component of public life. The Western-secular idea that public and private life needs to be organized separately and distinct from each other, militated against a foundational organizing principle of public life in India— Dharma. So central was dharma to the philosophical edifice of Hinduism that it conveyed simultaneously conceptions of righteous conduct, political duty, social organization and religion, all rolled into one.[60] It became synonymous with a moral force that could not be expunged from public life.

The ambition to fashion a national ethos that was distinctive (and unlike the institutions not borrowed from the Anglo-Saxon models) was shared by many founding fathers across the ideological spectrum. So they decided to be secular in a different sort of way with the state not separating itself from religion, but becoming a practitioner of *sarva dharma sambhaav* (translated loosely as 'equal treatment of all religions'). Institutionally it meant that the state would be equidistant from all religions, rather than *separate* from religion. Honourable as the chosen path may have been, it made for messy political outcomes. How could the state be neutral and liberate individuals from oppressive and religious hierarchies? How could the state be equidistant and yet protect minority rights and institutions? How could the state be neutral and yet be able to check majoritarian encroachments? What the Constitution left unsaid, our political culture transformed into a denouncement of the very principle that sought to treat all religions equally and respectfully.'

---

[60] So much so that, even a *nastika* religious practices (ones that denies the authority of the Vedas and divine origin theory) like Buddhism rests on the conceptual core of *dhamma* (the doctrine of righteous practice, taught by Buddha), while Jainism regards dharma as a *dharmaastikaay* (substance of reality).

As Tom Nairn stated in an influential article, nationalism can either be healthy or morbid: 'Both progress and regress are inscribed in its genetic code from the start.'[61] The retelling of Jagat Narain Lal's journey as a nationalist is an attempt to reveal these genetic codes. The idea of mixing religion with politics, of treating politics as a means to consolidate and represent identities, the idea of one's identity permeating one's political being, was always fraught for politics. A tension that was latent in 1950, gave way to a reneging that was clandestine and insidious pre-2014 and morphed into an unabashed denouncement of secularism in the era of ascendant Hindutva. The real and unarticulated conflict of Indian secularism is not between 'religion in public sphere' as opposed to 'religion only in private sphere', or between religion as a guide to public morality as opposed to religion only governing private morality. The conflict is between religion as faith and religion as nationalist ideology. Which is why, unlike Jagat Narain Lal (amongst many others like Gandhi, Malaviya, for instance) who would have traded secularism for sacralization of politics, Hindutva today stands for politics that is de-sacralized and for a religion that is politicized.

---

[61] Narain, *The Breakup of Britain: Crisis and Neo-Nationalism*, pp. 347–48; Quoted from Spencer and Wollman, *Nationalism* p. 95.

Afterword

Dear Dada,

The only memory I have of you is your prayer mat. It was square, brown and soft, patterned with motifs and fringed on the sides with tassels. I have no idea why I remember this, but in at least one sense it's a fitting memory. As I read your notes, diaries and memoir, written in impeccable English (truth be told, I had to use the dictionary twice) and masterly Hindi (again, I had to seek help for some of the idioms you used), I realized quite early on that the most meaningful and significant aspect of your identity was your religious and spiritual beliefs. In that sense, the prayer-mat memory becomes an apt repository of your being.

Your diaries and notebooks also made you my acquaintance. Ensconced in my secular habitat, I had no idea how matters of faith could be so compelling and so intensely charged that they could pervade every thought and mediate every action for a person. I see enough of its vulgar and caricatured manifestation now but they all lack your scholarly, philosophical and spiritual refinement. Through you, I at least now know that mixing religion and politics, while keeping one's soul intact, is a torturous path, riddled with personal dilemmas and suffering, no matter how much of 'good-faith' is involved.

Strangely, there's an odd assurance in the fact your nationalist imagination was often beset with self-doubt and question marks. For me they indicated an absence of dogma and zealous beliefs. That said, I still lack sympathy for your nationalist vision, that used religion to sacralize politics or even fashion a political self. It is a doomed project as you yourself realized every step of your political career. Perhaps that is why you eventually chose the dispassionate path of upholding civic virtues of shared values.

Enough said on your politics and nationalism. Since you do not know me at all, I wanted to acquaint you with my nationalist sensibilities too. Do you recall a diary entry of yours when Lala Lajpat Rai and you toured Assam (your diary was undated, but I surmised it would have been in 1927 after you joined the Independent Congress Party that Lala ji had founded)? How pained you were to see conversions of locals to Christianity! A year later you saw a similar conversion story being played out in the Chotanagpur areas adjoining Ranchi. I don't want to sit on judgement on your distress because we inhabit different philosophical worlds. I am too much of a rationalist to ever empathize with you, and you are too much of a spiritualist and a Vedantist to understand my mundane, material questions. But just so that you know, and perhaps in the process also find solace, here's a glimpse into what shaped my nationalism.

Let me start with something that'll make you happy. I have always been somewhat of a nationalist. I say 'somewhat' because nationalism is a loaded term now, or rather a burdened state of being that toggles between patriotism and jingoism, between pride and xenophobia, perhaps even between love and hate. Even when I began to understand the argument that nation states are born out of the trauma of dividing and demarcating, that boundaries separate and exclude not just territory but people, and that the birth of nation states is steeped in the blood of many, I would still secretly nurture a patriotic loyalty towards my country in a naïve, unshakeable sort of way.

My patriotic loyalty is by no means unique, Dada—many bleeding hearts may share similar feelings—but what makes it interesting (and it might surprise you a bit) is how it all started. After you died, Dad got a job in Bokaro Steel plant (then in Bihar, now Jharkhand). I was admitted to a Jesuit 'missionary' school, one of the pet peeves of your nationalist journey.

One of my more endearing school memories is of the morning trips to school on Republic and Independence days. Going to school on holidays, for some reason, was a particularly pleasurable exercise, notwithstanding the fact that it was mandatory for us to be there on these two days. This was the one 'mandatory' we didn't resist. Unfailingly, year after year, we'd be there to hoist the tricolour, and pay our respects to the country and to our founding fathers who gave us a free nation. Being a holiday, we were often driven to school in our school bus by our vice principal, Father Tom Keogh (a Jesuit; Australian by birth but Indian by home), as many of the regular bus staff would be enjoying their day off. We'd reach school, line up and stand in rows, look up reverentially at the flag being hoisted and sing the national anthem. And sometimes, depending on the status of my teenage hormones, I would even feel a lump in my throat as I did so. The anthem sung, we'd break up into groups of animated chatter; some of us would pick up the flower petals that the unfurled flag had showered (to be pressed later in books), greedily eat the laddoos that were distributed and feel the joyousness of just being part of that moment. And then the event would be over, and we'd be on our way home, once again being driven by Father Keogh.

The principal of our school was another Australian Jesuit, Father John Moore. If Father Keogh was the epitome of efficiency, charm and energy, Father Moore, the elder of the two, was a gentle, loving and generous soul. He'd preside over the morning assembly each day that would eclectically begin sometimes with

an inspirational poem in Hindi (for instance, *kranti ki mashaal ko/
desh ke jawan tu jalayeja . . .*), or with a spiritual, meditative prayer,
sometimes with Saraswati *vandana*, or with *Vande materam*,
sometimes with prayer to the Lord, and oftentimes with Tagore's
'Where the Mind Is without Fear'.

One Wednesday each month, we'd have an hour-long 'special
assembly' in the 'Chapel Hall', which Father Moore would
conduct. The assembly, mostly filled with school achievements,
announcements, accolades and applause would end with the Indian
national anthem. One of the things that would irk Father Moore
was the way we'd sing the anthem. Once he told us that we were
singing the anthem at a pace that was all wrong: 'it's too much
of a tuneless drawl', he said; 'it should take fifty-two seconds, no
less, no more.' He'd stand there in the hall, time us, and look at us
disapprovingly with an indulgently cross look if we got it wrong,
or reward us with a pleased smile if we got it right.

Here was a Jesuit school, Dada, that made *no* attempt to
proselytize us, to even 'inculcate' subtly. We could sing *saraswati
vandana* even in the chapel hall. Here were Fathers and Sisters who
were Christians, some even foreigners (doubly 'alien', 'non-native'
and presumed non-nationalists) who joined us in celebrating our
country's freedom and culture and who even acquainted us with
the niceties of our own nationalist ethos. Here was a culture of
toleration, secularism and nationalism that existed in undeclared,
unstated, quiet harmony.

You could argue that this was an oasis, an isolated pocket in a
small obscure steel city, but if you look back at your own school life,
college community or political life, you may find a similar story and
your own resonating instances. You recall Khurshaid Hussnain, your
first jail inmate, or Mazharul Haque and your trusting friendships
with them? You even made the beautifully and syncretically named
Sadaqat Ashram (by Mazharul Haque) as your political abode and
later went on to convert the premises into a university campus for
Bihar Vidyapith where you taught economics.

Let me share one more vignette from my life. The decade beginning 1990 saw the tumult of the 'Mandal clashes' whose brunt I personally faced one night. I was pregnant, travelling alone in an overnight train from Bokaro to Calcutta, when the train was gheraoed and attacked by pro-Mandal (so named after the recommendation of 'reservations' by the Mandal Commission) supporters. Men with crude country-made pistols, spears, bludgeons, shattered the window glass, stormed in and wreaked havoc and bloodshed in the compartments. Your great-grandchild and I survived the trauma, thanks to a gold chain and my engagement ring that I offered as a peace offering. Within a year or so, I was back in Delhi University, queuing up for jobs, losing some to 'reserved seats', a feature that continued in the coming years, but failing to ever make me resentful of 'reservations'. I knew that I was not the victim here.

But somewhere along the way everything changed. We, the Hindu majority, began to be made aware that we were victims in our own country. The idea that this nation, its 'first citizens', their faith, their temples their beliefs, their pride were under threat, was told and retold till it became part of our consciousness. Slowly but surely, from the podiums of politics and the portals of power, from the rath yatras and election rallies, a perception of victimhood steeped into our homes, offices, addas, social media (you'll never know what that is), textbooks and conversations within.

The rulers still divide and rule. But unlike your time (perhaps), a more sophisticated idea of persuasion is at work, in which the religious-majority is extolled to be a partner in the making of new India. Masses are enlisted as teammates and persuaded to become collaborators in a cycle of self-perpetuating myth that sanctions violence and exclusion. The myriad, everyday instances of majoritarian chauvinism assures that an open, public display, use or threat of violence is no longer aberrant or even particularly unlawful. On a good day in office, it might even pass off as the 'collective conscience of the country'. This kind of violence does not frighten us easily, but it is insidiously cunning because we slacken in our efforts to respond to it or to free ourselves from its grip.

I wonder what you would do today had you been around. Where would you have pitched your political tent? Religion in politics is no longer about expressing an 'Indian' ethic or practise of piety in the public sphere. Rather it is defined by a crude absence of civility that is not for the spiritual-hearted. Would you then have continued to retain faith in the saintly and spiritual idiom of nationalist politics? Or would you have retreated with your faith and spirituality into a private sphere? These are not just some of my questions. How much of faith in politics is good faith, and how much of it will enable us to define ourselves as an 'Indian' nation is an enduring question for an entire generation of citizens figuring out their burden of toleration.

Your granddaughter,
Rajshree
18 August 2021

Acknowledgements

Of all my writing endeavours, this perhaps has been the most challenging. My disciplinary training as a political scientist meant that I had to charter new territories, both as researcher and as a writer. But my interdisciplinary gene and learner's license made sure that I was on track after initial months of being lost in the archival woods.

The project was challenging in another sense too. I, as a fiercely secular person had to 'study' my very religious, very spiritual, very nationalist grandfather—Jagat Narain Lal. The object-subject relationship became not only complex but also, rather unexpectedly, interchangeable. I came face to face with many urgent emotions that not just enthralled, but also confronted and disturbed my own certainties. This deeply and variously 'personal-is-political' book, has been one heck of a journey, made possible with the kindness, generosity and guidance of a few good people whom I wish to acknowledge.

Foremost, my gratitude to the New India Foundation (NIF) for seeing promise in my book proposal—a political biography of Jagat Narain Lal. I am immensely thankful to them for the timely fellowship and for their very valuable support thereafter. In particular I'd like mention the very fantastic and very patient editor, Rivka Israel. Grateful thanks to my college, Janki Devi Memorial College (Delhi University) and principal Swati Pal, for backing my project and for sanctioning a year-long sabbatical which made this book possible.

I owe a deep debt of gratitude to Ramachandra Guha whose commitment to scholarship and mentoring is so wholehearted that it's a lesson all by itself. With an unsparing editorial pen and uncanny precision, he read page after page, guiding, appreciating, chiding and de-jargoning my draft. It was a real privilege to have him as a mentor. My sincere thanks to Niraja Gopal Jayal for the generosity of her spirit and for becoming a companion to this book, from its inception in my head to helping me through the maze of shortlisted titles. Her incisive intellectual analyses and her conduct as a scholar continues to be both formative and inspirational for me.

My heartfelt thanks to Pratap Bhanu Mehta for his friendship and kindness. His intellectual depth and generosity guided this book through many conceptual muddles, and his kindness through many moments of self-doubt and personal failings. My thinking about various issues and the desire to keep writing about them has grown through many conversations and readings of his work. Thanks are also due to him for putting me in touch with Deepa Bhatnagar, the director Ashoka Archives of Contemporary India. Owe her big thanks for personally overseeing the digitization of the some diaries and notebooks before they were donated to Nehru Memorial Museum and Library (NMML) in keeping with my family's wishes. Digitization meant that most of those brittle, faded pages could now be enhanced and made legible with the help of technology. In this regard, thanks are due also to Venu Madhav Govindu, author and biographer, who generously spared time to process and enhance the digitized files that made many of these diaries and notebooks legible to me.

Archival material for this book was sourced from Nehru Memorial Museum and Library, *Ideas of India* digital archives, Bihar State Archives, Bihar Assembly Library and Sinha Library, Patna. My sincere thanks to the Manuscript (Archives) and Reprography Divisions of NMML for their very enabling support in accessing Jagat Narain Lal papers and newspaper reports. To the Bihar State Archives, I owe much gratitude for their cooperation and for helping me navigate the archives. I was pleasantly surprised by how meticulously digitized and organized state archives are and how trained and helpful the staff was. The Bihar Assembly Library is part of a new building complex and all assembly records were comfortably and easily accessible there. Unfortunately, the Sinha library is in a state of utter disrepair and neglect. A library that's home to some rare collections, and that has witnessed history in the making, deserves better. A special word of mention for the *Ideas of India* Archive whose database, so painstakingly and absolutely stupendously indexes over three lakhs entries from over 250 English-language periodicals that were published between 1837 and 1947. It meant that magazines and journals like *The Modern Review, Indian Quarterly Register, Indian Annual Register*, to name a few, were available at a few clicks.

A big thank you is due to Rajesh Kumar, PhD scholar in 2019 (History department, Patna University) who helped me navigate the Bihar State and Assembly archives. His research assistance and support as a 'local guide' was invaluable.

Grateful thanks to my editor, Meru Gokhale at Penguin Random House India, who pushed me to sharpen the focus of the manuscript. Special thanks to Hina Khajuria for her patience, support and sharp copy-editing; and to the very creative Gunjan Ahlawat for an evocative cover. To the entire team at Penguin Random House India, a special round of thanks for backing my book.

My warm and heartfelt thanks to my friends and family—to my father, Shrish Chandra, Uncle Sushil Chandra, aunts Asha Sinha and Pratima Verma, for sharing their stories and conversations about their father. I will always regret that Pratima Phua did not live to see this book. She would have been particularly pleased to see how her own memoir of her father, Jagat Babu, served as a guiding light for this book. A special round of thanks to my extended family: to Mona Sinha for helping me translate some difficult parts; to Prabhat Chandra for the rare photographs; to Madhuparna Mitra who shares her privilege of 'US-academia-library-access' with a promptness and readiness that only a lifelong friend can. To all my friends who steadied my pen during a difficult period—to the Dolcitas, Banjos, VK friends; friends at and from college, you know who you are—gratitude and heartfelt thanks.

My loving thanks to my siblings Rashmi and Saurabh for their ideas, advice and solidarity; to my daughter, Niyati for sorting out the bibliography of this book which is always the bane of my life; to my son, Nikhil whose trips to NMML during the pandemic ensured an uninterrupted supply of archival material; to my in-laws who always take so much pride in my work; to my father whose unstinting faith in my abilities keeps me going; to my mother who has waited for this book more than anyone else. And finally, my deepest gratitude to my husband, Jaideep Ahuja, for helping me stay on the path that got me here. Thank you for helping me scan, sort, magnify, read texts, for the pitch-perfect title and for shining the torchlight each time it got dark.

It is likely that I have made mistakes while writing this book. Some of those would be inadvertent, but some 'errors' may be those that are perceived as such. So much of our nationalist history is mired in ideological binaries that it is possible that there's stuff in this book that doesn't fit received histories and their prevalent narratives. For both categories of mistakes, I assume full responsibility.

Bibliography

Books, Chapters in Books, Articles in Journals, Newspapers and News Portals

Aditi, 'Rajasthan Court Acquits All Accused Persons in Pehlu Khan Lynching Case [Read Judgment]', Bar and Bench, 15 August, 2019, https://www.barandbench.com/news/rajasthan-court-acquits-all-accused-persons-in-pehlu-khan-lynching-case-read-judgment,

Alam, Jawaid. *Government and Politics in Colonial Bihar in 1921–1937*, 1st edition (New Delhi: Mittal Publications, 2005).

Alqadar, Ambarien. 'What Does It Mean to Live Under the Constant Fear of Being Declared a Foreigner in Your Own Country? Personal Notes on Citizenship and Belonging', ThePolisProject. com, 22 July 2020, https://thepolisproject.com/what-does-it-mean-to-live-under-the-constant-fear-of-being-declared-a-foreigner-in-your-own-country-personal-notes-on-citizenship-and-belonging/?fbclid=IwAR2QRtg_Vk8psLNWAHbuMh_abye6CgolcXKLtsOAY3Tijryj2eTLLHHJce0#.XxkNG_gzbOS.

Anderson, Walter K. and Sridhar Damle. *The Brotherhood in Saffron: The Rashtriya Swayamsevak Sangh and Hindu Revivalism* (Gurgaon: Penguin Random House India, 2019).

Anderson, Benedict. *Imagined Communities: Reflections on the Origin and Spread of Nationalism* (London: Verso Books, 1983).

Ayde Rao, Shivaji. *The Message of Ashiana, Mazaharul Haq*, 1st edition (Chapra, Bihar: Mazharul Haque Memorial Board, 1962).

Bapu, Prabhu. *Hindu Mahasabha in Colonial North India, 1915-1930: Constructing Nation and History* (Routledge, 2013).

Bajpai, Rochana. *Debating Difference, Group Rights and Liberal Democracy in India* (Delhi: Oxford University Press, 2011).

Baru, Sanjaya. 'Developmental Hindutva', *Indian Express*, 14 April 2017, https://indianexpress.com/article/opinion/columns/developmental-hindutva-bjp-narendra-modi-democracy-4612194/

Barry, Brian. *Culture and Equality: An Egalitarian Critique of Multiculturalism* (Cambridge: Polity Press, 2001).

—'Statism and Nationalism: A Cosmopolitan Critique', *Nomos*, Vol. 41, (1999).

Bayly, C.A. *The Local Roots of Indian Politics: Allahabad, 1880–1920* (Oxford: Calrendon Press, 1975).

—*Recovering Liberties: Indian Thought in the Age of Liberalism and Empire* (Cambridge: Cambridge University Press, 2011).

Bilgrami, Akeel. 'Two Concepts of Secularism–Reason, Modernity and Archimedean Ideal', *Economic and Political Weekly*, Vol. 29, No. 28 (1994).

—'Secularism and the Moral Psychology of Identity', *Economic and Political Weekly*, Vol. 32, No. 40 (1997).

—*Secularism, Identity, and Enchantment* (Harvard University Press, 2014).

Butigan, Ken. *Pilgrimage through a Burning World, Spiritual Practice and Nonviolent Protest at the Nevada Test Site* (New York: State University of New York Press, 2012).

Bhargava, Rajeev. 'What Is Indian Secularism and What Is It For?', *India Review*, Vol. 1, (2002).

—'Reimagining Secularism, Respect, Domination and Principled Distance', *Economic and Political Weekly*, Vol. 48, No. 50, (2013).

—'Beyond Toleration: Civility and Principled Coexistence in Ashokan Edicts', in *Boundaries of Toleration*, ed. Alfred Stepan and Charles Taylor (Chichester, New York: Columbia University Press, 2014).

Bhatnagar, Gaurav Vivek. 'EC Hands Out Fourth 'Clean Chit' to Modi, but Uploads No Details on Website', Wire, 4 May 2019, https://thewire.in/politics/ec-fourth-clean-chit-narendra-modi.

Brown, Judith M. *Gandhi's Rise to Power: Indian Politics 1915-1922* (Cambridge: Cambridge University Press, 1972).

Carpenter, Daniel. 'Representation at a Visual Interface: Institutions as Encounters between Early American Government and Its Citizens', in *Anxieties of Democracy: Tocquevillean Reflections on India and The United States*, eds. Partha Chatterjee and Ira Katznelson (Delhi: Oxford University Press, 2012).

Chakravarty, Ipsita, 'How India's Founding Fathers Saw the "Nauseating Principle of Secularity of the State"', Scroll, 2 December 2015.

Chandra, Rajshree. 'Saffron Blind: The Political Project of Hindutva Is Incompatible with a Liberal Polity', *Indian Express*, 25 April 2017.

—'In Service of Politics: Hindutva Seeks to Surmount the Diversity of Hinduism", *Indian Express*, 4 January 2019, https://indianexpress.com/article/opinion/columns/hindutva-hindus-in-india-lok-sabha-elections-5522425/

—'Against Complacency', *Indian Express*, 6 May 2014, https://indianexpress.com/article/opinion/columns/against-complacency/

—'Activists' Arrests: The Exceptional Has Been Made the New Normal', Wire, 1 November 2018.

—'"Extraordinary" Laws are becoming Central to the Politics of Repression in India', Wire, 28 August 2018, https://thewire.in/rights/extraordinary-laws-are-becoming-central-to-the-politics-of-repression-in-india;

Chatterjee, Partha. *Nationalist Thought and the Colonial World: A Derivative Discourse* (London: Zed Books, 1986).

Chauhan, Siddharth. 'Legislature: Privileges and Process', *The Oxford Handbook of the Indian Constitution*, eds. Sujit Choudhry, Madhav Khosla and Pratap Bhanu Mehta (Oxford: Oxford University Press, 2016).

Choudhry, Sujit. 'Language', *The Oxford Handbook of the Indian Constitution*, eds. Sujit Choudhry, Madhav Khosla, Pratap Bhanu Mehta (Oxford: Oxford University Press, 2016).

Datta, K. K. *History of the Freedom Movement in Bihar*, Vol. 1. (Government of Bihar, Miscellaneous Official Publications, 1957).

—*History of the Freedom Movement in Bihar*, Vol. 2, Miscellaneous Official Publications.

Devji, Faisal. 'An Indian History of Toleration: Between the Secular and the Civilisational', *Open Magazine*, 2016.

Fozdar, Farida and Low, Mitchell. 'They Have to Abide by Our Laws and Stuff: Ethno-Nationalism Masquerading as Civic Nationalism'. *Journal of the Association for the Study of Ethnicity and Nationalism*, Vol. 21 (3) (2015).

Flood, G. *The Ascetic Self: Subjectivity, Memory and Tradition* (Cambridge: Cambridge University Press, 2004).

Friedman, Milton. *Capitalism and Freedom* (Chicago, London: University Chicago Press, 1962).

Foucault, Michel. 'Technologies of the Self' in *Ethics: Subjectivity and Truth* (3 vols.), Vol. 1, *Essential Works of Foucault, 1954–1984*, ed. Paul Rabinow (New York: New Press, 1997).

—'Technologies of the Self', in *Technologies of the Self: A Seminar with Michel Foucault*, eds. Luther H. Martin, Huck Gutman and Patrick H. (Amherst: University of Massachusetts Press, 1988).

—'The Masked Philosopher' in *Foucault Live (Interviews, 1961–1984)*, ed. Sylvère Lotringer (New York: Semiotext(e), 1996).

Gandhi, Rajmohan. *Rajaji: A Life* (New Delhi: Penguin Books India, 1997).

Guha, Ramachandra. *India after Gandhi: The History of the World's Largest Democracy* (India: Pan Macmillan, 2011).

—*Gandhi: The Years That Changed the World: 1914-1948* (Gurgaon: Penguin Random House India, 2018).

Ghosh, Papiya. *Muhajirs and the Nation: Bihar in the 1940s* (Delhi: Routledge, 2010).

—'The Virile and the Chaste in Community and Nation Making: Bihar 1920's to 1940's', *Social Scientist*, Vol. 22, No. 1/2, (1994).

Golwalkar, M.S. *We or Our Nation Redefined* (Bharat Publications, 1939).

—*Bunch of Thoughts*, 3rd edition, (The Hindu Centre, 2006), https://www.thehinducentre.com/multimedia/archive/02486/Bunch_of_Thoughts_2486072a.pdf

Gopal, Vikram. 'Would Have Lined Intellectuals Up and Shot Them If I was Home Minister: Karnataka BJP MLA', *Hindustan Times*, 27 July 2018, https://www.hindustantimes.com/karnataka/would-have-lined-intellectuals-up-and-shot-them-if-i-was-home-minister-karnataka-bjp-mla/story-fKylCymeza5sYwIlC7QsCJ.html.

Gordon, Richard. 'The Hindu Mahasabha and the Indian National Congress, 1915 to 1926', *Modern Asian Studies*, Vol. 9, No. 2 (1975).

Habermas, Jurgen. 'Struggles for Recognition in the Democratic Constitutional State', *Multiculturalism: Examining the Politics of Recognition*, ed. Charles Taylor, (NJ: Princeton University Press, 1994).

'Hindutva Unifying Factor: RSS Leader Krishna Gopal', *Economic Times*, 3 January 2020; https://economictimes.indiatimes.com/news/politics-and-nation/hindutva-unifying-factor-rss-leader-krishna-gopal/articleshow/73078791.cms

'Hinduism Not a Religion but a Way of Life, *The Hindu*, 2 April 2016; https://www.thehindu.com/news/international/hinduism-not-a-religion-but-a-way-of-life-modi/article7112383.ece.

Heimsath, Charles. *Indian Nationalism and Hindu Social Reform* (Bombay: Oxford University Press, 1964).

'I Don't Want to Become PM, Want to Be a Chowkidar, Says Narendra Modi', IndiaToday.in, video, 25 October 2013, https://www.indiatoday.in/india/video/narendra-modi-bjp-jhansi-rally-prime-minister-vs-chowkidar-423931-2013-10-25

'"India Is a Hindu Rashtra": BJP MP Ravi Kishan Bats for Citizenship Amendment Bill', News18.com, 4 December 2019, https://www.news18.com/news/politics/india-is-a-hindu-rashtra-bjp-mp-ravi-kishan-bats-for-citizenship-amendment-bill-2412227.html

'India Will become "Hindu Rashtra" by 2024, Says Uttar Pradesh's BJP MLA Surendra Singh', Firstpost, PTI, 14 January 2018. https://www.firstpost.com/india/india-will-become-hindu-rashtra-by-2024-says.

Ignatieff, Michael. *Blood and Belonging: Journeys into the New Nationalism* (New York: Farrar, Straus and Giroux, 1993).

Jaffrelot, Christophe. 'A De Facto Ethnic Democracy? Obliterating and Targeting the Other, Hindu Vigilantes, and the Ethno-State', *Majoritarian State: How Hindu Nationalism Is Changing India*, eds. Angana P. Chatterji, Thomas Blom Hansen and Christophe Jaffrelot (New York: Oxford University Press, 2019).

—'30 Years On: Is It "Game Over" for Mandal Politics', *Indian Express*, 22 August 2020.

—'What's Left of the "Mandal Moment", Politically and Socially, Now?', *Indian Express*, 30 August 2020.

Jayal, Niraja. 'Citizenship', *Oxford Handbook of the Indian Constitution*, eds. Sujit Choudhry, Madhav Khosla and Pratap Bhanu Mehta (New York: Oxford University Press, 2016).

Jha, Shefali. 'Secularism in the Constituent Assembly Debates: 1946-1950', *Economic and Political Weekly*. Vol. 37, No. 30 (2002).

Kaviraj, Sudipta. 'Modernity, State, and Toleration in Indian History: Exploring Accommodations and Partitions', in *Boundaries of Toleration*, eds. Alfred Stepan and Charles Taylor (New York Chichester, West Sussex: Columbia University Press, 2014).

Kesavan, Mukul. 'Experiments in the Politics of Sadomasochism', *Telegraph*, 20 July 2020. https://www.telegraphindia.com/opinion/the-bjp-government-s-experiments-in-the-politics-of-sadomasochism/cid/1699989.

Khan, Adil Hasan. 'Politics and Piety in India: Re-learning Traditions of Civility', *Third World Approaches to International Law Review*, 12 June 2020.

Králová, Jana. "What Is Social Death?", *Contemporary Social Science*, Vol. 10 (2015).

Kymlicka, Will. *Multicultural Citizenship: A Liberal Theory of Minority Right* (Oxford: Oxford University Press, 1996).

Lal, Jagat Narain. 'Why Jagat Narain Lal, Once a Hindu Mahasabha Member, Saw Nehru as a Fellow Patriot', Wire, 2019.

—*Light unto a Cell* (Bombay: Hind Kitab Ltd., 1947).

—*Light unto a Cell*. ed. Manish Sinha (Patna: Janaki Prakashan, 2019).

Lobetti, Tullio Fredrico. *Ascetic Practice in Japanese Religion*. (London, New York: Routledge, 2014).

Mandal, Saumen. 'Tarakeswar Satyagraha: A Historical Event Revisited', *Proceedings of the Indian History Congress*, Vol. 74 (2013).

Mason, Andrew. *Community, Solidarity and Belonging: Levels of Community and Their Normative Significance* (UK: Cambridge University Press, 2000).

Mehta, Pratap Bhanu. *The Burden of Democracy* (Gurgaon: Penguin Random House India, 2017).

—'Babble of Babel', *Indian Express*, 2 November 2006, http://archive.indianexpress.com/news/babble-of-babel---------------/15801/

—'The Real Contest for India', *Indian Express*, 22 May 2014, https://indianexpress.com/article/opinion/columns/the-real-contest-for-india/

—'Being Free to be Free', *Open Magazine,* 12 August 2015, https://openthemagazine.com/voices/being-free-to-be-free/

Miller, David. *On Nationality* (Oxford: Clarendon Press, 1995).

Mishra, Basanta Kumar. 'India's Response to the British Offer of August 1940', *Proceedings of the Indian History Congress*, Vol. 40 (1979).

'Mohan Bhagwat, 130 Crore Indians Are Hindu Society', *The Hindu*, 26 December 2019; https://www.thehindu.com/news/national/130-crore-indians-are-hindu-society-mohan-bhagwat/article30397898.ece.

'Muslims and Christians Will Be Wiped Out of India by December 31, 2021: BJP Leader Rajeshwar Singh', SabrangIndia.com, 14 December 2014; https://sabrangindia.in/article/muslims-and-christians-will-be-wiped-out-india-december-31-2021-bjp-leader-rajeshwar-singh.

Nair, Neeti. *Changing Homelands: Hindu Politics and the Partition of India* (Cambridge, Harvard University Press, 2011).

Nandy, Ashis. *The Intimate Enemy: Loss and Recovery of Self Under Colonialism* (Delhi: Oxford University Press, 1983).

Nietzsche, Friedrich. *The Genealogy of Morals: The Complete Works*, Vol. 13, trs. Horace B. Samuels, ed. T.N. Foulis, (Edinburgh, London, 1913).

Patel, Hitendra K. 'Aspects of Hindu Mobilization in Modern Bihar', *Proceedings of the Indian History Congress*, Vol. 65 (2004).

Pattabhi Sitaramyya, Bhogaraju. *History of Indian National Congress*, Vol. 2, (S. Chand, 1969).

Pamuk, Orhan. *Other Colours: An Essay and a Story* (London: Faber & Faber, 2007).

Prasad, Rajendra. *Mahatma Gandhi and Bihar: Some Reminiscences* (Delhi: Prabhat Prakashan, 2015). —*Mahatma Gandhi and Bihar: Some Reminiscences* (Hind Kitab, 1949).

Ramanujan, A.K. 'Three Hundred Ramayans: The Essay Delhi University Deemed Unfit for its Students', *Open Magazine*, 28 October 2011, https://openthemagazine.com/art-culture/three-hundred-ramayanas/

Raza, Syed. 'Mazharul Haque: A Pioneer of the Sadaqat Ashram and Bihar Vidyapith', *Proceedings of the Indian History Congress*, Vol. 70, Indian History Congress (2009–2010).

Roy, N.C. 'The Growth of Linguistic States in the Indian Federation', in *Essays on Indian Federalism*, ed. S.P. Aiyar and U. Mehta, Bombay, New York, Allied Publishers, 1965.

Roy, Debayan. 'Supreme Court Issues Notice in Fresh Petitions Challenging Citizenship Amendment Act, Tags Matter with Other Pending Pleas', Bar and Bench, 20 May 2020, https://www.barandbench.com/news/litigation/supreme-court-issues-notice-in-fresh-petitionschallenging-citizenship-amendment-act-tags-matter-with-otherpending-pleas.

Russo, Chandra. *Solidarity in Practice: Moral Protest and the US Security State* (Cambridge: Cambridge University Press, 2018).

'RNG Awards: Need to Reflect on Emergency So That No Leader Dares to Repeat It, Says PM Narendra Modi", *Indian Express*, 3 November 2016; https://indianexpress.com/article/india/india-news-india/rng-ramnath-goenka-awards-need-to-reflect-on-emergency-so-that-no-leader-dares-to-repeat-it-says-pm-narendra-modi-3734545/

Savarkar, V.D. *Hindu Rashtra Darshan* (Karnavati: Akhil Bharat Hindu Mahasabha, 19th Session of the Akhil Bhartiya Hindu Mahasabha, 1949).

—*Hindutva: Who Is a Hindu*, 5th edition (Bombay: Veer Savarkar Prakashan, 1969 [1923]).

Sinha, Manish. 'The Dilemma of Jagat Narain Lal, Congress or the Hindu Mahasabha: Some Excerpts from Unpublished Letter of Jagat Narain Lal to Dr Moonje from Hazaribagh Central Jail, March, 1932', *Proceedings of the Indian History Congress*, Vol. 76 (2015).

Sharma, Padmasha. 'Communal Award and the Indian National Congress', *Proceedings of the Indian History Congress*, Vol. 33 (1971).

Spencer, Philip. & Wollman, Howard. *Nationalism: A Critical Introduction* (California, Delhi: Sage Publications, 2002).

Srivatsan, R. 'The Concept of "Seva" and "Sevak" in the Freedom Movement', *Economic and Political Weekly*, Vol. 41, No. 05 (2006).

Tamir, Yael. *Liberal Nationalism* (New Jersey: Princeton University Press, 1995).

Tava, Francesco. 'Sacrifice as a Political Problem: Jan Patočka and Sacred Sociology', *Metodo*, Vol. 6, No. 2 (Sdvig Press, 2018).

Taylor, Charles. 'The Collapse of Toleration', *The Guardian*, 17 September 2007.

Tejani, Shabnum, 'Re-Considering Chronologies of Nationalism and Communalism: The Khilafat Movement in Sind and its Aftermath, 1919–1927', *South Asia Research*, Vol. 27 No. 3, 2007.

Tiwari, Ravish. 'Mohan Bhagwat's Silence on Golwalkar telling: Edits Anti Muslim Remark', *Indian Express*, 20 September 2018, https://indianexpress.com/article/india/mohan-bhagwats-silence-on-madhav-sadasiva-golwalkar-telling-edits-anti-muslim-remark-5365537/

Tharakeshwar, V.B. 'Competing Imaginations: Language and Anti-colonial Nationalism in India", *Interrogating Reorganisation of States: Culture, Identity and Politics in India*, eds. Asha Sarangi and Sudha Pai (Delhi, London: Routledge, 2011).

'Union Minister Makes Controversial Statements at Pro-CAA Program, Congress Says BJP's Real Face on CAA Stands Exposed', *New Indian Express*, 12 January 2020; https://www.newindianexpress.com/nation/2020/jan/12/union-minister-makes-controversial-statements-at-pro-caa-program-congress-says-bjps-real-face-on-c-2088692.html

Valantasis, Richard. *The Making of the Self: Ancient and Modern in Asceticism* (Oregon: Cascade Books, 2008).

Varshney, Ashutosh. 'Modi on Balance: What to Overlook, What to Watch Out for, in the Prospect of a Modi Government', *Indian Express*, 29 April 2014.

Verma, Pratima. *'Jagat Narain Lal: Bihar ke Ananya Vibhuti'* (Bokaro: Seema Press, 2004).

Vivekananda, Swami. 'The Ideal of Karma Yoga' in *The Complete Works of Vivekananda*, Vol.1, Ch.8., Advaita Ashrama. Available at https://www.ramakrishnavivekananda.info/vivekananda/volume_1/karma-yoga/the_ideal.htm. Last accessed July 30, 2021.

Wakankar, Milind. 'Body, Crowd, Identity: Genealogy of a Hindu Nationalist Ascetics'. *Social Text* 45 (1995).

'Will Remove Every Single Infiltrator, except Buddhists, Hindus And Sikhs: Amit Shah', *Indian Express*, 11 April 2019, https://indianexpress.com/elections/will-remove-every-single-infiltrator-except-buddhists-hindus-and-sikhs-amit-shah/

Wills, Lawrence M. 'Ascetic Theology before Asceticism? Jewish Narratives and the Decentering of the Self', *Journal of the American Academy of Religion*, Vol. 74, No. 4 (2006).

Weil, Simone. *First and Last Notebooks*, trs. Richard Rees (London: Oxford University Press, 1970).

Weiner, Myron. 'India: Politics of Scarcity: Public Pressure and Political Response in India', *India Quarterly: A Journal of International Affairs* Vol. 19(2) (1963).

Archival Records

National Archives of India: Dr. Rajendra Prasad Papers
Bihar Legislative Assembly Debates: 1952–1960

Bihar State Archives
Government of Bihar and Orissa, Political Dept.
Emperor v. Jagat Narain Lal, Section 124A IPC, Govt. of Bihar & Orissa, 1927
Govt. of Bihar and Orissa, Govt. of India, Fortnightly Report 1920 Home Department (Political) Files. 1920–1925
Confidential Report Bihar Special Branch, 8 March 1921
Bihar and Orissa Political Special Files, 1921

Indian National Congress Archives
Indian National Congress, Resolutions 1934–36
Indian National Congress, Report of the General Secretaries, March–October 1940

Government Reports
Report of the Linguistic Provinces Commission (Delhi: Government of India Press, 1948)
Report of the Hindu Religious and Charitable Endowments Committee United Provinces (Allahabad: The Superintendent, Government Press, United Province, 1931)

Magazines, Newspapers
Young India, 1921–22
The Hindu, 1925–130
Leader, 1923
Searchlight, 1921–1942
Motherland, 1922–24

Ideas of India—Rediscovery of India Archives
Indian Quarterly Register, Vol.2, No.3 July–Dec 1927
The Modern Review. Vol 44, Nos 1–6, July–Dec 1928
The Indian Annual Register, Vol.5. 1921

Nehru Memorial Museum and Library
Jagat Narain Lal Papers, NMML archives: Speeches and Writings
Jagat Narain Lal Papers, NMML, Notebooks

Jagat Narain Lal Papers, NMML, Letters and Correspondence
B.S. Moonje, Papers and Letters
AICC Papers, Jawaharlal Nehru to Jagat Narain Lal, September
1936

Constituent Assembly Debates
    CAD, Volumes 1, 3, 7, 8,9, 10, 11